FOOD INSECURITY AND THE SOCIAL DIVISION OF LABOR IN TANZANIA 1919–85

Food Insecurity and the Social Division of Labor in Tanzania, 1919–85

Deborah Fahy Bryceson
Senior Member of the Cross-Cultural Centre for Research on Women
Queen Elizabeth House
University of Oxford

St. Martin's Press New York

First published in the United States of America in 1990
Printed in Great Britain

Library of Congress Cataloging-in-Publication Data

Bryceson, Deborah Fahy.
Food Insecurity and the Social Division of Labor in Tanzania, 1919–85/
Deborah Fahy Bryceson.
p. cm.
ISBN 0-312-04073-3
1. Food supply–Tanzania. 2. Labor supply–Tanzania.
3. Tanzania–Economic conditions. I. Title.
HD9017.T32B79 1990
338.1'9678–dc20 89–29437
CIP

To My Parents

Contents

List of Tables

List of Figures

List of Abbreviations and Acronyms

BRALUP	Bureau of Resource Assessment and Land Use Planning
CCM	Chama cha Mapinduzi (Revolutionary Party)
CIDA	Canadian International Development Agency
CDR	Centre for Development Research
DC	District Commissioner
DO	District Officer
DSM	Dar es Salaam
EA	East Africa
EAAFJ	East African Agricultural and Forestry Journal
EAAJ	East African Agricultural Journal
EARC	East Africa Royal Commission
ECB	Economic Control Board
ERB	Economics Research Bureau
FAO	Food and Agriculture Organisation
GSD	Grain Storage Department
HBS	Household Budget Survey
HMSO	His/Her Majesty's Stationery Office
IBRD	International Bank for Reconstruction and Development
IDS	Institute of Development Studies
ILO	International Labour Office
IMF	International Monetary Fund
IRA	Institute of Resource Assessment
JASPA	Jobs and Skills Programme for Africa
KILIMO	Ministry of Agriculture
KNCU	Kilimanjaro Native Cooperative Union
LegCo	Legislative Council
MDB	Marketing Development Bureau
NAFCO	National Agricultural Farm Corporation
NAPB	National Agricultural Production Board
NESP	National Economic Survival Programme
NMC	National Milling Corporation
OECD	Organisation for Economic Cooperation and Development

PC	Provincial Commissioner
PMO	Prime Minister's Office
PPR	Price Policy Recommendations (or Review)
PWD	Public Works Department
RH	Rhodes House
SAP	Structural Adjustment Programme
SCOPO	Standing Committee on Parastatal Organisation
SIDA	Swedish International Development Agency
TANU	Tanganyika African National Union
TECSA	Tanganyikan European Civil Servants Association
TFNC	Tanzania Food and Nutrition Centre
TNR	Tanganyika Notes and Records
TRDB	Tanzania Rural Development Bank
TT	Tanganyika Territory
UDSM	University of Dar es Salaam
UNICEF	United Nations International Children's Emergency Fund
UNIDO	United Nations Industrial Development Organisation

Acknowledgements

This book was written, amidst other work commitments, between 1981 and 1989, and, in an expanded form, was submitted as my D.Phil. thesis at Oxford University. Because of the book's long gestation, I have innumerable people to thank for their advice and support.

Professional contact and intellectual stimulation came from many quarters. During my first year in Oxford I was a Research Associate at the Food Studies Group, Queen Elizabeth House. My thanks to the United Nations University for funding my year there and to Roger Hay and his colleagues for providing the initial encouragement to write on the topic. The academic environment of Oxford, afforded me exposure to many new ideas. The Political Economy of Developing Countries seminars at Queen Elizabeth House in particular provided a stimulating forum for discussion. I would like to make special mention of Judith Heyer, Richard Palmer-Jones, Gavin Williams and, more latterly, Megan Vaughn in this context. Luis Parra and Peter Winchester were generous in relating their practical experiences in the Third World at a point when I was formulating my ideas on clientage. I am particularly endebted to the late Roger Freeman who put a great deal of time into developing a statistical computer programme to fit my needs. I am also extremely grateful to M. Mulokozi, Richard Palmer-Jones, Paul Collier and Andrew Coulson, the latter of the University of Birmingham, for giving me comments on some of my draft chapters.

I have found Britain's libraries, especially those in Oxford, a real treat after years of book hunger in Dar es Salaam. The help I received from the library staffs of Rhodes House, the Institute of Commonwealth Studies, Queen Elizabeth House and the Institute of Economics and Statistics is greatly appreciated. I would like to express my gratitude to John Iliffe of St John's College, Cambridge for allowing me access to his private collection of source material on Tanzania.

The people who have helped me with data collection in Tanzania are far too numerous to mention individually. I am grateful to them all especially the staffs of the Tanzania National Archives and the Bureau of Statistics, notably Mr Mkai and Mr N.K. Mbalilaki for making the findings of the 1976 Household Budget Survey available to me prior to its publication. At the Ministry of Agriculture, Mr R.A. Gommes of the Early Warning and Crop Monitoring Programme and Mr T. Banda of the Marketing Development Bureau were very helpful.

My greatest intellectual debt has to be traced back to my friends during the nine years I spent at the University of Dar es Salaam. These include: Henry Bernstein, Bernard Joinet, Marjorie Mbilinyi, Kemal Mustafa, Phil Raikes, Salvatore Rugumisa, Ulla Vuorela and to my former colleagues at the Institute of Resource Assessment, notably Han Bantje, Kjell Havnevik and Finn Kjaerby, all of whom helped me through discussion and debate to understand the changing nature of rural Tanzania during the late 1970s when so much was happening so quickly. Since 1981, thanks to the inconvenience endured by Han Bantje, I have received stacks and stacks of Dar es Salaam *Daily News* which have kept me reasonably informed of events. Special mention goes to Sophie and Abdullah Mustafa, for their warm hospitality and friendship during my visits to Dar es Salaam.

Ajit Singh and Selina Cohen deserve my heartfelt thanks for all the kindness and common sense they have offered me over the years. In addition, Ajit Singh's perpetual disagreement with me over the nature of clientage has given me the means of, I hope, arguing my case more rigorously.

My parents' encouragement throughout was critical to the completion of this book and it is for this reason that I dedicate the book to them. My son, Yenan, provided a counterbalance. His impatience and lack of regard for his mother's work kept the undertaking in perspective. Similarly, John Howe, husband and colleague, exhorting me to move on to other things, kept the pressure on in the final stretch.

I am deeply endebted to Gavin Williams for his wisdom in supervising my thesis. The penetrating comments of Terrence Ranger and Paul Richards, as thesis examiners, saved me a great deal of agonizing over how to edit my thesis for publication. Megan Vaughn and Rosemary Thorp also gave me helpful guidance in this regard.

Lastly, I want to express my gratitude to Tanzania as a country and to Tanzanians as a people whose coping strategies under material insecurity have taught me that human social inventiveness is not stifled by lack of material opportunity.

Part I
Food Supply in Pre-Industrial Societies

Paradoxically, countries that are primarily agrarian in nature tend to be the most vulnerable to deficits of staple foods. Tanzania is one of them. Roughly 85 per cent of Tanzania's population live in rural areas, and most derive a livelihood directly from the soil, yet the country has experienced repeated shortfalls of food supplies during this century.

Tanzania's current food insecurity can be likened to the situation experienced in pre-industrial eighteenth-century Europe. Virtually all countries on the eve of industrialisation face a similar dilemma, namely, how to generate a food surplus for the growing proportion of the population who are engaged in non-agricultural activities in addition to ensuring rural food supplies.

This section reviews classical and recent literature on the topic of food supply in transitional societies.

1 The Population/Food Production Capability Balance at the Outset of Industrialisation

In comparing the writings of Malthus, Ricardo, Preobrazhensky and W.A. Lewis, the dynamic character of the population/food production capability balance over the last two centuries becomes evident. Malthus and Ricardo were early-nineteenth-century British political economists analysing the country that was the first to industrialise and that was favoured by a simultaneous evolution of agrarian and industrial productivity. Preobrazhensky, on the other hand, was writing in the Soviet Union during the 1920s when the majority of the Soviet population (80 per cent) was still living in rural areas and the country's manufactures were not competitive in the world market. Finally, W.A. Lewis has been writing since the 1950s about the difficulties of industrialising predominantly agrarian Third World economies. All of the authors addressed the food constraint in the process of industrialisation and national development.

1 MALTHUS: THE 'NATURAL ORDER' OF THE PRE-INDUSTRIAL FOOD ECONOMY

Malthus was virtually blind to the possibility of technological transformation and changing social relations either in the sphere of food production or in human reproduction. National populations were doomed to live on the knife-edge of physical survival unless moral restraint, i.e. the postponement of marriage, was exercised. He assumed that the population would double every 25 years in the absence of positive or preventive checks.[1]

Malthus's disagreement with Ricardo over the Corn Laws led him to elaborate his premise of restricted agricultural growth relative to population increase, which has come to be known as the law of diminishing returns. Cherishing rural society against urbanisation and market forces, Malthus represented the tail-end of physiocratic thought. He assumed that value ultimately derived from the land and supported the landlord class's high rents, which were seen as synonymous with the expansion of national wealth.

In his opposition to the new industrial order, Malthus argued that declining food prices would lower the level of wages and would cause a glut of industrial production because there would not be enough working-class purchasing power for buying industrially-produced goods.

2 RICARDO: EXPANDING FOOD SUPPLY THROUGH INTERNATIONAL TRADE

Adhering to Malthus's theories of population growth and the law of diminishing returns, Ricardo was, however, an exponent of a new order, that of urban-based industrialists. Like Malthus, he desired the expansion of national wealth, but it was to be facilitated by increasing profits of capitalist industrialists rather than higher rents.[2] Contrary to Malthus, he held the view that supply created its own demand.[3] An increase in food imports would lower the cost of food and wage levels and make possible the proliferation of industrial production for the enhancement of national wealth, although it would be injurious to landlords and farmers in the short run.

Thus, high food prices were neither desirable nor unalterable. Ricardo admonished Malthus for not drawing the logical conclusion from the law of diminishing returns; some countries with more fertile land than England were producing food at lower costs and it was quite logical to import food from them, just as a country does not hesitate to cultivate its most fertile land prior to resorting to less fertile land. Thus each country could reap the benefits from its 'comparative advantage' in trade.

Britain had the option to import grain because she was highly competitive in the export of manufactured goods. By the start of the industrial revolution, Britain had already developed a fairly complex market economy. The proportion of the population living in settlements of over 5000 people in 1801 is estimated at 25 per cent. Virtually all rural producers participated in labour or commodity markets.[4] The social division of labour was relatively highly developed.

3 PREOBRAZHENSKY: EXPANDING FOOD SUPPLY THROUGH STATE APPROPRIATION FROM THE PEASANTRY

Preobrazhensky was a Bolshevik intellectual and active in Soviet policy debates of the 1920s. His book, *The New Economics*,[5] was aimed at providing a realistic assessment of the Soviet Union's prospects for industrialisation in the absence of most of the conditions that had made the industrial revolution possible in Britain.

Industrialisation required an increasing supply of peasant production both in the form of grain to feed a growing industrial working class and urban population and in export crops to earn hard currency for the import of foreign machinery. Preobrazhensky pointed out that the Soviet Union could not expect to gain through any comparative advantage in the international market as Britain had, nor did it have colonies to exploit. Thus he advocated 'primitive socialist accumulation', which involved extracting surplus from the peasantry through state control of produce marketing and price setting at a level that was below the world market price, but above a minimum at which peasants would not have incentives to extend cultivation. Preobrazhensky saw the role of the state as mediator between the peasantry and the international market as the ultimate control. Peasant grain production was to expand rapidly such that grain export would become increasingly important.

Despite the optimism of Preobrazhensky in believing that primitive socialist accumulation could proceed on a non-coercive path, there were forebodings of possible problems in his characterisation of both local traders and the peasantry. Local traders were viewed as 'parasites', whose appropriation, contrary to the forces of primitive socialist accumulation, did not lay the basis for industrialisation and higher productivity in rural areas, even though it was admitted that they could operate at smaller costs per unit of circulation than state trading due to their low overheads and the underlying personal trust of employer and employees in the trading concern. The peasants themselves were seen as nascent capitalists. Preobrazhensky quotes Lenin approvingly regarding the need to replace the peasantry with modern large-scale production.

Preobrazhensky was criticised by Bukharin and Stalin for claiming the need to exploit the peasantry and was expelled from the party in 1927, a year after his book was published. Under pressure, Preobrazhensky recanted in 1934. Nonetheless, he was put to death in the purge of 1937. Ironically, Stalin implemented the policy of primitive socialist accumulation in an extreme and highly coercive form beginning in 1928 with the requisition of grain, followed by forced collectivisation a year later. By 1934, most of the land and the peasantry were collectivised.

Since then, the Soviet Union has become an industrial nation but still retains a large rural sector. In a 1971 survey, 70 per cent of rural household food needs were met by their own production.[6] Overall, Soviet agriculture has not succeeded in generating grain surpluses big enough to feed its urban areas. Not unlike Britain in the 1870s, the Soviet Union in the 1970s was relying on North American imports of wheat to make up its national deficit each year.

4 W.A. LEWIS: EXPANDING FOOD SUPPLY THROUGH INTERNATIONAL TRADE AND TECHNOLOGY TRANSFER

In light of several countries' successful industrialisation under a variety of conditions and combinations of state and market forces, Arthur Lewis analyses the economic growth made by the tropical countries since the 1880s.[7] He argues that the tropical countries had two options, either to imitate the industrialisation process of the developed countries or to trade with them. Since their colonial governments did not encourage industrialisation and the countries lacked developed markets, an entrepreneurial class and other vital social institutions, the latter course was followed in virtually every case. An even greater impediment was their low level of agricultural productivity.

While not openly opposed to state-led industrialisation, Lewis sees industrialisation as not only an economic and political phenomenon, but also a profoundly sociological one, involving far-reaching structural changes in social organisation. He assumes that the market is the institution most capable of nurturing the requisite changes, in conjunction with state support.

The food production capability/population ratio is an essential part of Lewis's theoretical framework and is analysed through a historical comparison of world migration patterns and their consequences for international commodity markets. At the turn of the century, about 13 million Europeans settled in the temperate zone frontier areas of Canada, Argentina, Chile, Australia, New Zealand and South Africa and roughly 50 million Indian and Chinese left their countries to work on plantations in the colonial tropics of Asia and Africa. The difference in opportunity costs of labour between the two groups was very large. An Asian farmer produced roughly 700 lb of grain per acre while his European counterpart produced 1600 lb per acre and cultivated more acreage. Lewis estimates that the European produced roughly six or seven times more than the Asian farmer. These facts were reflected in the terms of trade of the developing world. Both sets of destination countries were unindustrialised, yet the tropical countries received lower prices for their export crops and displayed a lower standard of living than the temperate frontier zones because of their relatively unlimited supplies of Chinese and Indian labour willing to work for anything above the baseline earnings of 700 lb grain. The temperate countries, on the other hand, had greater grain yields and no labour reserves.

As productivity has continued to improve in food production in the industrialised countries over the last two decades, the prices of their non-food exports do not decline with the price of food in the world market because agricultural incomes are linked to the relatively rigid level of urban incomes. In the tropical countries, on the other hand, export crop prices decline because imported food is being substituted for locally grown staples such that more peasant farmers resort to growing export crops and through competition with one another drive export prices down.

The industrialised countries have a comparative advantage over tropical countries in both manufactures and agricultural products. One might assume that it is therefore unwise for tropical countries to engage in international trade. Lewis argues otherwise. Even though the developing countries have a disadvantaged trading position relative to the less populous industrial world, the market does allow them a means of lifting themselves out of stagnant subsistence peasant production. There are two aspects to the improvement. The market is a channel for technological transfer between the industrial and agrarian nations and the means by which material infrastructure, notably a transport network, is provisioned; secondly, it is the medium through which entrepreneurship, middle-class professionalism and social institutions more conducive to an industrial society are fostered.[8] This social theme is emphasised very strongly by Lewis and distinguishes him from today's mainstream economists who prefer quantitative model-building and relegate social factors to the status of externalities.[9]

While Lewis argues for participation in the international trade, he sees such participation as a stage of growth rather than the ultimate solution. The ultimate aim is to effect an increase in agricultural productivity large enough to sustain an industrial revolution. Thus an agrarian revolution and an industrial revolution are inseparable, both representing technological change and the advancement of the social division of labour. International trade is only a means to that end.

2 The Relationship Between Population, the Social Division of Labour and Food Supply

In the works of the four political economists reviewed in the preceding chapter, the balance between food production capability and population is formulated in various ways. Malthus sees 'food production capability' (fpc) as an independent variable with a fixed upper limit. This is because he equates fpc with land availability. Population is posited as the dependent variable. Ricardo, Preobrazhensky and Lewis offer different interpretations of fpc. None of them accepts a fixed upper limit. Ricardo reformulates fpc as food supply resulting from land availability and food import capability. National development of technology and the social division of labour determine food import capability. Preobrazhensky constructs fpc as a combination of advances in technology and the social division of labour, notably the development of state marketing of peasant produce and eventual large-scale state production of food. Lewis sees fpc in the same light as Ricardo, emphasising technology and the development of the social division of labour rather than land availability. In contrast to Preobrazhensky, both Ricardo and Lewis see the market as primary in encouraging the development of the social division of labour.

Ricardo, Preobrazhensky and Lewis, however, still agree with Malthus that food supply and not population is the independent variable. In contrast, Durkheim and Boserup are outstanding proponents of the notion that population is an independent variable with technology and the social division of labour as dependent.

1 DURKHEIM: POPULATION DENSITY AND THE SOCIAL DIVISION OF LABOUR

Durkheim never addressed the works of Malthus, yet his thesis in *The Division of Labor in Society*[1] directly contradicted the central tenet of Malthus. For Durkheim, increases in population density are related to the enhancement of the social division of labour. Durkheim advanced the proposition that 'The division of labor varies in direct ratio with the volume and density of societies, and, if it progresses in a continuous manner in the course of social development, it is because societies become regularly denser and generally more voluminous.'[2] With the increase in population density, human needs proliferate and control over the means of production deepen. Durkheim sees this as giving rise to increased specialisation of labour primarily due to the struggle for existence of the human collective.

The Division of Labor in Society is commonly regarded as the blueprint for most of Durkheim's future work, specifically its discussion of social morality and the division of labour. He sought to explain why 'the individual, while becoming more autonomous, depends more upon society.'[3]

Durkheim's definition of the division of labour extends beyond Adam Smith's notion of economic interdependence and task allocation to social consensus and moral rules of conduct. In the first part of the book Durkheim portrays ancient society virtually without the social division of labour. Coercive authority structures and law demand complete social conformity, a situation referred to as 'mechanical solidarity'. In contrast, modern society encourages an ever greater division of labour which is moulded by restitutive rather than coercive law. What results is an 'organic solidarity' built upon social consensus.

In the second part of the book Durkheim argues that the division of labour exists in pre-market societies in the form of a division of labour and relations of dependence based on sex and age within the family. He criticises Spencer's notion that the division of labour arises out of deliberate rational foresight. According to Durkheim, the division of labour evolves from the human need for order, harmony and social solidarity in the struggle for human survival. Maintenance of the division of labour is not solely a matter for the governing state; social consensus itself acts in this capacity exerting pressures to conform. Objectively and subjectively, each individual is dependent on the social division of labour for his survival and social cohesion arises therefrom.

The elaboration of the division of labour in modern society involves the development of professionalism, i.e. occupational identities distinct from one's territorial or familial identity. Occupational morality is at the very root of a highly developed social division of labour.

> The rules of occupational morality and justice . . . are . . . imperative. . . . They force the individual to act in view of ends which are not strictly his own, to make concessions to consent to compromises, to take into account interests higher than his own. Consequently, even where society relies most completely upon the division of labor, it does not become a jumble of juxtaposed atoms, between which it can establish only external, transient contacts. Rather the members are united by ties which extend deeper and far beyond the short moments during which the exchange is made. Each of the functions that they exercise is, in a fixed way, dependent upon others, and with them forms a solidarity system. Accordingly, from the nature of the chosen task permanent duties arise. Because we fill some certain domestic or social function, we are involved in a complex of obligations from which we have no right to free ourselves.[4]

In *Professional Ethics and Civic Morals*,[5] Durkheim elaborates his views on occupational morality. Professional ethics are categorised as intermediary between family morals and civic morals, defined as 'a code of rules that lays down for the individual what he should do so as not to damage collective interests.'[6] Rights and obligations are specific to each occupational grouping and 'can be established neither by the scientist in his study nor by the statesman; it has to be the task of the groups concerned';[7] a moral particularism, which arises out of the fact that modern economic life is too vast and too complex. The effectiveness of professional ethics depends on 'the greater the stability and the better the organisation of the professional groups themselves. . . . When they [professional ethics] fail, it is because the cohesion of the group is at fault, because as a group its existence is too shadowy and the rudimentary state of its ethics goes to show its lack of integration.'[8]

Durkheim did not directly consider the effect of the division of labour on food production, but did recognise that the division of labour is disrupted under conditions of material duress. During a famine, the division of labour contracts as less essential functions are foregone to ensure the essential one, that of provisioning adequate food supply.[9] This is a point that will be considered in greater detail in the chapters to follow.

While there is a tremendous amount of conceptual fuzziness in *The Division of Labor in Society*, its optimism regarding human adaptability to the imperatives of survival represents an important contrast to Malthus.

2 BOSERUP: POPULATION INCREASE AND TECHNOLOGY

In her book *The Conditions of Agricultural Growth*, Boserup sets out to counter Malthus's central premise that land availability was the constraint determining food supply.[10] She argues from evidence of existing Third World agricultural practices that the human response to land shortage is the adoption of more productive tools which serve to intensify land and labour usage. The succession from shifting cultivation with digging sticks to hoes, to more intensive agricultural techniques with shorter fallow periods and ploughs, progressing to permanent mixed agriculture, was overlooked by Malthus who lived in an economy where permanent agriculture was the norm. Population growth actually serves to develop the agrarian economy technically and often materially, rather than impoverish it as Malthus argued.

The underlying assumption behind Boserup's theory is that increasing land productivity has historically been bought at the cost of labour intensification. Generally, agrarian non-market societies are unwilling to intensify their labour expenditure until population pressure and human survival needs make it imperative.[11]

In Boserup's analytical framework, population is the independent variable and is positively correlated with the dependent variable, namely, technological development in food production. Boserup shares Durkheim's optimism towards the beneficial effects of high population densities, but her stress is on the effects of population increase on technology rather than the division of labour. Labour intensification requires a restructuring of the division of labour and she clearly illustrates this with respect to women's participation in agricultural production under different agricultural regimes.[12]

In *Population and Technology*,[13] Boserup traces the effect of population growth on the development of technology and material culture. Food supply was a constraint on the growth of urban settlement and its concomitant, the elaboration of the division of labour. Ancient and medieval cities arose not so much in areas known for higher than average agricultural productivity, but rather in places where there was a particularly high density of rural population in close proximity. It is the absolute rather than the relative surplus of grain that accrued in subsistence agricultural systems that was critical to urban development in ancient medieval times.

Boserup cautions that the positive relationship between population and technological development does not persist in a coherent form once the impact of industrialisation and the world market begins to act on an agrarian economy. Transport technology and the operation of the market brings agricultural innovations to rural populations that may be adopted for other reasons than population pressure. The forces of modernisation on the part of a state bureaucracy or a particular ruling class are decisive. Nonetheless, Asia is more likely to develop faster technologically than Africa, because of its denser rural population who face land shortages and dispossession of their means of rural livelihood. The process of proletarianisation combined with a long urban tradition are more conducive conditions for industrialisation than those prevailing in the more sparsely populated African continent.

In reviewing the present Third World food problem, Boserup seems in agreement with Lewis. Cheap food imports from the developed countries' more technologically advanced and higher grain-yielding systems cause a displacement of Third World food production and heightened export crop production that leads to lower prices. Nonetheless, like Lewis, she does not conclude that the situation is futile. With the right policies and perhaps more importantly, the right 'administrative technology' a simultaneous agrarian and industrial revolution is within the reach of the developing world. 'Administrative technology' is an awkward phrase that seems to have been devised to keep the technology theme of her book consistently in the forefront. It actually denotes the social division of labour, particularly the modernising cadre involved in government decision-making and development projects.[14]

3 VARIATION ON THE CLASSICAL PROBLEM: FOOD INSECURITY AND THE SOCIAL DIVISION OF LABOUR

It is apparent from the broad sweep of history that agricultural technology does advance as population increases, but not without setbacks and painful delays, causing ill-health and early death for countless numbers. The classical economists and their followers were concerned with suggesting state and market strategies for rectifying the imbalance between food production capability and food demand by a growing population. They assumed that the state and market were viable social institutions capable of serving as the organisers of the society's agricultural work effort. It is only Lewis who throws some shadow of doubt onto the situation with his emphasis on institution-building. Some developing countries clearly do not have entrepreneurs and market rationality or a state and modernising cadre strong enough to give sufficient impetus to technological development. There are other social institutions that are determining technology choice in these societies. And the question to be answered is why, despite the formalistic presence of the state and market in these societies, there is relatively little content to their operations. What is holding back their effectiveness?

Insight can be derived from being more analytically precise about the division of labour. Durkheim defined the division of labour as the economic interdependence of specialised producers and the ideologically cohesive force of occupational morality. I have chosen to define it as the combination of economic interdependence through labour specialisation, function-based morality and social institutions. The occupational moralities can then be more precisely identified relative to their role in the societies' social institutions. As social institutions, the market and state are clearly pivotal, but there are others, notably, in the Tanzanian case, clientage networks and households, each of which has its own morality.

But how does food production capability relate to this expanded notion of the social division of labour? The interaction of food production capability and population is mediated by technology and the social division of labour. While the long-term tendency is for food production capability to respond to population growth, nonetheless, in the short-term, restricted food production capability is a constraint on the quality if not the quantity of population. In other words, population growth may proceed under food supply constrictions, but the standard of living and dietary intake will suffer.

It is interesting that almost all the authors reviewed assumed that restricted food supply would engender positive human efforts to increase food production and distribution. Malthus, however, viewed such efforts as futile because of the limits of land availability. Durkheim, on the other hand, acknowledged the destructive effects of famine on the social division of labour, but did not extrapolate its consequences.[15]

In general, Malthus's gloomy outlook has fortunately been proven wrong as technological developments in agricultural productivity have unfolded, but in specific contexts there appears to be certain short- and medium-term bottlenecks in the development of technology and the division of labour that arises not out of any God-ordained limit, but rather from human action and social organisation. In this book it is argued that the phenomenon of food insecurity, in and of itself, can act as a limiting factor on food supply. This may seem tautological, but when seen in the context of a cycle its significance becomes clearer. Food insecurity defined as the inadequacy of the quantity and quality of food consumption, as well as its irregularity over time, can lead to the contraction and ineffectiveness of the institutions that might serve as positive spurs to the enhancement of food production and distribution. In so doing, food insecurity acts as the independent variable holding back the development of the division of labour and technology that could bring about an increase in food production. Figure 2.1 depicts the cycle of food insecurity and contrasts it with the schemas of the three other authors considered in this section.

Food insecurity, arising from the vicissitudes of the weather, has profoundly influenced the development of the division of labour in Tanzania. Food insecurity leads to small-scale, risk-averse tactics on the part of all economic agents who are reacting to very basic material uncertainty, i.e. whether or not they and their households will have a sufficient supply of food. The moral content and the social organisation of the division of labour have evolved around persistent food insecurity.

The household is the main unit of production. Peasant households continue to grow their own food rather than depending on market supply and specialising in production. A productive effort centred on household members' labour is linked to pro-natalist attitudes and high fertility. The resultant population growth exerts intensified pressure on food supply. Distribution of food outside the household is increasingly channeled through clientage networks as material uncertainty grows. With domination of household and clientage networks, the proliferation of functional groups is restricted to that made possible by face-to-face accountability or household ties. A circularity sets in whereby this particular configuration of the division of labour and social organisation can serve to perpetuate or even heighten food insecurity, by its limited scale, its barriers to outside innovation and to the free flow of food between deficit and surplus areas through market channels, as well as the consequent impediments to the development of food production technology.

The low density of the agricultural population and a severe lack of transport infrastructure contributes to the dominance of the household and clientage networks over the state and market. Formally the

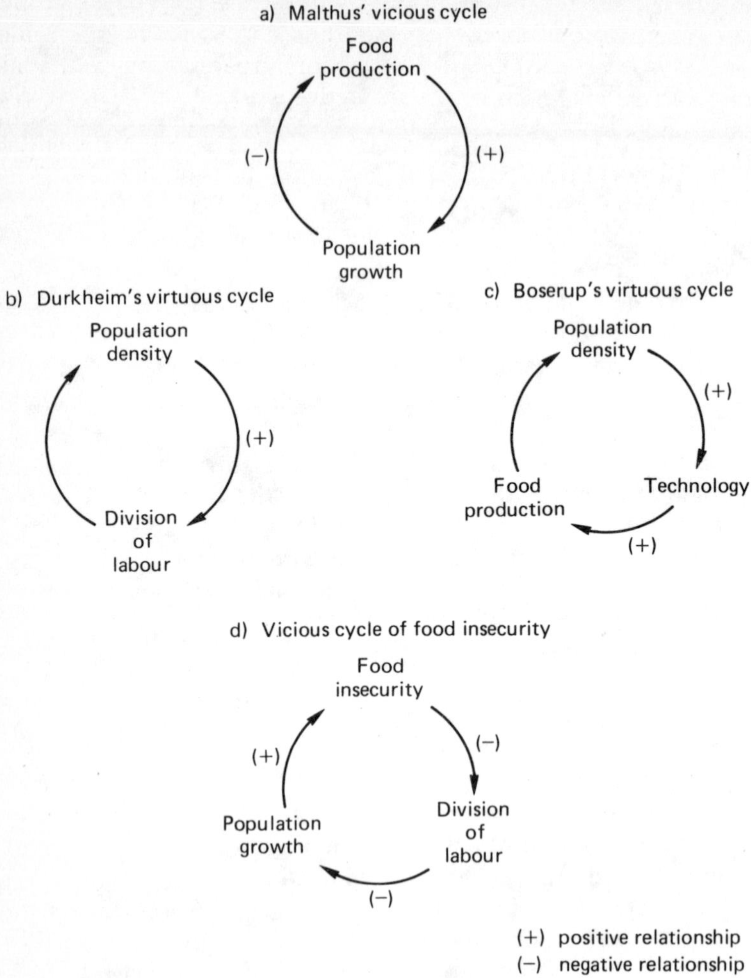

FIGURE 2.1 *The inter-relationships between food supply, population change and the division of labour*

market and state exist, but their operation is modified by the household and clientage networks, which lend them their substantive social, economic and moral content.

Food insecurity arising from low, erratic food output is an impediment to Tanzanian national development in the transition from rural agrarian to urban industrial society. This tendency should be seen in the context of contradictory forces at work. On the one hand, there exists embryonic economic accumulation and social change leading towards an expanded division of labour, urbanisation, industrialisation and the evolution of the 'collective worker' whose work discipline is akin to Durkheim's notion of occupational morality. On the other hand, there are social forces responding to the material insecurity which take the form of personalistic strategies of the extended household and clientage networks aimed at ensuring household survival.

Summary of Part I

Essentially, food insecurity retards development of functional social groups and the organisational structure of the market and state relative to the household and clientage networks, owing to the prevalence of risk-averting, household-based strategies of all functional groups as opposed to maximising strategies of market or state agents. Food insecurity causes a reduction in the scale of the division of labour and impedes the development of the state and market. Households and clientage networks, smaller in scale and based on face-to-face interaction, encroach on state and market functions and tend to dominate under the duress of shortfalls of basic essentials such as food. With technological stagnation and a division of labour in agriculture restricted to that primarily based on sex and age within the peasant household, the age-old peasant need for household labour power influences women's fertility decision-making. Population increases, facilitated by improvements in health arising from imported medical technology. The combination of increased population exerting more food demand on a stagnant agriculture, the restricted social division of labour, and the fluctuation of weather, serve to heighten food insecurity, and so begins another round of the vicious cycle of food insecurity.

Part II
The Peasant Household, the Environment and Food Insecurity, 1919–85

In rural Tanzania, the primary unit of production and consumption is the peasant household. Food self-sufficiency is usually the peasant household's foremost productive aim.[1] Cereals and root crops constitute the bulk of the rural diet.[2] Food insecurity will be discussed exclusively in terms of these staple foods.

Because of the country's geographical and ethnic diversity, a wide variety of cereals and root crops are consumed. The most recent national household budget survey records rural household consumption in order of value as follows: maize (46 per cent), rice (12 per cent), sorghum/millet (10 per cent), bananas (8 per cent), cassava (6 per cent), sweet potatoes (5 per cent), barley (2 per cent), potatoes (2 per cent), wheat (1 per cent), and other assorted starches (7 per cent).[3]

In this section, peasant household production, demographic change and the incidence of food insecurity will be situated in their environmental context.

3 Physical Determinants of Food Insecurity and Settlement

East Africa has been identified as an area of the world particularly prone to food shortfalls.[4] Tanzanian peasants have a profound appreciation of the ecological constraints. Their farming practices are highly risk-averse. Three main physical constraints hamper if not threaten agricultural output: erratic rainfall, pest attack and rapid depletion of soil fertility.

1 RAINFALL

Except for the well-watered highland areas, which constitute only a small portion of Tanzania's land surface area, peasant cultivators have had to adopt farming practices that are conducive to low and seasonally erratic rainfall. Roughly 55 per cent of Tanzania receives less than 750 mm rainfall annually on a regular basis, an amount considered to be the minimum required for most forms of crop cultivation.

In addition to low total amounts of rainfall, much of the country is transitional between a unimodal and bi-modal rainfall pattern making rainfall highly variable from year to year. The seasonal concentration of rainfall makes early planting of utmost importance.[5] If the rains are delayed, replanting, sometimes repeatedly, becomes necessary.

2 PESTS AND PLANT DISEASES

Pest attack and plant diseases are often temperature and humidity-dependent, causing adverse weather and infestation to coincide. Food crop loss due to disease and pest attack in the field cannot be estimated, while post-harvest storage losses are reckoned at 20–30 per cent.[6] Chemical control of pests and plant diseases is not practised by most farmers and was virtually absent in African farming before the 1950s. The cultivation of mixed crop stands in numerous plots was the farmer's main and sometimes only means of preventing plant diseases and insect attack.

The plant diseases that most seriously affect grain and root crop yields in the field are streak- and mosaic-disease and the parasitic weed, striga. Pests are seemingly endless in number and range in size from elephants to microscopic mites. Of the insects, locusts have probably caused the most drastic losses, especially in the 1930s. Army worms are like locusts, harmless in small numbers, but multiplying quickly with increased temperature, decimating crops. Others, such as the banana borer and nematodes, spread more gradually over several years as a result of neglectful crop husbandry, to become a major drain on crop yields. The protection of ripening grain crops against bird attack requires constant vigilance in the field in the final stages of plant growth. Quelea quelea birds are particularly troublesome and in some areas during dry years can invade in vast, undeterrable numbers.

Once food crops are harvested and stored they are subject to fungus and further insect attack, being particularly prone to weevils. Often peasants' storage methods have been blamed; storage in the rafters of the house or in simple containers made of local materials offer little protection from insect and rodent attack. Exhortations to peasants to improve their grain storage and to shell maize instead of storing it on the cob have been made to try to check the rapid spread of a new pest, the insect locally referred to as 'scania', which causes severe damage to stored maize.[7] Native to Central America, this insect is believed to have been introduced with some American food aid imports in the mid-1970s.

In the 1950s, pesticides were beginning to be sold in village shops.[8] Peasants started using pesticides on cash crops, notably coffee and cotton. Virtually no research has been done on the ecological effects of pesticides in Tanzania, although some researchers suspect damage to human health and the environment are taking place as a result of haphazard usage by poorly informed farmers.[9] For example, the banana borer is now rampant in Kagera region as a result of its acquired resistance to dieldrin insecticide.

3 SOIL FERTILITY AND FARMING PRACTICES

It was only after World War II, when soil surveys and experimentation become part of a research programme under the auspices of the newly-formed East African Agriculture and Forestry Research Organisation (EAAFRO), that colonial authorities appreciated how very different tropical soils were from soils in temperate climates.[10] High temperatures and low rainfall encourage rapid rates of oxidation which result in a low humus content in the soil and a consequent clayey soil texture rather than the desired crumb-like structure of temperate soils. Hardpans, reduced water-holding capacity and soil acidity are common. Tropical downpours, often short in duration but of a very high intensity, compact the soil, causing drainage problems and leach the soil of nutrients. Rapid exhaustion of soil fertility is the net outcome of these physio-chemical processes.

It is difficult to isolate soil as a purely physical factor when farming practices are so influential in its maintenance. African farming practices have evolved around the soil fertility constraint. In Tanzania, the majority of land falls into a shifting cultivation regime whereby cropping of three to four years must be followed by fallow periods of over twenty years to restore the natural fertility of the soil. The farming practices of the Gogo of Dodoma, the numerous tribes inhabiting the vast miombo woodlands, the Mashokora cultivation of the coast, the Makuwa of Tunduru, and the Makonde thicket system of Ruvuma exemplify shifting cultivation. Fallowing of such a long duration results in a highly extensive form of agriculture, in which households are either widely dispersed through the countryside or are aggregated but subject to periodic relocation as land becomes exhausted. 'Shifting cultivation' has become the generic term for such farming practices and is associated with low population densities in the drier, tsetse-infested parts of the country. Permanent and semi-permanent cultivation, on the other hand, is found in the wetter, more fertile highland areas, with the notable exception of Sukumaland, or 'cultivation steppe', where a cattle/cropping complex has evolved, capable of supporting a large population density. Bananas are the staple of the highland areas in all but the coldest areas.[11] The Chagga of Kilimanjaro, the Haya of Bukoba, the Kara of Ukara island, the Nyakyusa of Rungwe, the Matengo of Songea, the Sambaa of the Usambaras, and the Luguru have all developed intensive forms of permanent agriculture.[12]

In the 1930s, the colonial government first became concerned with the problem of soil erosion, particularly in the arid Kondoa region of Central Province.[13] Over the years, more and more areas of soil degradation associated with population pressure were identified and the problem was attributed to three main factors: reduction of the fallow period, the expansion of populations into unfamiliar soil/ecology zones where their accustomed farming practices were not well-suited, and cattle overstocking. It was felt that traditional African farming practices, particularly shifting cultivation were undergoing rapid change without the requisite adjustments to safeguard soil fertility.[14]

4 PEASANT RISK AVERSION

Tanzanian peasant agriculture is primarily devoted to subsistence food production and exhibits a variety of cropping patterns and practices finely tuned to compensate for the precariousness of the physical environment.

In the absence of reliable statistics on annual production, it is impossible to measure the effect of rainfall variation on total grain production over time or space. However, net grain import/export statistics do exist for the period under review. They provide a long and consistent record of Tanzania's grain supply situation from which inferences can be made about domestic grain production. Table 3.1 lists net import/exports of maize, rice, sorghum/millet and wheat between 1920 and 1984.

Table 3.2 provides national summary data on rainfall by year and Table 3.3 correlates this data with net grain import/export figures. The results show a significant correlation for the most recent period between 1970 and 1980, particularly for maize. This might suggest that food imports and by inference grain production, are more sensitive to rainfall fluctuation after national independence in 1961, and that peasant farming is becoming more rather than less physically vulnerable. There is no evidence of a decline in rainfall over time; the mean annual rainy season precipitation for all fifteen stations for the three successive 21-year periods was 923, 981 and 972 mm.

Given the unreliability of rainfall, risk-averting farming practices are found throughout Tanzania, whatever the degree of cashcropping and cattle-owning. The most important one is intercropping. In the 1971 Agricultural Census, 52 per cent of all food crop hectarage was reported as intercropped.[15] One of the most common crop combinations is a grain and a legume, such as maize and cowpeas. Agronomists acknowledge that intercropping is a sound practice. Different root depths are good for water balance, legumes are nitrogen-fixing and thereby enrich the soil, and most importantly, combining crops

TABLE 3.1 *Net imports/exports of maize, rice, millet/sorghum and wheat by year, 1920–84 (quintals)**

Year	*Maize*[+]	*Rice*	*Millet/ sorghum*	*Wheat*[§]	*Total grain*
1920	5470	8518	136539	–8633	141894
1921	10753	24299	119342	–9191	145203
1922	18965	3928	102083	–12142	112834
1923	3905	26971	62096	–11520	81452
1924	22474	27090	80607	–15093	115078
1925	–15288	11010	33871	–22028	7565
1926	–30826	10891	29592	–26980	–17323
1927	–26474	20680	36792	–34067	–3069
1928	–9012	21642	78725	–40495	50860
1929	–49731	–23567	48207	–48105	–73196
1930	–61300	12531	18107	–54301	–84963
1931	–10452	33487	53663	–39359	37339
1932	26082	50512	42610	–32704	86500
1933	–29429	60849	28966	–38769	21617
1934	–77854	59829	27854	–40462	–30633
1935	–107176	46307	36625	–44152	–68396
1936	–100032	61506	36188	–51288	–53626
1937	–74488	85707	42637	–49120	4736
1938	–138755	78464	18500	–44477	–86268
1939	–133040	95785	57780	–33982	–13457
1940	–38143	151749	22706	–30215	106097
1941	–90693	179424	10100	–24365	74466
1942	–96086	180860	13979	–25298	73455
1943	–18810	47580	–5264	–24527	–1021
1944	–27287	44769	112	–141449	–123855
1945	–186110	21219	38050	–25703	–152544
1946	–290874	713	–65897	3380	–352678
1947	–43152	26625	32552	136	16161
1948	–112784	65673	–134485	–47143	–228739
1949	1055	28201	759	–3	30012
1950	–455001	–29730	–3822	–159276	–647829
1951	21646	8884	–40828	–140023	–150321
1952	84979	–5461	–19961	–166069	–106512
1953	–524677	–725	–8571	–187862	–721835
1954	–190249	–6450	2394	–184377	–378682
1955	358004	8011	–121988	–173665	70362
1956	1107630	11596	–56830	–145983	916413
1957	88226	–12284	–15637	–201170	–140865
1958	214864	11460	–59322	–285227	–118225
1959	316877	–10310	–40018	–206351	60198
1960	704188	22144	62904	–298611	490625
1961	–434730	7393	5774	–284741	–706304
1962	–496043	–4466	–80189	–311591	–892289

TABLE 3.1 *continued*

Year	*Maize*[+]	*Rice*	*Millet/ sorghum*	*Wheat*[§]	*Total grain*
1963	–177418	5912	–67823	–224965	–464294
1964	339675	27866	–19082	–283083	65376
1965	828	–22565	24848	–379686	–376575
1966	–165479	–121563	37208	–255890	–505724
1967	–54572	–29494	76630	–292814	–300250
1968	273767	–150950	13936	–480188	–343435
1969	32389	–80168	33826	–184619	–198572
1970	190115	–67829	72810	–319192	–124096
1971	4716	–58474	89690	–240353	204421
1972	–1438200	–4255	30408	–418237	–1830280
1973	–244006	–6631	41815	–83553	–292375
1974	–482843	–711626	6640	–1026980	–2214810
1975	–2404640	–639777	–47720	–1351360	–4443500
1976	–745566	–87835	–341	–149691	–983433
1977	–271601	–520729	–57	–580806	–1373190
1978	362927	–471815	99968	–751683	–760603
1979	159204	–253087	136449	–328538	–285972
1980	–2514030	–1026770	22311	–440681	–3959170
1981	–1552520	–450558	–72	–596892	–2600000
1982	–1330750	–1033110	–9935	–686959	–3060750
1983	–1210018	–638467	0	–110962	–1959447
1984	–1068028	–257738	0	–463128	–1788894

NOTES
* Negative number denotes net imports.
+ Includes maize flour: 1.0526 maize equivalent
§ Includes wheat flour: 1.3333 wheat equivalent
SOURCES
1. Tanganyika Blue Books 1920–45.
2. Tanganyika Trade Reports 1946–8.
3. East African Trade Reports 1949–76.
4. Tanzanian Trade Reports 1977–84.

with different water requirements mitigates the possibility of a total harvest failure.

Because of differences in soils and micro-climate effects, farmers prefer to cultivate several scattered fields rather than one large holding to minimise the risk of crop failure. The 1971 Agricultural Census recorded that 54 per cent of all holdings were fragmented into more than one field.[16]

Cattle overstocking, the bane of the agricultural officer, is another risk-averting practice on the part of the individual farmer. The

TABLE 3.2 *Annual rainfall variation, 1920/21–1980/81*

Year	Arusha	Bagamoyo	Bukoba	DSM	Dodoma	Iringa	Kigoma	Mahenge	Mbeya	Musoma	Mwita	Tabora	Tanga	Tunduru	Utete	National rainfall indicator+
	*Rainfall Stations' Annual Variation:**															
1920/21	n.a.	n.a.	2	n.a.	n.a.	31	n.a.	n.a.	n.a.	n.a.	n.a.	n.a.	n.a.	n.a.	n.a.	17
1921/22	–16	–75	–190	–70	n.a.	178	–159	–3	n.a.	–58	n.a.	–37	14	–30	–4	–38
1922/23	54	–134	–146	–182	–53	–64	–25	33	n.a.	–57	n.a.	113	–25	–39	n.a.	–44
1923/24	–18	–81	–36	–85	–64	–41	–59	2	n.a.	n.a.	n.a.	25	48	–132	–22	–39
1924/25	–186	–32	–106	–150	–90	–126	–43	–173	n.a.	–55	n.a.	–146	–181	108	–157	–103
1925/26	107	36	32	93	42	–61	175	–29	n.a.	77	n.a.	257	8	–189	–40	39
1926/27	–37	–70	–71	–52	23	93	69	–20	n.a.	81	n.a.	28	–57	–106	–56	–13
1927/28	–69	52	82	150	–145	33	–202	–110	n.a.	–149	n.a.	30	28	–59	–106	–36
1928/29	–130	–149	–78	–43	15	–59	–152	–147	–114	–123	–79	–97	–25	22	–80	–83
1929/30	59	14	–35	69	165	150	–12	78	123	24	111	107	–3	84	74	67
1930/31	22	69	45	28	–90	–82	–30	–7	n.a.	–60	–87	6	98	–82	–49	–16
1931/32	114	82	–73	88	–47	5	124	38	n.a.	–94	–33	20	–5	21	76	23
1932/33	–105	–198	–99	–102	49	–82	30	12	3	–75	–90	–29	53	–83	–1	–48
1933/34	–87	8	–96	2	18	110	–270	–37	–61	–161	138	–66	2	11	68	–28
1934/35	75	25	–125	11	–74	33	56	222	–3	–97	–91	20	–28	–41	–138	–10
1935/36	89	33	–9	134	68	177	–18	80	165	132	49	–3	277	86	46	87
1936/37	16	–46	–28	–16	79	125	15	–34	–16	158	–20	41	–74	67	3	18
1937/38	3	44	63	38	25	–48	–98	–150	–89	–102	–36	13	79	–121	68	–21
1938/39	57	18	96	75	–104	–50	30	–142	–126	–85	1	–56	117	–19	28	–11
1939/40	48	131	–63	59	31	65	30	24	24	–9	–3	–9	10	112	–30	28
1940/41	–163	–109	–126	–152	67	–4	–71	2	–26	–89	–46	–47	–42	6	–81	–59
1941/42	250	284	162	n.a.	219	161	147	5	74	37	–5	180	48	–11	194	125
1942/43	–56	–71	–50	77	–70	4	–166	–72	–24	14	8	–33	89	28	165	–10
1943/44	5	19	–21	–62	–33	–40	–134	–23	–69	–47	–188	–139	48	–63	64	–46
1944/45	64	–15	160	–17	156	289	58	142	33	40	198	–17	74	196	140	100
1945/46	–3	–86	–187	–74	–51	–130	66	–62	–122	–83	–196	9	–91	–149	–224	–92
1946/47	169	118	161	134	231	101	6	–27	57	35	11	108	115	237	184	109

TABLE 3.2 *continued*

Year	Rainfall Stations' Annual Variation:* Arusha	Bagamoyo	Bukoba	DSM	Dodoma	Iringa	Kigoma	Mahenge	Mbeya	Musoma	Mwita	Tabora	Tanga	Tunduru	Utete	National rainfall indicator+
1947/48	–40	101	37	–6	–65	37	–87	–47	–30	46	–93	–25	–51	91	48	–6
1948/49	26	–2	–167	–97	–73	–188	27	–85	–170	–189	–128	–224	–15	–79	–104	–98
1949/50	124	157	22	–79	13	–127	137	–54	98	105	63	–65	–27	–5	n.a.	26
1950/51	–46	–104	–73	–38	24	62	10	–47	–21	–26	–49	147	–27	–31	–30	–17
1951/52	61	65	132	–115	7	70	74	42	65	75	107	–27	52	65	–20	44
1952/53	–76	–41	54	–34	–204	–124	–48	–42	–180	–156	–106	–172	75	–135	n.a.	–85
1953/54	n.a.	–9	–33	120	–105	–46	–41	–55	–271	104	–57	–81	6	13	–86	–39
1954/55	n.a.	–15	12	175	–30	–15	74	–23	–10	–21	n.a.	–106	66	30	141	21
1955/56	–105	–3	–84	–8	1	21	42	113	50	31	–5	–50	–166	243	–67	1
1956/57	–26	–44	–103	79	15	140	–36	–19	86	82	–4	–9	57	–18	91	19
1957/58	20	–37	–103	–117	119	25	–125	17	–63	–36	–49	–44	31	46	–9	–22
1958/59	–66	–65	–65	n.a.	35	–89	10	–99	–25	62	–123	–68	–8	62	–120	–40
1959/60	n.a.	–105	47	–72	199	4	141	36	147	188	164	144	–42	40	–52	60
1960/61	n.a.	–22	119	–100	–131	n.a.	–35	n.a.	–46	–60	–108	0	–115	–147	–30	–56
1961/62	64	268	122	253	146	85	219	233	191	359	244	305	n.a.	n.a.	145	203
1962/63	–33	–33	81	19	–81	–59	144	n.a.	–24	29	74	163	n.a.	84	64	33
1963/64	246	5	101	75	119	–10	18	111	45	93	49	174	90	40	217	92
1964/65	–181	–117	–53	–129	–34	–117	–40	–50	40	–74	–59	–85	–199	–107	n.a.	–86
1965/66	7	198	81	34	–83	–109	16	153	–51	81	64	–5	39	–212	–74	9
1966/67	–119	100	37	–84	–119	108	–155	–163	135	–76	134	–7	–77	–55	n.a.	–24

1967/68	137	135	180	35	231	199	79	142	148	53	94	109	146	318	37	136
1968/69	–71	n.a.	130	16	–173	–112	21	–58	–49	99	–45	–88	–75	27	49	–24
1969/70	0	–61	–106	n.a.	–11	25	–31	–84	14	42	–114	–10	–133	–37	–142	–46
1970/71	–31	–54	11	–32	67	–154	17	–49	175	–2	5	–38	–106	29	–73	–16
1971/72	–20	90	61	109	–2	13	92	–71	–29	–84	69	–129	–39	11	–40	2
1972/73	–7	–19	239	68	70	–61	–42	10	26	19	97	–100	113	–26	9	26
1973/74	n.a.	–3	32	–140	–25	n.a.	91	42	–71	69	36	–19	–143	–71	–40	–19
1974/75	n.a.	–113	–62	–53	–99	14	–190	–161	–39	–105	–78	–98	–157	–13	45	–79
1975/76	–146	–69	60	27	–80	–107	12	164	–23	–104	56	16	–26	–16	–64	–20
1976/77	–54	–143	–86	–132	–74	–108	–1	–22	–94	–101	–160	–7	–158	–34	–190	91
1977/78	186	61	107	113	–13	–7	99	86	34	81	8	56	187	45	–19	68
1978/79	n.a.	156	124	253	68	–51	86	283	221	143	155	n.a.	234	5	204	145
1979/80	n.a.	–132	–40	–52	31	–60	–70	n.a.	–6	–17	115	–13	–109	32	–41	–28
1980/81	–120	–22	–70	–47	–101	–27	109	98	–107	26	n.a.	81	n.a.	–41	28	–15

NOTES

* The residual resulting from the subtraction of the rainfall station's overall mean from the annual rainy reason rainfall total divided by the rainfall station's rainy season standard deviation. In other words, the deviation of the annual rainy season rainfall total from the overall rainy season mean expressed as a percentage of the standard deviation; a positive value representing greater than average rainfall.

$$\frac{x - \bar{x}}{\text{s.d.}}$$

\+ The mean of all the rainfall stations' annual percentage residual values as calculated above.

SOURCE

Compiled from Tanzania Meteorology Department rainfall statistics.

TABLE 3.3 *Spearman's rank correlation coefficients for the annual national rainfall indicator⁺ and net grain import/export, 1920–82*

Net grain import/export unit	*Years:* 1920–82	1920–29	1930–39	1940–49	1950–59	1960–69	1970–1980
All grain	.009						
All grain per capita	.017	–.176	.224	–.006	.539	–.115	.636**
All grain per urban resident	.040	–.176	–.224	–.030	.515	–.115	–.536
Maize	.102*	–.272	.091	–.309	.515	.024	.736***
Rice	.030						
Wheat	–.147						
Millet/sorghum	.014						

NOTES
+ See notes to Table 3.2.
* Significant at the 0.10 Level, One-tailed 'T-test'.
** Significant at the 0.05 Level, One-tailed 'D-statistic'.
*** Significant at the 0.01 Level, One-tailed 'D-statistic'.
SOURCES
National Rainfall Indicator compiled from Tanzania Meteorology Department rainfall statistics.
Grain figures as listed in Table 3.1.

accumulation of cattle is not only a means of bridewealth payment and wealth display but also an important precaution against crop failure and famine. In the event of food shortage, cattle are readily bartered or sold.[17] Cattle overstocking is a classic case of the isolation paradox. Each individual household benefits from cattle ownership, while the aggregate suffers from destruction of the resource base. What agricultural officers rarely acknowledge is that often numbers of cattle per person are declining as population and total cattle numbers increase. From the perspective of the peasant household they are not aggrandising cattle but merely trying to maintain long-established safety margins of per capita cattle ownership.

In agri-business management terms, intercropping, fragmentation of holdings and cattle overstocking are irrational because they do not optimise output and earnings. Peasant farmers however, must make their first priority that of producing their households' basic consumer needs. Having to contend with great rainfall variability means taking precautions that may reduce yields and jeopardise the physical environment in the long run.

The other ubiquitous feature of peasant household farming systems is food self-sufficiency. Even in areas where cashcropping is very well-developed, peasant households generally aim to provision their own staple food needs.[18] The extent to which they succeed varies regionally depending on climate. In periods of economic prosperity, some reliance on market supply of food may develop. In a few areas, poorer households resort to market purchase of basic foodstuffs.[19] But these are exceptions to the general rule; Tanzanian peasants have been and still remain largely self-sufficient producers of their basic food needs.

5 SETTLEMENT PATTERN AND POPULATION DENSITY

At the time of the 1978 census the total population of Tanzania numbered 17.0 million, of which 87 per cent lived in the rural areas. In the inter-censal period between 1967 and 1978, the population growth rate was 3.3 per cent per annum. Tanzania's overall population density is fairly low when compared with most non-African Third World countries. At the time of the 1978 census it was 18.7 persons per sq. km, but rural population densities ranged between 1.0 and 233.6 persons per sq. km between districts.

To a large extent, Tanzania's harsh physical environment has determined the settlement pattern and imposes continuing constraints on peasant cultivators. The two most important factors influencing the regional pattern of human settlement and defining the boundaries of agricultural zones are rainfall and tsetse fly. Tsetse is the carrier of trypanosomiasis, which causes sleeping sickness in cattle and man. Tsetse thrive in miombo woodland, amidst wild game that act as vectors. Such a plant/animal complex arises in uncultivated areas of moderate rainfall. The extent and boundaries of tsetse fly infestation have varied over time as the balance between human populations, vegetation type and wild game populations have changed. The violent upheavals of the nineteenth-century slave trade and German colonial conquest caused considerable human depopulation and movement that gave the tsetse fly room to advance. Throughout the British colonial period and to the present, over half of the country has been infested. The areas of high rainfall have high population concentrations and have remained unaffected. Tsetse makes the presence of human settlement in moderate rainfall areas difficult, so areas of low and unreliable rainfall are far more densely populated than might otherwise be expected. Cattle-keeping is practised extensively in these semi-arid areas and makes possible the support of above-average population densities.

The regional pattern of settlement has remained roughly the same for fifty years. Population is concentrated in the highlands of Bukoba, Kilimanjaro, Tanga and Mbeya, the cultivation steppe of Mwanza/Shinyanga, and finally the Mtwara region, where moderately high rainfall is associated with maritime rather than orographic rainfall. In between these far-flung concentrations, corridors of settlement crisscross; a corridor from the southwest to the northeast originating in Mbeya, Rukwa and Ruvuma passing through Iringa and Dodoma intersects with an east/northwestwards corridor from Dar es Salaam, along the Central rail-line to Lake Victoria, which dips down to Kigoma on the northern most tip of Lake Tanganyika. There is another corridor running north/south along the coast from Mtwara to Tanga. Three sparsely populated areas stand out: the arid area of Arusha in the north, the two large tsetse-infested areas centered around Tabora in the west and Lindi and Songea in the south (see Figure 3.2).

With regard to the 1931 population distribution, Gillman made the observation that two-thirds of the country's population was concentrated in one-tenth of its land surface in the highlands and cultivation steppe, whereas 62 per cent of the land was virtually uninhabited.[20] The remaining third of the population lived in the savannah and coastal hinterlands practising shifting cultivation.

With population growth of the last 30 years, one sees some spilling out into the sparsely populated and uninhabited areas Gillman referred to. The largest relative growth has taken place in the geographically unfavourable tsetse areas of Tabora, Lindi/Songea and arid Arusha.

Regional variation in levels of agricultural intensity is strongly related to the level of population pressure on the land. Table 3.4 shows district and regional over- and under-population relative to the carrying capacity of the land based on Moore's calculations[21] and Table 3.5 lists the percentage incidence of various farming practices by region according to the 1971 Agricultural Census. Table 3.6 provides the Spearman's Rank Correlation Coefficients for regional over/under-population and farming practices. The incidence of cattle-keeping, agro-pastoralism and use of ploughs gives the strongest positive correlations with the population measure. Fertiliser usage, tractors and mulching also correlate. The association between population pressure and agricultural intensification, that Boserup so incisively identified,

FIGURE 3.2 *Map – Tanzania, regions and districts, 1978*

TABLE 3.4 *Over- and under-population* by region and district, 1967*

Region/ district	*(A)* *Area (km²)*	*(B)* *Population density*	*(C)* *1967 population*	*(D)* *Population as % of regional total*	*(E)* *Population rating⁺*
ARUSHA	82098	7.1	578022	100	O Net 12%
Arusha	2978	61.0	181764	31	O
Masai	63063	1.7	106892	19	U
Mbulu	16057	18.0	289366	50	M
COAST	32117	13.0	419107	100	U Net 100%
Bagamoyo	9842	11.9	117547	31	U
Kisarawe	8936	20.2	180536	28	U
Rufiji	13339	9.1	121024	41	U

TABLE 3.4 *continued*

Regions/ districts	*Area (km^2)*	*Population density*	*1967 population*	*Population as % of regional total*	*Population rating*
DODOMA	41310	16.6	685821	100	O Net 100%
Dodoma	16576	17.9	297440	40	O
Kondoa	13208	16.1	212195	32	O
Mpwapwa	11526	15.3	176186	28	O
IRINGA	56845	11.8	668159	100	U Net 100%
Iringa	28619	8.1	230881	50	U
Mufindi	7117	16.6	118467	13	U
Njombe	21109	15.1	318811	37	U
KAGERA	28456	22.9	650571	100	U Net 27%
Biharamulo	10878	7.5	81854	12	U
Bukoba	8029	46.7	374988	58	M
Karagwe	6700	14.5	97407	15	U
Ngara	2849	33.8	96322	15	M
KIGOMA	37039	12.2	452074	100	U Net 54%
Kasulu	9324	12.8	207611	46	M
Kibondo	16058	8.5	136918	30	U
Kigoma	11657	9.2	107545	24	U
KILIMANJARO	13210	47.4	625858	100	O Net 76%
Kilimanjaro	5310	89.7	476223	76	O
Pare	7900	18.9	149635	24	M
LINDI/MTWARA §	82748	12.2	1007381	100	U Net 23%
Kilwa	13852	7.1	97957	10	U
Lindi	9454	24.1	228062	23	M
Nachingwea	42735	1.9	80482	8	U
Masasi	8936	23.9	213683	21	U
Mtwara	3756	30.4	114345	11	U
Newala	4015	68.0	272852	27	O
MARA	21756	24.3	528713	100	M Net 100%
Musoma	17871	19.0	340177	64	M
N. Mara	3885	48.5	188536	36	M
MBEYA/ SUMBAWANGA**	83140	11.5	956574	100	U Net 63%
Chunya	27066	2.0	53618	6	U
Mbeya	18519	9.9	180208	19	U
Mbozi	9583	15.4	147489	15	U
Rungwe	5180	69.5	359971	38	M
Sumbawanga	22792	9.4	215288	22	U
MOROGORO	73039	9.0	659842	100	U Net 71%
Kilosa	14245	13.6	193810	29	M
Morogoro	19296	15.1	291110	44	U
Ulanga	39498	4.4	174922	27	U

MWANZA	19677	51.9	1020080	100	O Net 64%
Geita	9065	41.0	371407	36	M
Kwimba	6087	50.2	305516	30	O
Mwanza	3885	60.3	234080	23	O
Ukerewe	640	170.7	109277	11	O
RUVUMA	61255	6.4	393043	100	U Net 100%
Mbinga	8418	13.7	144098	37	U
Songea	34059	4.4	151390	38	U
Tunduru	18778	5.2	97555	25	U
SHINYANGA	50761	17.7	899468	100	O Net 20%
Kahama	19943	7.4	147628	16	U
Maswa	21368	20.2	430916	48	M
Shinyanga	9450	34.0	320924	36	O
SINGIDA	49341	9.3	457938	100	O Net 23%
Iramba	7900	23.3	183962	40	O
Manyoni	28620	2.8	80157	18	U
Singida	12821	15.1	193819	42	M
TABORA/ MPANDA++	121989	4.4	541859	100	U Net 44%
Nzega	13727	22.0	302017	56	M
Tabora	62419	2.9	179039	33	U
Mpanda	45843	1.3	60803	11	U
TANGA	26808	26.5	710002	100	O Net 46%
Handeni	13209	10.1	133235	19	M
Korogwe	3756	37.4	140306	20	O
Lushoto	3497	60.2	210484	30	O
Pangani	1425	19.9	28426	4	U
Tanga	4921	40.1	197551	29	M

NOTES

* 'Over-', 'under-' and 'moderately populated' districts represent the ratio between Moore's computed carrying capacities and the actual 1967 population:

O – 'overpopulation', ratio under 0.80
M – 'moderately populated', ratio 0.80–1.49
U – 'underpopulated', ratio over 1.50.

\+ The regional population rating is arrived at by multiplying proportional district populations, column (D), by coefficients of +1, 0 and –1, for over-populated, moderately populated and under-populated, respectively, then adding the totals.

§ Lindi and Mtwara regions were combined in 1967.

** Mbeya region included Sumbawanga district in 1967. Sumbawanga later became part of Rukwa region.

++ Tabora region included Mpanda district in 1967. Mpanda later became part of Rukwa region.

SOURCES

Compiled from:

1. Moore, J.E., 'Rural Population Carrying Capacities of the Districts of Tanzania', *BRALUP* Research Paper No. 18 (1971) p. 15.
2. Tanzania, *1967 Population Census*, vol. 3.

TABLE 3.5 *Farming characteristics and practices by region, 1971*

Region	*Sex ratio of adult family workers*	*Percentage of holdings using:* Irrigation	*Modern fertiliser*	*Farmyard manure*	*Compost*	*Green manure*	*By-products*	*Mulching*
Arusha	101	3.9	24.1	34.0	4.9	1.4	35.2	12.2
Coast	80	0.1	1.2	0.0	0.1	1.9	32.6	0.0
Dodoma	84	0.0	5.2	28.4	0.1	0.0	12.1	0.2
Iringa	81	2.8	5.2	8.6	0.2	2.7	33.3	4.6
Kagera	69	0.0	5.2	8.7	5.6	7.0	45.7	32.0
Kigoma	68	0.0	0.1	16.8	10.9	0.0	59.4	0.2
Kilimanjaro	67	32.7	3.7	47.4	3.1	2.3	39.0	24.5
Mara	82	0.5	1.9	3.0	0.2	0.0	48.9	0.7
Mbeya/ Sumbawanga	87	4.3	8.6	4.3	2.9	1.9	46.3	1.1
Morogoro	79	1.5	0.6	0.0	0.0	0.0	84.8	0.0
Mtwara/ Lindi	85	0.6	1.3	0.0	0.0	0.8	34.7	6.5
Mwanza	95	0.8	8.9	5.8	1.5	6.2	32.0	5.0
Ruvuma	85	0.5	17.9	3.2	3.1	17.5	48.9	0.8
Shinyanga	102	2.3	13.5	5.6	3.4	0.7	46.6	0.3
Singida	86	0.4	19.5	17.7	0.0	4.4	46.9	0.0
Tabora	97	0.1	18.1	19.6	1.1	8.3	42.5	3.4
Tanga	83	5.1	2.1	7.1	2.0	2.8	69.4	2.0
TOTAL	85	3.2	7.4	11.0	2.1	3.1	44.5	5.9

Region	Per agricultural worker: Hoes	Ploughs	Carts	Tractors	Oxen	Donkeys	Cattle
Arusha	0.88	.0421	.0048	.0017	.1415	.0215	5.80
Coast	1.26	–	–	.0012	–	–	0.03
Dodoma	1.92	–	–	–	.0143	.0055	2.43
Iringa	1.44	.0288	.0023	.0010	.0323	.0031	0.80
Kagera	1.72	–	.0023	.0041	–	–	0.44
Kigoma	1.08	–	–	.0009	–	–	0.35
Kilm.	1.40	.0012	.0132	.0079	.0065	.0022	0.87
Mara	3.35	.1366	.0050	.0006	.2993	.0061	2.98
Mbeya	1.19	.0050	.0034	.0016	.0649	.0017	0.85
Morogoro	1.25	–	–	.0019	–	–	0.23
Mtwara/ Lindi	1.20	–	.0042	.0008	.0047	.0060	0.01
Mwanza	1.38	.0162	.0007	.0027	.0515	.0096	1.77
Ruvuma	1.46	–	.0052	–	–	–	0.10
Shinyanga	1.13	.0737	.0119	.0036	.1982	.0012	2.08
Singida	1.24	.0399	.0068	–	.1140	.0120	2.91
Tabora	1.32	.0687	.0024	.0013	.1857	.0028	2.45
Tanga	1.11	.0002	.0007	.0018	.0004	.0009	0.55
TOTAL	1.68	.0266	.0062	.0020	.0641	.0044	1.41

SOURCE
Tanzania, *Agricultural Census of Tanzania 1971/72*, vol. I, *Peasant Farming* (DSM: Bureau of Statistics, 1979), Tables 6, 7, 15, 17.

TABLE 3.6 *Spearman's rank correlation coefficients of regional over-/under-population and farming characteristics and practices*

Farming characteristics and practices	*Regional over-/under-population*	
	All regions	*All regions except Dodoma and Singida*$^{+}$
Sex ratio of adult family workers	.194	.196
Holdings per capita usage of:		
Irrigation	.140	.393
Modern fertilisers	.262	.243
Farmyard manure	.583***	.489*
Compost	.093	.345
Green manure	–.031	.039
By-products	–.180	–.034
Mulches	.223	.488*
Regional per capita number of:		
Hoes	.039	–.111
Cattle	.600***	.600**
Oxen	.412	.482*
Ploughs	.447*	.448*
Tractors	.248	.625***

NOTES
+ Omitted because extreme semi-aridness puts special constraints on agricultural intensification.
Two-tailed 'D-statistic' Significance Levels
* .100
** .050
*** .020
SOURCES
As listed in Tables 3.4 and 3.5.

is strongly reflected in Table 3.6.[22] High population densities and plough agriculture co-exist.

Evidence from the colonial period seems to support Boserup's thesis that the transition from shifting cultivation to plough agriculture arises from exigencies of population growth.

4 Characteristics of the Peasant Household Farming Unit

Before colonial rule was established in the 1890s, Tanzania was a collection of local tribal agrarian economies loosely bounded by long-distance trade in hunting and gathering products, notably ivory, salt and copal. The smallest unit of economic endeavour was not the household, but rather the lineage or, in the case of some tribes, the age-grade. After the establishment of colonial rule this gradually changed. Colonial economic policy aimed at a higher level of economic production and circulation than that which could be sustained on the basis of hunting and gathering. Agriculture was to become pivotal to commodity production, in addition to being the foundation of subsistence production. Agriculturalists and pastoralists were drawn into commodity exchange through the imposition of taxes, and in this way a peasantry was created. The unit of tax collection was the residence of the reproductive couple referred to as the 'hut', and peasant households began to displace lineages as the primary unit of social organisation. The social force of lineages and age-grades was to continue, but as units of economic reckoning they would become increasingly subsidiary and supportive to strategies of survival and accumulation based on the smaller household unit.

As a production unit, the peasant household is relatively small and based on familial relations. Because it serves as a unit of human reproduction and consumption, its productive, reproductive and consumption strategies all interlock. It has a great deal of autonomy over its labour resources, but the state is involved in defining its access to land and capital.

1 THE HOUSEHOLD LABOUR FORCE

Tanzanian peasant agriculture is premised on household labour. In the past and continuing to the present, relatively few peasant households have hired in labour. During the colonial period, although migrant wage labour was prevalent in many areas, there is not much evidence of wage labour being employed on peasant holdings. Traditional forms of labour exchange were more common. Until 1925, chiefs could call on their subjects to perform labour service.[1] Amongst the peasant producers, communal labour parties were often called for harvesting and strenuous work of an infrequent nature.

In the post-independence period, peasant wage labour is found in some areas, but it is by no means widespread nor deeply entrenched. The 1971 Agricultural Census records only 0.4 per cent of all peasant agricultural labour as other than household labour.[2] In a more recent 1980 survey of 20 villages in 8 regions by Collier *et al.*, 90 per cent of the labour force gave their main or only occupation as farming and only 1 per cent of total agricultural labour was allocated to non-household, non-communal farm work.[3] Since the hiring of labour has been actively discouraged by the post-colonial government, these survey figures may be subject to under-reporting. Nonetheless, in comparing Tanzania with the rest of the Third World, or even with neighbouring Kenya, the relative absence of a labour market in the peasant sector is striking.

In 1978, the average rural household size was 5.0, ranging from 3.7 to 6.3 between regions.[4] The household labour force is characterised by a division of labour on the basis of age and sex. Task allocation varies somewhat between tribal groups but most areas fall into Boserup's 'female farming' category.[5] Generally, men are expected to clear the land and assist in planting, while women provide the bulk of hoeing and weeding work. In those areas where ploughs have been adopted, women are sometimes found ploughing, but more significantly the larger acreages that can be farmed with ploughs increases the time women must devote to weeding.[6]

Fifty-four per cent of the rural household labour force was female in 1971.[7] Studies of various rural areas of Tanzania have revealed that women are generally working longer hours than men.[8] Detailed labour time studies have been concentrated in the Kagera Region (West Lake). Men's yearly labour expenditure in crop production was 84 per cent of that of women in Rald and Rald's 1969 village survey.[9] During the day, men distributed their activities proportionately between agricultural work (45 per cent), leisure (44 per cent) and social activities (11 per cent), whereas the corresponding figures for women were 59 per cent, 29 per cent and 12 per cent. Historically, men have had a stronger presence in cashcropping throughout Tanzania while women have held greater responsibility for food crops.

2 THE HOUSEHOLD FERTILITY PATTERN

Children's contribution to the household workload and their responsibilities to aged parents, makes each child an asset to the household. Female fertility is held in high esteem. Motherhood is considered to be the most important role a woman could ever fulfill, and through it she gains social recognition and status. Traditionally it was considered natural for women to give birth to a child approximately every three or four years throughout her childbearing years. For two to three years after the birth of a baby, lactation in conjunction with sexual abstinence were moral imperatives aimed at safeguarding women from pregnancy and ensuring their babies' health. Recent census data suggests that a natural fertility regime continues to prevail. The total fertility rate for the rural areas of Tanzania was reported as 7.4 and 6.4 children, and the mean average age of first marriage was 17.9 and 17.1 years, in the 1967 and 1978 censuses respectively.[10]

Kocher attempted to identify determinants of rural fertility within the framework of neo-classical demand and supply models, measuring the relative costs and benefits of children in Kilimanjaro and Lushoto peasant households. His findings showed that fertility had a highly significant, positive correlation with infant mortality, suggesting that women do try to compensate for the death of a child.[11]

Rural infant and child mortality rates were 141 and 113 respectively in 1978. Life expectancy was 41 in 1967 and 44 in 1978.[12] The gradual decline in mortality rates and the persistence of high fertility has resulted in rapid population growth in the rural areas.

It is debatable when Tanzania's present rural population growth began.[13] Authorities tend to think that the population stagnated or even declined during most of the German colonial period, as a result of violent upheaval and pestilence. An upswing probably occurred in the 1920s.[14] Since then growth has been steady and seems to have accelerated in the 1960s.

3 HOUSEHOLD LAND

Peasants' rights to land have been subject to unwritten customary law for most of the period under study. Their actual access has been largely conditioned by the degree of under- or over-population existing in their locality. There has been little landlessness in rural

Tanzania, although many areas are supporting relatively high population densities. In the last two decades, rural over-population has been eased by a high urban migration rate.

Tanzania's land tenure policy has been eclectic during the British colonial and post-colonial periods. In the 1923 Land Ordinance, the entire territory was declared 'public land', with the exception of that land that had been alienated as freehold during the German period (roughly 1 per cent of the total).[15] The government conferred two types of tenancy on public land: leasehold private rights of occupancy for a term not exceeding 99 years and rights of occupancy to tribal communities. The latter were entrusted to 'native authorities' headed by local chiefs under a system of indirect rule. The native authorities guaranteed usufruct rights to peasant cultivators. However, by the 1950s, landlord and tenant relationships had appeared in the densely populated areas of Kilimanjaro, Upare, Ukerewe, Bukoba and Usukuma.[16]

In 1963, the post-colonial government converted existing freehold into leasehold, which for the most part pertained to non-Africans. Peasants' land rights were left in the sphere of unwritten customary law, despite the dismantling of the power of the local chiefs with the abolition of the Native Authorities. Peasants' customary usufruct rights were upheld but the local conferring agency was left ambiguous throughout the 1960s and early 1970s. The 1975 Village Act specified peasants usufruct rights and vested the Village Council with the powers of land allocation, transfer and land use planning. More recently, the Ministry of Agriculture has proposed that Village Councils grant 33-year leaseholds to villagers with a stipulation that these cannot be bought or sold but rather revert to the Village Council when the land is not being used.[17] This measure is designed to meet the criticism that the law did not ensure peasants' security of tenure and was therefore a disincentive to peasant investment in land improvement.

The 1971 Agricultural Census recorded the average peasant holding as 1.3 ha; 32.3 per cent being under 0.5 ha. Seventy-two per cent of all peasant land was 'owned or held owner-like' under customary law, whereas only 4 per cent of the land was rented, another 3 per cent was owned or held owner-like under government tenure and the remainder existed under more than one form of tenure.[18] During the villagisation programme of the mid-1970s which nucleated peasant settlements a great deal of re-allocation of land took place. Collier *et al.* record the average size of household holding in the pre- and post-villagisation period at 2.1 and 1.9 ha respectively.[19] According to their findings, the distribution of land between households before and after villagisation has not altered significantly. Fifty-eight per cent of those who owned less than 0.5 ha in the pre-villagisation period had not increased their holdings whereas 70 per cent with more than 5 ha before retained that amount after. The Gini coefficient of land concentration was a low 0.35 in the post-villagisation period, with landlessness reported as negligible.[20]

4 HOUSEHOLD NON-FARM ACTIVITIES

Collier *et al.*'s village survey found only 10 per cent of total labour allocated to off-farm activities.[21] Other studies support this low figure.[22] Beer-brewing is by far the most important non-farm cash-earning activity of rural households, except in coastal Islamic areas. For many rural women, brewing is their only means of gaining cash in an otherwise male-dominated village economy.[23] The existence of other non-farm activities tends to be limited by the low purchasing power of the villages. Periods of rural prosperity sustain an array of non-farm activities. During the mid-1950s in Bukoba, Reining found men spending a lot of time in secondary occupations, whereas in the depressed period of the early 1980s male and female farmers reported spending only 3 per cent and 1.5 per cent of their waking hours engaged in building, handicraft skills, trading and other non-farm activities.[24] Access to urban markets is another stimulus. In Rufiji district, which is proximate to the Dar es Salaam market, 60 per cent of the rural economically active population was engaged in crafts and extractive industries for market sale.[25] In more prosperous Kilimanjaro villages, 50 per cent of cash incomes is derived from non-farm production of goods destined for sale to Moshi and Arusha urban residents.[26]

Generally, except for beer-brewing and the non-farm activities of rural areas exceptionally well-connected to urban markets, most peasant households are engaged almost solely in plant and animal husbandry activities. Only during the relatively few interludes of this century when peasant agricultural commodity production experienced an economic boom owing to favourable terms of trade and weather conditions has the village division of labour been able to specialise and expand.

In summary, Tanzanian households have tended to provision their own subsistence, while participating to a greater or lesser degree in agricultural commodity production. The development of land and peasant labour markets varies over the country, but overall they are still at an embryonic stage, in part because the post-colonial government did not encourage their development and, more significantly perhaps, because population densities did not reach critical levels. The rural division of labour is based primarily on age and sex, which determines not only the allocation of the household workload, but also access to household resources.

5 The Incidence of Household Food Inadequacy

The occurrence of famines in Tanzania's history should not be over-dramatised relative to the incidence of malnutrition and seasonal hunger. Nutritionists studying famine-affected populations in Tanzania have sometimes observed with surprise that the level of malnourishment of children in famine areas is not much lower than the country-wide average.[1] Far too little is known about the identification and measurement of stages of caloric stress, let alone their consequences for the future health of the surviving victims. Famine should be viewed as an accelerated worsening of food inadequacy on a wide-spread basis rather than a sudden and sharp decline.

1 TYPES OF FOOD INADEQUACY

1.1 Malnutrition

Malnutrition is defined as a chronic state of under-nutrition caused by a deficient intake of calories and/or proteins arising from a continuously inadequate supply of food. The problem of malnutrition was not officially recognized until the late 1930s, when under the instigation of the Colonial Office, East and Central African governments began to investigate its incidence. Jerrard and A.T. and G.M. Culwick called attention to the monotony of the peasant diet and its low protein content.[2] Their findings were reinforced by the poor state of nutrition and general health of the African conscripts recruited during World War II, many of whom could not pass their physical examinations.[3]

Concern with the nutritional well-being of children and pregnant mothers did not appear until the 1950s. From then on, numerous village surveys documented growth stunting and wasting amongst children, and a high incidence of protein calorie deficiency in under-fives.[4] In addition to low or inadequate food intake, intestinal parasites are often identified as causes of children's poor nutritional status.[5]

Most of the social factors cited in the literature as being associated with children's malnourishment are related to the intra-household sexual division of labour and resource allocation: namely, men's higher calorie and protein intake relative to the rest of the household arising from their customary claims to bigger and more meaty portions of the household's cooked meals,[6] father's use of cash for drinking and eating out,[7] high female fertility,[8] male disapproval of women using family planning,[9] and male outmigration.[10] The female work load and the irregularity of meals has been identified by many as a very significant problem.[11] A recent UNICEF study argues that the irregularity of meals is in fact meal infrequency, which has an especially detrimental effect on children under four, whose small stomachs make it impossible for them to ingest large quantities of food at any one meal. Thus infrequent feeding results in inadequate total calorie consumption.[12] Low birth weight is also related to women's heavy workload. Women perform agricultural work throughout their pregnancies; the consequent low birth weight babies face higher risks of infant mortality. The UNICEF study pinpoints the severity of the female work load as the single most important factor causing infant malnutrition and mortality.[13]

Women's responsibility for household food production arises from their traditional central role in agriculture whereas men were the hunters, cattle herders and warriors. As economic and political changes deprived men of their hunting and military activities, cash-crop production filled the void, but not entirely, men enjoyed far more leisure time than women, whose working day included child-care and domestic duties in addition to their agricultural work. The deepening sexual division of labour has meant that women find it difficult to feed their children three meals a day; mid-day meals are generally forsaken, agricultural field work making them a locational impossibility.[14]

Aspects of inter-household stratification of wealth or inadequacy of village resources are cited as causes of child malnutrition less frequently. Significantly, when they are mentioned they refer to areas of dense settlement and pronounced cashcropping, especially Kilimanjaro. In these areas, the lack of cattle, land shortage and consequent lack of variety in diet have been stressed as causative factors.[15]

1.2 Seasonal hunger

Seasonal hunger is a cyclical dip in dietary intake, causing a temporary state of under-nutrition or exacerbating a chronic state of under-nutrition. Many areas have two harvests, others only one, but the cycle of food availability coupled with labour expenditure in the agricultural calendar creates identifiable periods of caloric stress. Usually the most stressful time is during the rainy pre-harvest season, when low food stocks, higher incidence of infections and parasitic diseases and peak labour demand for planting and weeding all converge.

The phenomenon of seasonal hunger was identified as the major problem of peasant food supply in the first Tanganyikan government document regarding nutrition.[16] Surprisingly little attention has been given to seasonal hunger since then.

Seasonal caloric stress is reflected in birthweights. Tanzanian peasant women whose last trimester of pregnancy takes place during the rainy season have a higher probability of giving birth to an underweight child not only because of low food stocks but also as a result of the practice of working in the field right up to the time of delivery. Bantje documents the monthly pattern of birthweights in Rufiji over a period of seven years. Birthweights tend to be lowest at the beginning and end of the rainy season in February and June, which coincides with peak labour expenditure on rice planting and harvesting.[17]

1.3 Famine

The famine record is fairly well documented for the British colonial period thanks to district annual reports and the compilation of mission records by Brooke.[18] It is more difficult to know exactly how widespread and frequent food shortages were during the first fifteen years of post-colonial rule, before the Prime Minister's Office began keeping systematic records of famine relief.

Food shortages occurred every year in one or another parts of the country. The 1920s seem to have suffered the least hardship, although this may merely be a reflection of the less complete records for that early period. The 1930s was a difficult decade for the coast from Tanga to Lindi, whereas Dodoma was hard-hit in the 1940s. In the 1950s, rural food deficits were less frequent, and although the 1960s began with severe famine on the coast and in Dodoma, rural food supplies over the rest of the decade were not problematic, except in the Rufiji valley where flooding took its toll. The 1970s and the 1980s were not so kind. Severe rural shortages were experienced in several places each year.

While Mascarenhas argues that food shortages tended to increase over the colonial period as more and more land and labour was devoted to cashcropping, Brooke contends that those areas which developed strong cashcropping were diversifying their economy and were in a position to purchase food when their food crops failed.[19] The bulk of the evidence seems to support the latter view. However, increasing population density relative to carrying capacities of the land (see Table 1.4) is probably the most important determinant of an area's vulnerability to famine. The widespread tendency to switch over from the highly drought-resistant sorghums and millet to higher yielding but less-drought resistant maize is often cited as a significant factor in increasing liability to famine in the more arid regions.[20]

2 THE INCIDENCE OF FAMINE BY AGRICULTURAL ZONE

Gillman identified five main types of land occupation and associated agricultural patterns which are used in the following to delineate regional patterns of famine and peasant response.

2.1 Banana cultivation of the highland zone

Food shortages are least likely to occur in the highland zone due to the higher rainfall and the heavier reliance on cashcrops, notably coffee. In Kilimanjaro, food shortages have been extremely rare, save for in the drier Rombo district where farmers resort to specialisation in finger millet for beer-brewing and seek wage labour in other parts of the mountain during times of scarcity.[21] While drought is less frequent, altitude does not afford escape from locusts; migratory locusts were responsible for food shortages in the Usambara mountains in 1927, 1933 and 1944.[22] As population pressure becomes more acute, the size of holdings shrinks. In the Usambaras, cropped area per family has declined over time. In the Mlalo Basin in 1947 the average family holding was 1.38 ha, whereas in the late 1970s only about 25 per cent had over 1 ha; many had less than a half ha.[23] As household holdings contracted, bananas were replaced successively with potatoes, maize and then cassava, because of environmental depletion and expansion into new areas not suited to other food crops. In Kilimanjaro and Bukoba there has been a tendency for population to spread out into the drier plains where the bananas are replaced with maize as the staple. Food risks increase.

2.2 Rice cultivation of the floodplains

Many river valleys are relatively underpopulated because of the catastrophic flooding that occurs, especially in their upper reaches. The Rufiji delta area, however, is densely populated and since the mid-1930s has experienced food shortages about one in every three years.[24] The extension of land under cultivation and deforestation have been blamed for an increase in run-off and the consequent rise in flood levels over the past fifty years.[25]

The disastrous flooding of 1968 led the government to relocate the valley's residents in villages on the plateau; the first area to be 'villagised'. Bantje argues that this has in fact heightened the incidence of food shortage in the upper reaches, where increased distance to fields has made it difficult to protect crops from animals and led to smaller plots as more time is taken up in commuting between home and field.[26]

Historically, migration out of the district in search of food has been a very common famine response. In 1940, an estimated 50 per cent of upstream householders were temporarily absent.[27] The area has always had a close association with Dar es Salaam and food appeals tend to be directed as much at urban as rural relations. The impassability of the roads during the rains has often been an impediment to effective famine relief. Over the decades, Rufiji district has been subject to depopulation, migration to Dar es Salaam being the major drain.

2.3 Millet and maize agro-pastoralism of the cultivation and semi-cultivation steppe

Agro-pastoralism is widely practiced in Sukumaland, Mbulu and the drier semi-cultivation steppe area of Dodoma and Kondoa. Cattle lend an additional margin of safety against food shortage, as they can be slaughtered for family consumption or otherwise sold when the need arises. But cattle overstocking has often been identified as the reason for soil erosion, environmental degradation and ultimate increased liability to food shortfall.

In Sukumaland (Shinyanga and Mwanza), the 1940s was a decade of severe food shortages. Mounting population pressure and fears of environmental deterioration led to the implementation of the Sukumaland Development Project. From the mid-1950s to the mid-1970s, Sukumaland was relatively free of food shortages.[28] Food shortages have been acute recently, due to poor weather and the depradations of the scania weevil. Farmers prefer to over-sell their maize, rather than take their chances storing it.[29]

Crop failures have been frequent in Mbulu and Kondoa district, both of which are areas experiencing over-stocking and hemmed in by tsetse fly. Maize is the main staple. Wheat was encouraged as an alternative staple by colonial authorities in Mbulu after World War II, but it has developed more as a cashcrop than a food crop.[30]

Severe food shortages and famines have become a way of life for the Gogo semi-pastoralists of Dodoma, Manyoni and Mpwapwa districts.[31] There is scarcity of food in some part of Gogoland almost every year. Rainfall is very low and unreliable.

Colonial authorities were quick to notice that Gogo acreages were too small to afford them adequate grain for household consumption. Colonial efforts to make the Gogo people raise their agricultural production included: the requirement that each taxpayer place half a bag of grain in a tribal famine reserve and the planting of minimum acreages of one acre per adult, half an acre per child. A viable cashcrop suitable to the semi-arid climate of Dodoma has never been found. Over-sale of food crops is common.[32]

Trading cattle for grain in the surrounding districts has been the usual first response to food shortfall. Thiele argues that such cattle sales have had a differentiating effect on households, leaving some households without any cattle and forced to seek wage labour. Following World War II, Gogo increasingly resorted to migrant wage-labour on sisal plantations, on the Groundnut Scheme, and on the commercial maize farms of Iringa's rich peasants during the 1950s. More recently, in the aftermath of villagisation, village differentiation has occurred and Gogo from less well-endowed villages work on the farms of more prosperous neighbouring villages in exchange for grain or in those villages close to Dodoma town engaged in commodity production destined for urban sale, e.g. charcoal production, tomato cultivation, etc.[33]

Latham's nutritional survey of Dodoma and Kondoa in the second year of a famine (1962/63), showed a rate of only 9.2 per cent protein calorie malnutrition in under-fives and the number of other signs of malnutrition were not much greater than in other parts of Tanzania free from famine conditions. He attributed this to the timely distribution of famine relief.[34]

2.4 Maize and millet shifting cultivation of woodland and wooded grassland areas

Woodland and wooded grassland of the east, south, southwest and west cover over two-thirds of the country, most of it tsetse-infested. The population density is low, especially in Tabora and Rukwa, where large tracts of land were completely unpopulated until recently. Maize is the major staple, although it is not suitable for some of the drier areas. Some districts, notably Handeni in Tanga region, have recurrent famine approaching the Dodoma-syndrome. Records of food supply in Bagamoyo for 34 years under British colonial rule reveal five years of famine, nine years of moderate to severe food shortage and eleven years of unsatisfactory food supply.[35]

Peasant responses to food shortage are similar to other regions. In some areas, cashcropping helps to tide people over in lean years. This is especially true of the cashewnut production of the south. In Tanga, many men have resorted to working in the sisal plantations. Drought-resistant cassava is grown extensively especially in coastal and southern areas, although it has been persistently rejected in Handeni, where droughts are frequent because it is felt that the year-round nocturnal vigilance needed in protecting it from wild pigs and baboons is not worth the effort.[36] Finally, bush foods, wild fruits and roots are eaten in this zone more than any other because of their abundance.[37]

2.5 Pastoralism

The largest group of pastoralists, the Masai, inhabit the rift valley in Arusha region. Other small pockets in Coast, Tanga, Dodoma and Singida are inhabited by a related group of pastoralists, the Baraguyu. Both the Masai and the Baraguyu have practiced fairly pure forms of pastoralism in the past with a diet primarily of milk, blood and meat. Recently, however, amongst the Masai, maize has become an important part of the diet for many, sometimes household-grown, but more often purchased, and it can now form up to 50 per cent of the diet. This change is attributed to a shortage of grazing land and to cattle diseases causing a shortage of milk.[38]

Kjaerby records the same process of increasing reliance on maize amongst the Barabaig of Northern Tanzania, but dates its origin as far back as the 1930s, when drought and trypanosomiases killed off a large number of cattle at the same time as pressures of population growth were being experienced. Numbers of cattle per capita declined from 4.3 in 1934 to 2.3 in 1965.[39] Pastoralism is suited to arid environments and famine relief has been infrequent historically. Nonetheless, as pastoralists have become more reliant on maize, food insecurity has arisen from the inadequate and sporadic supply of maize meal in the local shops. During the droughts of the mid-1970s onwards, pastoralists have not been as easily availed of famine relief as cultivators because of the long distances to distribution points and the unsympathetic response of the local bureaucracy whose ethnic connections are with the cultivating tribes.

Summary of Part II

Can Malthus' gloomy outlook be rejected in the case of Tanzania? The Tanzanian population has quintupled between 1919 and 1985. Has agricultural production increased concomitantly? Comparison of fragmentary yield data suggests that yields per hectare have remained roughly constant.[1] With the increasing number of non-food producers, i.e. the greater proportion of the rural population under 15 who are not fully involved in field production and the escalating numbers of urban dwellers, it is likely that staple food output per capita has declined, even though the food output per producer may have remained roughly constant or even increased.

There is no way of knowing total output of staple food from year to year, given the largely subsistence nature of production and the lack of records on food passing through unregulated markets. Food imports, therefore are used as a proxy. Figure 5.1 plots 7-year moving averages of net food production import/export per capita between 1921 and 1982. The annual values show a strong downward tendency, beginning with a 3.5 kg per capita net export in 1921 and ending with a net import of 15.8 kg in 1982, with fluctuations in between. Continuing with the use of the three 21-year intervals previously established for analysing rainfall data, between 1920 and 1940 net imports and exports fluctuated gently with a mean average of 0.4 kg net export per capita. During World War II and through the 1950s, the trend line first took a nose dive down to 4.9 kg net import then improved to 10.6 kg net export before sliding to a 7.1 kg net import. Fluctuations were much greater than the previous period, with an overall deficit position of 1.3 kg. The period since independence has experienced, except for the first few years, a very marked decline to as low as 28.7 kg net import per capita with an overall average of 7.5 kg net import. This suggests that food production capability is at an all-time low.

In this section, it has been argued that the physical environment, especially low and erratic rainfall, causes a continuous threat of food shortfalls. While there is no evidence of a declining rainfall trend or an increase in its fluctuation over time, correlations between annual grain imports and rainfall suggest that Tanzania has become more sensitive to annual rainfall fluctuation, especially with respect to maize, the main staple food (see Table 3.3).

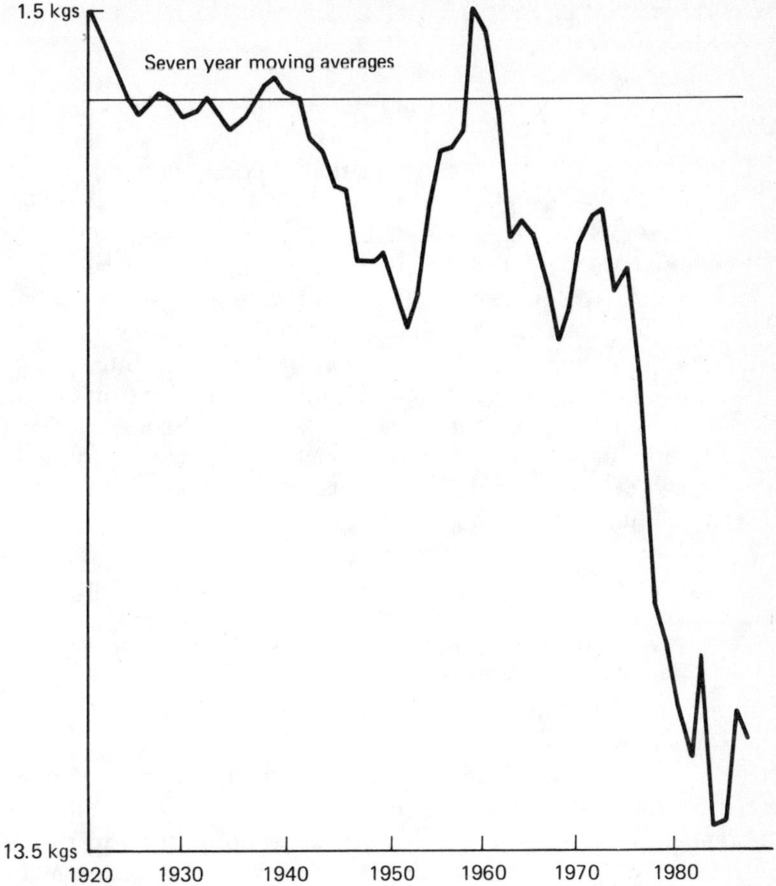

Source: Table 3.1 + population censuses

FIGURE 5.1 *Net grain import/exports per capita, 1921–84*

Tanzanian peasant farmers contend with an uncertain physical environment which, at the present level of technology, sets limits on labour specialisation and market development. The material uncertainty that the physical environment imposes profoundly affects the form and content of peasant household decision-making. Food becomes an axiomatic concern and food self-sufficiency is given precedence in household production. Household members' roles in the labour process are ascribed to them on the basis of age and sex.

Women are held more responsible for household food production than men.

Areal population densities have largely been shaped by the effort to avoid the most adverse physical environments in terms both of low rainfall and tsetse infestation. Food crop cultivation presents a very dynamic picture. While risk minimisation regarding household food needs has been the underlying theme in Tanzanian peasant food systems, as population densities increase the need for greater production per unit of land has led to an increasing reliance on maize, a crop more sensitive to low rainfall than the traditional sorghums and millets. In those areas experiencing extreme population pressure, even higher-yielding cassava has been adopted, but often at the expense of nutritional adequacy. Population pressure has given measurable impetus to labour intensification and technological development, notably the adoption of plough agriculture. With these innovations, the traditional female tasks of weeding and harvesting tend to mount within the household production unit.

The drastically increased population density that the growth of urban areas represents is a less direct pressure on the peasant household, and it remains to explore just how responsive peasant households are to it. In comparing population growth and food import figures, it is evident that Tanzanian agriculture has not been able to keep up with the food demand exerted by urban growth.

Peasant households' food insecurity was discussed in terms of three types of food inadequacy: malnutrition, seasonal hunger and famine, and evidence was provided of the within and between household differences in their incidence. Available evidence seems to suggest that women and children are most affected by malnutrition and seasonal hunger. Regional variation is very pronounced with the populous, northern, export crop-producing areas tending to experience less malnutrition and to some extent less famine than the more remote and sparsely populated southern and western parts of the country which are more tightly bound in a syndrome of food insecurity with attendant high infant mortality and fertility.

Two apparent paradoxes arise from these findings. If women perform the bulk of food production, why should they and their children experience the worst incidence of malnutrition and seasonal hunger? Why aren't women looking after their interests in intra-household food distribution? Secondly, and at an aggregate level, how can Tanzania experience a high rate of population growth under conditions of food insecurity? If ill health and child mortality abound, why is fertility outstripping mortality?

The paradoxes are related, being micro and macro-level outcomes of the convergence of production, consumption and human reproduction logics in the peasant household. Beginning at the micro-level within the household, the deepening sexual division of labour has imposed an extremely heavy workload on women and bears directly on the widespread incidence of malnutrition amongst children and infants. Taxing work and inadequate nutrition during pregnancy results in low birthweight babies whose vulnerability to infant and child mortality is high. Women's agricultural work infringes on breastfeeding and household food preparation thereby contributing to children's malnourishment. Women compensate for the high rates of infant and child mortality by giving birth to large numbers of children. High fertility expands household food demand which in turn exerts pressure on household labour, notably female labour. And so the vicious cycle continues with the population expanding and providing few incentives for capitalisation of agricultural production due because of the availability of household labour.

As this cycle proceeds at greater or lesser intensities in peasant households throughout the country, aggregate population growth is fuelled by food insecurity in the form of a high level of infant and child malnutrition and associated mortality. On the other hand, food insecurity in the form of famine and deaths arising therefrom have probably declined since 1919 relative to pre-colonial and German times as a result of state and market intervention.

The possibility of Malthusian cataclysm is remote; rather, the Boserup effect of agricultural innovation following the attainment of localised critical population densities is evident, but it appears that after the adoption of new technology, such as a new cropping pattern, mulching, and ultimately ploughs, rural populations are not stabilising immediately but are continuing to grow on the knife-edge between chronic and intense food insecurity, alleviated by out-migration to the towns or less densely populated rural areas. As long as technological innovation is achieved in conjunction with the deepening of the household sexual division of labour, rapid population growth can be expected to continue.

Part III
Extra-Household Social Institutions and Food Insecurity: State, Market and Clientage Networks, 1919–50

So far I have concentrated on the issue of food insecurity within the peasant household. The focus in the rest of the book will be on the evolution of the social division of labour outside the peasant household, namely labour specialisation in the national economy, extra-household social institutions, and their associated occupational moralities and forms of accountability. In this section, a categorisation of Tanzania's extra-household social institutions precedes a review of each institution during the period between 1919 and 1950.

6 Defining Extra-Household Social Institutions

In Chapter 4, the peasant household was examined in terms of its functions: production, human reproduction and consumption. Its consumption function is generally considered definitive, with household membership delimited on the basis of a shared cooking pot. As with all social categories, this standard definition of the household is an over-simplification of reality. It abstracts from the complexity of familial residential relations, giving precedence to consumption over production and human reproduction as well as inferring a relatively static view of the Tanzanian household that obscures the household's evolution from lineages and clans.[1] Nevertheless, the 'household' is a useful category, representing a social grouping that is the locus of concrete activities performed on a daily basis involving all of Tanzania's population. Delineating and defining Tanzania's other major social institutions is a more difficult task that requires methodological clarification.

1 DEFINING THE STATE AND THE MARKET

The state and the market are standard categories used to denote the functions of distribution, exchange, power mediation and welfare generation outside the basic household unit. However, in a society where households predominate, the household naturally assumes many distributional and welfare functions otherwise held by the state and the market. Furthermore, it is debatable whether the phenomena that are labelled state and market operations in Tanzania always adhere to standard definitions of the market and the state.

The 'state' refers to a bureaucracy adjudicating and administering according to impersonal, fixed legal norms. Bureaucratic officials are specially trained with powers that are strictly delimited. They work in a clearly established system of super- and sub-ordination that demands their full working capacity to the exclusion of other forms of gainful employment.[2]

The classical definition of the 'market' is exchange in which money price is determined by impersonal forces of demand and supply; buyers and sellers are dependent upon market exchange for their livelihood; and market prices crucially influence the allocation of resources and production. Profit maximisation is the guiding principle. Market competition generates a tendency for marginal returns and costs to equalise between competitors.

The material context of nineteenth-century Europe, which gave rise to definitions of the state and the market outlined above, was quite different from that prevailing in twentieth-century Tanzania. Tanzania is less urbanised and industrialised than Western Europe of that era. Chapter 3 emphasised how human control over the physical environment is very limited for the vast majority of Tanzanian residents and living conditions are insecure, particularly with respect to staple foods. The provisioning of basic material needs is persistently uncertain and extra-household exchange and power relationships reflect this. In a country where transport and communications are poor and material uncertainty with regard to the essential requirements of life is great, impersonal exchange and power relations of the market and state are largely precluded. Personal appeals and inter-personal cooperation or conflicts over resources appear in their place, not mediated directly by profit calculations or legalistic considerations. Rather, they are responses to survival imperatives.

These imperatives give rise to the social institution of clientage, whose importance is greatest where and when the material context is most uncertain. The social processes generated by clientage are different from that found where society is dominated by a state and a market.

It is vital to distinguish the differences in institutional configurations between societies especially between industrial and primarily agrarian societies. It is unlikely that, given Tanzania's particular material context, the categories of the market and the state can exhaustively explain the dynamics of the society. On the other hand, it would be gratuitous to discard them as categories. Tanzania is part and parcel of the twentieth-century world economy, albeit on its periphery. As a transitional society, rapidly undergoing a process of de-agrarianisation and urbanisation, Tanzania evidences elements of state and market operations in their classical form, especially in relation to the presence of state and market agents transplanted from other countries, and more latterly the impact of foreign education on nationals. The behaviour of these state and market agents is conditioned by their previous training and environment or the continued influence of another external context of reference which renders them relatively impervious to the inter-personal relations of the more materially insecure society they live in.

Section 2 focuses on the anomalous exchange and power relations of clientage whose function, structural form and content are categorised as those of a distinct social institution which interacts with, but is not subsumed to, the state and the market.

2 DEFINING CLIENTAGE

Clientage is premised on the peasant household as the basic unit of production and consumption. The social content of clientage is the relationship between peasant producers, on the one hand, and monopolist appropriators on the other. The monopolists control access to scarce resources and 'modern goods' that can provide the means of *improved* production or an enhanced standard of living. Appropriation takes place through networks of clientage such that the monopolist patrons can become clients to one another as well, since they control different goods or services and must therefore seek access to each other's resources.

Clientage relationships are conditioned by the fact that peasants retain direct access to the means of production and hence prove difficult to control directly. Monopolists have the means of achieving some degree of control over the peasantry through their control over other scarce resources and the means of *improved* production and consumption.

Generally, the patron's control over scarce goods and services arises from his strategic position *vis-à-vis* the formal state and market. Patrons are often formally agents of the state or the market, but their personalistic prestige-seeking behaviour displaces the behaviour of the professional bureaucrat or profit-minded merchant. The social relations between the producers and the monopolists and between the monopolists themselves are epitomised by non-market personalised exchanges in which the client assumes a dependent status that alleviates his material insecurity, while the monopolist patron assumes dominance which enhances his prestige and power. The patron pursues conspicuous consumption in place of productive accumulation and investment; displays and distribution of wealth attract clients. The clientage relationship is constrained neither by communally-enforced moral obligations nor state-guaranteed legal rights. It is subject only to face-to-face accountability. Hence the patron's mobility and scope for escape from the personal pressures exerted by his clients is an important factor in determining the coherence of the network.

Appropriation by unequal exchange in the market and by state taxation provides the context in which personalised exchange proliferates, since the rates of extraction rarely strike a balance between what clients can afford and what the state and merchant capital extract. Clientage relations can evolve into a fine-tuning mechanism through which the rate of extraction from the productive base and the pattern of distribution of surplus through the various levels of the network of channelled surplus are adjusted.

The clientage practices of state and market agents arise in the interstices of the state and the market, and expand to the detriment of the fabric of state and market operations. In some cases they more or less dissolve these structures and replace them with clientage networks, through which commodities, goods and services are channelled to and from the peasants.

Clientage networks form delicate branching chains which are easily broken and difficult to reconnect immediately. The networks are subject to constant imbalance, even though they arise from the need for balance. Monopolists tend to hoard goods, services, commodities, money and prestige, thus serving to reinforce the scarcity and irregularity of resources. Many monopolists have a vested interest in the stops and starts in the flow of products, services and information. Restricting information flows creates confusion and an aura of public unaccountability in which discretionary activities can proliferate. Forces outside the network, namely natural hazards and fluctuations of world market prices, constantly impinge on it, rendering the network even more fragile.

The clientage network is a poor distributive system because its tendency towards expansion and incorporation is not built around the continuous supply of commodities, goods and services for the purpose of accumulation and investment, but rather around the monopolists' attempt to aggrandise clients by increasing their own command over scarce resources. Productive accumulation and financial investment occur as fortuitous by-products rather than as the motivating force and necessary outcome of clientage practices. Financial investment and the savings behaviour it involves are anathema to clientage. Instead clientelistic 'social capital' investment is the organising principle which serves to maximise power and prestige but does not necessarily provide viable incentives for increased production and a resultant widening of the provision of goods and services through the distributive network.

Clientage's material context arises, on the one hand, out of an agrarian economy which is subject to wide fluctuations in production and, on the other hand, from the influence of the capitalist world market, international relations between nation-states and the technological advances achieved in the industrial world. The means for improved production and enhanced living standards that the monopolists channel usually originate in the industrial nations of the world.

Both the agents and the goods and services channelled by these agents are intimately entwined with the agents and operations of the state and the market, such that it may seem confusing or even pointless to distinguish clientage networks. However, since the logic of clientage is so different from and often in direct conflict with that of the state and the market, it is necessary to analyse and trace the development of clientage as a separate institution if we are to understand the nature of food insecurity and the constraints on the development of the social division of labour in Tanzania.

3 PERIODISING SOCIAL INSTITUTIONS

Most work on Tanzania is periodised on the basis of the state's transformation from a British colony to a politically independent state in 1961. This is a very formalistic periodisation which, nonetheless, is treated as a profound break by most authors. Ironically, there is little evidence that the material context of the state changed radically between the colonial and post-colonial periods.

The development of the market with respect to staple foods can be divided into four stages: the dominance of Asian merchant capital, 1919–41; a state-regulated market, 1941–57; the decline of Asian merchant capital and the rise of the African cooperatives, 1957–73; and parastatal marketing, 1973–85.

The development of clientage is more difficult to periodise since it comes to permeate state and market channels without any clear symbol to denote its presence. Despite the ubiquity of clientage relations in extra-household affairs, clientage logic and practices are embodied in particular organisational forms at different times which do not preclude the incidence of clientage elsewhere but which nonetheless typify its specific characteristics for each period. Thus the development of clientage networks can be divided into three stages coinciding with the rise and fall of three organisational forms, namely, the Native Authorities, 1919–50; the cooperatives, 1950–73; and the parastatals, 1973–85.[3]

During the 66 years under study and especially since 1950, the tendency has been for the state and the market to be engulfed gradually by clientage networks. For this reason, the stages of clientage development rather than those of formal state and market development are used as the basis for periodisation in this book. Between 1919 and 1950, the state, market and clientage were identifiably separate social institutions interacting with each other. From 1950 to 1973, there was a tendency for clientage networks to undermine the operation of the market, whereas the state retained its separate identity. Finally, from 1973 to 1985, the gradual merger of state and market operations into those of clientage took place.

7 The British Colonial State

1 COLONIAL STATE STRUCTURE AND POLICY

Tanganyika Territory, previously German East Africa, was a League of Nations mandated territory awarded to Great Britain after World War I in 1919. The territory's central administration, headquartered in Dar es Salaam, consisted of a Secretariat, High Court, Treasury and various technical departments, e.g. agriculture, labour, public works, etc. The Secretariat was composed of a Governor appointed by the Colonial Office and an Executive Council meeting once a week with day-to-day business presided over by the Chief Secretary. A Legislative Council convened three times a year. Both councils were made up of departmental heads and unofficial members appointed by the Governor who acted in a primarily advisory role to the Governor.

Tanganyika was divided into eight provinces headed by Provincial Commissioners who had the responsibility of ensuring that the Secretariat's policies were being carried out by the district administrations under their jurisdiction. There were roughly forty districts with a district commissioner in charge, supported by one or two other district officers in addition to police and technical officers, of whom the most important were the agricultural officers.

In 1926, Tanganyika's second governor, Cameron, elaborated a policy of 'indirect rule' whereby selected chiefs and other traditional authorities were delegated executive and judicial powers at the tribal level under the purview of the district administration. Indirect rule through Native Authorities was the cheapest way of governing.[1] For district administrators, it placed a buffer between them and the peasantry. The state's rural policies were first communicated to the chief, who either facilitated or impeded their implementation. A district colonial official's essential duties were to ensure the payment of taxes and the avoidance of famine.

Economic policy was directed at spurring peasants to produce a surplus over and above their immediate household food needs. The surplus was to take the form of cashcrops, be it food or export crops, or alternatively wage labour. Districts distant from the rail lines were more likely to fall in the latter category. The peasant surplus was not to be had at the expense of famine. In Governor Cameron's words: 'The natives in some localities in the Territory are exposed to periodical famine and it is the duty of the Agricultural Department to ameliorate this state of affairs; to save a native community from famine is more important that the export of many bales of cotton'.[2]

In effect, the territorial policy towards peasant production was one of household food self-sufficiency with male cash earning on the side, in the form of either cashcrop production or migrant labour. Throughout the thirty-year period under review, the lack of funds for developing productivity in peasant agriculture posed a dilemma for district administrators who had to formulate locality-specific policies that were capable of nurturing a delicate balance between subsistence food production and cash-earning activities. Failure to do so, and consequent tax default and/or food shortages, reflected the impossibility of the task, given the weather for that year and the area's potential under the prevailing level of agricultural technology. Most actively involved in this task were the District Administrative Officer and the District Agricultural Officer.

2 DISTRICT ADMINISTRATIVE AND AGRICULTURAL OFFICERS

In a number of ways, the district administrative and agricultural officers were archetypal Weberian bureaucratic agents. Operating within an office hierarchy based on written documentation, they were appointed officials with a strong professional identity and bureaucratic impartiality. Their posts consumed all their working energies and were the source of considerable social esteem.

Recruitment was highly selective with the tacit entry qualifications being a British public school and Oxbridge education.[3] A district administrative officer was responsible for the overall well-being of the district, which involved not only tax collection and peasant food supply, but also maintaining law and order, acting as a judicial officer and supervising infrastructural building such as roads and water supplies, health and educational services. Most of his duties were carried out in conjunction with the Native Authorities using Native Treasury funds.

The district agricultural officer's brief was to organise, improve and standardise African agriculture and assist in non-African agriculture in an advisory capacity upon invitation. They were expected to spend twenty days a month on safari, holding village *barazas*[4] and visiting peasants in their *shambas*.[5] The Agricultural Department was grossly understaffed. In 1927, for example, only 14 districts had agricultural officers.

Famine prevention was the agriculture department's most basic concern, especially during the drought and locust-ridden 1930s.

> It is the first duty of the department to work towards the production of adequate supplies of food for local consumption. With the possible exception of the highland areas, any part of the Territory, in any year, may suffer a partial or almost complete failure of the rains. When this occurs a shortage of grain foods is likely to arise. Furthermore the possibility of locust depredations must be taken into account, such crops as maize, sorghums and rice are particularly vulnerable to this pest. The anti-famine policy is simple; it consists of the planting of adequate areas of such root-crops as cassava and sweet potatoes, both of which are drought resistant and are not damaged by locusts to any appreciable extent. Provision exists in the Native Authority Ordinances to enforce the planting of anti-famine crops wherever necessary.[6]

All district officers worked on a 'tours of service' system. Tours lasted two and a half to three years usually followed by a home leave of six months, allowing officers and their families to return to the UK. This usually resulted in fairly brief postings of only two to three years in any one district. The Secretariat favoured frequent transfers with an interspersal of desirable and hardship postings. This system was criticised for never allowing district administrative personnel to get to know a place well enough to make a positive impact.[7]

The work of the district administrative and agricultural officers was frustrating, strictly delimited in terms of the resources at the officer's disposal and highly impersonal and distant from the peasants that were supposed to be served by British mandated administration. After World War II, A.J. Wakefield, the former Director of Agriculture, had this to say:

> the work of the Agricultural Officer was very impersonal. Almost everything we thought should be done was passed on by the Chief as an instruction to the whole community. If an officer had a strong personality and the Chief had confidence in his knowledge and

judgment, good progress could be achieved. But in this we did not think so much of the man and the well-being of his family as the prevention of famine in an area; the growing of cash crops so that taxes could be paid. (Administrative Officers were concerned with the percentage of tax collected in an area, and not what prevented the individual from meeting his obligation). All our work was pre-conditioned by the necessity to balance the territorial budget and to maintain law and order.[8]

3 OCCUPATIONAL MORALITY/ACCOUNTABILITY: FOOD AS A BUREAUCRATIC WELFARE CONCERN

It has been argued above that the district administrative and agricultural officers were bureaucratic agents. Was their behaviour on the job impersonal and impartial with regard to peasant food security? Famine prevention and relief measures were embodied in the Native Authority Ordinance of 1921, the Native Foodstuffs Ordinance of 1924, and Circular No. 33 of 1930. The former two dealt with preventive measures including planting orders and restrictions on trade and beer-brewing, whereas the latter laid out detailed famine relief procedures beginning with the precautionary measures of surveying village and regional food reserves, submission of annual district food reports, and advance identification of relief public works, specification of famine relief distribution, its financial accounting and, finally, the post-famine relief report that had to be submitted to the central government.

District officers' domestic supply of food was problematic. What was considered a 'reasonable diet for a European' was sporadically unavailable or absent virtually all the time in some desolate and remote up-country stations.[9] The tropical climate and the scarcity of refrigerators made it impossible to keep stores of many types of food.

Nonetheless, the uncertainty of district officers' food supplies did not seriously interfere with their peasant food security duties for several reasons. First of all, there was a notion of the separateness of European foods and African foods, particularly in relation to staples; Europeans preferred wheat flour as opposed to Africans' *sembe* maize flour, sorghum/millet or plantains. Second, district officers had a varied number of sources of supply which tended to be far more reliable than those of peasants. District officers' families frequently moved into a station bringing with them a large stock of imported tinned goods.[10] Households in the remoter stations often arranged to receive monthly food parcels from Dar es Salaam shops containing staples such as wheat flour, sugar, baby milk and cheese. One district officer's wife in Rufiji did not hesitate to send a runner to Dar es Salaam over a hundred kilometres away to bring back condensed milk, potatoes and shoe polish when the household ran out of these items before schedule.[11] In other areas, local Asian *dukas* sold these items. Wives of district officers often kept kitchen gardens and many officers were avid wild game hunters. When it came to purchasing vegetables, meat and dairy products in local African markets, it is interesting to note that the 'just price' principle rather than market supply and demand often operated. The 'just price' tended to be quite low and some Europeans insisted on paying more for their African-produced milk and eggs out of embarrassment whereas others, adherents of the backward-sloping supply curve theory, felt higher prices would cause labour shortages as African target earnings were achieved more quickly.[12]

Famine prevention measures were basic and usually did not require funding, being merely the loud and long exhortation to plant cassava and sweet potatoes. Famine relief measures were of an urgent nature and very few officers dared getting sidetracked onto other matters in the midst of a famine. Peasant food security was the lynchpin of district policy, to ignore it was to commit gross negligence.

The most notable incidence of administrative negligence which prevented the timely delivery of famine relief supplies occurred in Bugufi in 1929, when an estimated 500 peasants died. An official enquiry[13] into the actions of Biharamulo's District Officer, and Bugufi's Assistant District Officer, revealed that the newly placed Assistant District Officer had been preoccupied with constructing a sub-district headquarters and having been misinformed by the District Officer that in Bugufi the word *njaa*[14] meant a shortage of beer rather than food. It was not until he encountered corpses on the road that he realised the seriousness of the situation and started the machinery going for famine relief. The District Officer had a great deal to answer for, having ignored the chief's written notification of impending food shortages four months before the outbreak of the famine.[15]

Aloofness rather than conflicting interests seemed to be the basis of administrative officers' neglect in famine relief work. The primary problem was slow detection of food shortages. Commenting on the late discovery of a food shortage in Dodoma district in 1941, the Director of Agriculture remarked:

> it appears no proper information with reference to the crops reached the Provincial Commissioner until at least four months after he should have been fully informed as to the food prospects and I can see no avoidance of similar conditions unless officers of the Administration are in a position to get round their districts and away from the main roads more frequently. . . . the Administration is no longer in touch with the ordinary native . . . and . . . in certain cases for prolonged periods of the year there is in effect no real continuous contact with the people.[16]

Famine prevention and relief epitomised the paternalism of the colonial government and struck a deep responsive chord in officers. Most officers saw themselves as superior in intellect and culture to the African peasant populace. Their duty to the peasantry was defined by the British Empire's civilising mission. This outlook is pointedly described by Rowe in an interview he had with Tawney, both having been district administrative officers in Tanganyika:

> [We were] members of an alien administrative service, a colonial service with its own tradition. You and I and hundreds of others knew the form expected of us. We hoped to be able to think at the end of our service we had done something to help the country we were serving in and its people, but the people who we really had to satisfy were our masters, who were of our own race, our own traditions, our own outlook. We knew that as long as we were doing our stuff honestly and really trying, we would be backed by our Civil Service masters up to the Governor and, if necessary up to the Secretary of State.[17]

8 The Asian Market

1 ASIAN MARKET STRUCTURE

Some Asian families can date their ancestors' arrival in Tanzania to the late eighteenth century, but it was not until the mid-nineteenth century that Asians began displacing Arabs as the principal merchants and financiers of the Zanzibari ivory caravan trade. In 1921, Indians numbered 9411.[1] Thereafter, under British colonial administration, heavy immigration, combined with a natural growth rate estimated at between 2 and 3 per cent, brought their total number to 46 254 in 1948; almost a five-fold increase over 27 years.[2]

Apart from a few Asians who had large-scale sisal plantation holdings, Asian businesses were mainly in wholesale and retail trade and transport. It was estimated that in 1939 Asians held 50 per cent and 60 per cent of the import and export trade and 80 per cent of transport services in addition to 90 per cent of town property and 17 per cent of non-African agricultural land.[3] Asian businesses were family concerns, very often run as a partnership between brothers or other close kin, and employing family relations for virtually all non-manual jobs. Businesses evolved around the mutual obligations of the patriarchal joint family as it had existed in Western India. The solidarity of the Asian communities strengthened business activity, provided meeting places for the exchange of trade information and helped to ensure the fulfillment of obligations and the recovery of loans between members of the community.[4]

Asian commercial concerns were vertically and horizontally integrated. Wholesalers and sub-wholesalers were frequently retailers, and at all levels of the marketing chain trade in consumer goods was combined with agricultural produce buying. There were several reasons for this. First of all, Tanganyika's large territory and poor rail and road conditions caused transport costs to be exhorbitantly high. It was imperative to arrange that lorries and rail cars had return loads when sending a shipment of consumer goods to an area. Second, produce buying was the axis of all trading activities. Retail and wholesale margins were comparatively small on consumer goods relative to the greater margins but higher risks of produce buying. Third, markets for consumer goods were extremely small. For many consumer items, the market was limited to the time immediately after the harvest when peasant farmers had just sold their produce and had money in their pockets. This seasonality of supply and demand put enormous stress on the poor transport and communications network and frequently led to unplanned surpluses or shortages and wide price fluctuation. Diversified trading helped to ease the normal volatility of such trading conditions. High margins at one time of the year in particular products could help to smooth out the losses incurred in another product during lulls in trade.[5]

There were a number of factors that could make the system vulnerable to monopoly. The network of *dukas*[6] in up-country areas was not dense, peasants could not compare the prices in several different shops, and since they were usually illiterate and often unaware of the range of different qualities in a product line, it could make it easy for a *dukawallah*[7] to charge monopoly prices. In the cases where there were a few shops in a trading centre to choose from, competitive pricing might be minimal if merchants had communal ties and practiced price collusion. These were always the fears of the colonial administration, and in some areas they were well-founded. In the Southern Province, where transport was particularly difficult, oligopolistic practices were pronounced.

Ironically, it was in fact the effects of 'too many' rather than 'too few' traders that district administrations usually complained about. Throughout the 1920s and especially the 1930s, district administrators reported that numerous, under-capitalised traders were trading with the peasants and they were usually doing so on barter terms, which undermined the peasants' ability to pay tax in cash and, it was charged, left the peasants vulnerable to unscrupulous deals.[8]

Despite the accusations levelled at the Asian rural marketing system by the colonial administration and the peasant resentment towards it, it is apparent that the Asian marketing system was reasonably competitive, allowing for the extremely difficult transport and communications. It was a highly cost-conscious system; there were low overheads from using family labour, spending little or no time or money on book-keeping and accounting and operating from very inauspicious premises and storage facilities. Traders from various religious communities often inhabited the larger settlements and this engendered competing prices for peasant produce and consumer goods. Asian trading firms tended to remain small rather than amalgamating into large monopolistic concerns because businesses were usually restricted to family labour and therefore limited by the size of the family. Finally, the notion of a 'just price' operated on various standard articles of basic consumption which benefited the peasant as a consumer. Certain basic foodstuffs like sugar and maize meal had a conventional price and it was an imprudent *dukawallah* that tried to charge over and above that amount.[9]

2 THE DUKAWALLAH

Despite the importance of the *dukawallah* in the political economy of Tanganyika and the strong imagery surrounding him, there is a dearth of documentary evidence. To colonial officials and peasants alike he was the embodiment of profit-seeking greed,[10] whereas to the Asian population he was the most vital node in the trading network, living a hard-working, frugal life which was lonely and materially unrewarding in itself, but a necessary first step on the road to commercial success.

The first up-country *dukawallahs* settled along the Central and Tanga rail-lines. As trunk roads were built in the period between the wars they settled further afield. The larger rural settlements, or what were then called 'small towns', of over 2000 people were where they built their shops and adjoining houses of sun-dried bricks and corrugated iron roofs. Generally, their immediate family and perhaps some more extended family members lived with them. The *duka* was a full-time occupation for virtually everyone in the family; wives, sons and daughters were all in attendance. The working hours were long; customers were served anytime between 7 am and 10 pm.

Prices were arrived at through a process of bargaining on all but the most basic goods, such as sugar, rice, maize meal and soap. The price that the *dukawallah* agreed to was contingent on his stocks, the other purchases or sales being transacted with the customer, whether his need for cash was pressing at that moment and how urgently the customer desired the article. It is this process of bargaining which seems to have been the basis of suspicion on the part of African peasants and colonial officials. It was, however, an almost inevitable form of market transaction, given the volatility of supply and demand in the market and the transport and supply constraints operating on the *dukawallah*.

3 OCCUPATIONAL MORALITY/ACCOUNTABILITY: FOOD AS A BUSINESS

The *dukawallahs*' role in rural food supply depended largely on the degree to which peasants relied on purchased food and the number of rural waged labourers working on private estates in the area. Peasant households were almost entirely self-sufficient for staple foods.[11] Trade in food provisions was restricted mainly to the sisal estate areas where all the *dukas* stocked the basic maize meal, beans, rice and sugar. These items sold at conventional prices, which varied somewhat regionally because of different transport costs. Profit margins on foodstuffs tended to be small; merchants were compensated for this by their fast turnover rate and by the wider margins on other less basic items such as tinned food and piece goods.

How did the *dukawallah* react to a local harvest failure and a consequent food shortage or famine situation? In a number of ways, the *dukawallah* and his family occupied a very similar position to that of the district official. Both were outsiders, only partially dependant on the local supply of food, and practising different culinary traditions from African peasants. Because an Asian's food habits were conditioned by ritualist purity and food taboos were an important aspect of communal identity, his dietary intake was culturally insulated from those of the African and the European populace and of members of other religious sects.

The staple foods Asians consumed were rice, wheat and atta flour. Since *dukawallahs* were frequently in touch with traders in the larger towns and in Dar es Salaam, the supply of these products for home consumption was generally assured, regardless of the state of the local harvest, and therefore would not have conflicted with the food supply of the local peasantry during famines. But beyond the Asian *dukawallahs*' immediate household food concerns, his trading interests were in many respects directly at odds with peasant food security.

Acute shortages of goods will engender high prices in markets anywhere. In Tanganyika, colonial officials did not desire the free interplay of market forces, branding escalating prices as commercial malpractice. The reasons for this were two-fold. First of all, the buyers were considered commercially inexperienced and naive and persistently prey to overcharging. Second, supply was relatively inelastic because of poor transport and weak integration of commodity markets with factor markets. The inadequacies of an embryonic market were equated with market agents' wrong-doing in the minds of colonial officials. The *dukawallah* was accused of numerous unfair trading practices including underweighing/overweighing in his favour, bartering goods and using his two-way trade with peasants to his advantage, and advancing consumer goods to peasants on agreement that they sell their harvested produce to him at a price he knew to be undervalue.[12] The colonial administration was particularly concerned about these practices during famines and food shortages.

When conditions of intense food insecurity prevailed in the rural areas, the state's famine relief programme was a highly effective curb on skyrocketing food prices. If famine relief was distributed free, as was reluctantly done in some cases, and the quantities of relief were adequate to cover demand, the *dukawallah*'s market evaporated.[13] Even when peasants had to pay for the food it was generally at cost or subsidised, making it difficult for the *dukawallah* to compete. On occasion, merchants were asked to facilitate distribution in one or another ways because of their strategic position in rural transport and commodity distribution, but in these cases they were under more than usual surveillance and it would have been highly unwise for them to act in other than a circumspect fashion.[14]

Thus the *dukawallah*, whose motivation and morality was profit maximisation, faced the superimposition of accountability to the state when it came to the matter of peasant food security. Since the staple food trade was never a product line offering great profit, owing to its limited market and the 'just price' conventions surrounding it, it appears that the local *dukawallah* largely conformed to state dictates in this regard and could rarely be directly implicated in the incidence of rural famine.

9 Native Authority Clientage

1 THE HISTORY AND STRUCTURE OF NATIVE AUTHORITIES

Prior to colonial penetration, Tanzania was composed of a welter of tribal[1] groupings displaying a wide array of organisational forms that embraced a kingdom, dozens of matrilineal and patrilineal chiefdoms, and age-grade societies as well as acephalous populations which did not cohere as corporate units until the superimposition of the colonial state made it expedient to do so.

In most societies, both the leadership and the collective groupings they led tended to be unstable. The combination of shifting cultivation with hunting and gathering practices gave rise to considerable geographical mobility and segmentary processes. Frequent leadership changes were a natural outcome of the fluidity of the groupings.

Leaders were the interceding agencies between the people and their ancestors. Appeals to ancestors were made in the hopes of securing favourable natural conditions for the survival and well-being of the tribal group. Ensuring crop and human fertility were the goals and the measures of good leadership. Related to this, leaders had the responsibility of preventing the tribe's devastation in war. Failure of the rains, locust invasion, defeat in war, were all signs of a leader's lack of rapport with the ancestors, and could trigger the installation of a new leader.[2]

Under German colonial rule the form of tribal authorities was altered and their content distorted when and where it was not conducive to bureaucratic administration. Most importantly, the colonial administration did not allow the continuation of frequent changes of leadership which would cause discontinuities in the execution of administrative orders. Over time, colonial backing was given to the evolution of lifelong hereditary rulers with clear patrilineal succession, contrary to the dynamics of traditional tribal rule.[3] In so doing, tribal leadership became increasingly accountable to the colonial administration rather than to tribal membership.

The British policy of indirect rule consciously aimed at striking a balance between tribal authorities' local and bureaucratic accountability. On one hand, they sought to restore 'authentic' traditional rulers to power, on the other hand they unthinkingly perpetuated the system of hereditary rule and could not resist trying to standardise traditional authority and impose chiefdoms on all tribal areas regardless of their original organisational form or history of leadership succession. There were several tribes where chiefdomship was a subversion of the nature of leadership, since it imposed political functions on leaders who had previously been restricted to performing a magico-religious role.[4]

British colonial administration had no desire to retain an authentic content to the operations of the Native Authorities. Most colonial officials were of the opinion that traditional society had tolerated autocratic excess.[5] All forms of traditional tribute were outlawed in 1926 and chiefs and sub-chiefs received a salary paid from their Native Treasury, its amount stipulated by the central government according to the rank and the size of the chiefdom. The aim was to create an authority with legitimacy in the eyes of the peasants which was capable of collecting tax and implementing government policies at the local level efficiently. The machinery to do so was the Native Treasuries and the Native Courts. Chiefs were nominally in charge of both, but educated clerks were managing their day-to-day operations and the district officer was the overseer of everything, particularly the Native Treasury.

2 RAINMAKERS, CHIEFS AND CLERKS

Because the Native Authority was endowed with both old and new functions and had been cast in a traditional mould, it is not surprising to find that its personnel and their activities represented a continuum of old and new aspects of the society, illustrated by the links between the rainmaker, the chief and the clerk.

Whatever the organisational form of the pre-colonial tribal society, the rainmaker was pivotal. In the acephalous groups, the ritual powers of the rainmaker provided a centre of gravity, whereas in the more hierarchical societies the chief's primary duty to his people was to have on hand or otherwise be an effective rainmaker, performing rituals that accorded with the dictates of the ancestors.[6]

In the British colonial government's search for authentic tribal leaders, the local rain magicians were frequently selected.[7] Throughout the British colonial period, there is evidence for a number of areas that peasants continued to believe in the efficacy of rain ceremonies and judged chiefs on the basis of their fulfilment of ritual duties to the ancestors rather than their administrative performance and fiscal rectitude.[8]

While the British were eager to harness the legitimacy derived from tribal leaders' magico-religious role, their aim was to gradually transform the nature of the chiefs' elite status from one rooted in traditional beliefs and honour to that of an educated bureaucratic elite. This was to be accomplished through the education of chiefs' sons. The Tabora Boys' school was Tanganyika's equivalent of Eton.

Elitism was further encouraged through the government's incomes policy. The government stressed that chiefs were not salaried civil servants requiring incentive increments; rather, the income a chief was given was a commutation of tribute, or in other words a stipend 'to enable him to maintain his position and meet the necessary expenses of his office',[9] the level fixed according to the size and wealth of the population in his area.

The wealth of the chiefs relative to their people was considerable. In terms of formal salary, the 1929/30 figures for the Native Treasury of the Sukuma Federation show chiefs' salaries and pensions constituting 48 per cent of the total salary bill, with the far more numerous headmen receiving only 27 per cent, and clerks, messengers, tribal dressers and sanitary labourers accounting for the remainder.[10] Since Native Authority personal emoluments were usually over two thirds of total expenditure, taxpayers received negligible services for their tax money.

According to Mitchell, the Secretary of Native Affairs, tribute had been commuted to a fixed salary because the development of a market economy upset the balance between the people and their chief and subverted the nature of tribute.

> [Traditionally,] the people paid a tithe of their produce or stock, and gave their labour to hoe the Chief's fields and gather his harvest, to fetch him firewood and make and tend his game and fish traps. In a subsistence economy there was little risk of abuse in that, for there was no market to which surpluses could be sold. But as soon as stock, maize, groundnuts, rice and the rest of it became saleable for cash to merchants a very different state of affairs came into existence and in fact there were avaricious Chiefs whose demands on their people amounted to extortion. One who had

perhaps about 100 000 people under him was found to have sold a surplus in one year worth £10 000; at the then prevailing produce prices that was clearly a great deal too much.[11]

The fact that the chiefs were accorded an elite status, but that chiefly rivalry had been built into the system at the time of selecting chiefly personnel and differentiating their salaries, meant that chiefs felt compelled to compete with one another in ostentatious consumption.[12] As early as 1921 chiefs in Bukoba were reported as having cars.[13] While the government attempted to keep competitive consumption in check by stipulating that chiefs must not incur liabilities for expensive articles without the sanction of the Provincial Commissioner,[14] nonetheless, chiefs had a tendency to get indebted to local Asian traders, who felt confident that the chiefs would not be willing to make their debts known to the district officer.[15]

In return for the elite status accorded them by the colonial government, chiefs had to serve as the intermediaries between their people and district officers. In the eyes of the colonial government, the efficacy of this arrangement depended on: first, the degree to which the people recognised their chief as a legitimate leader; second, the chief's understanding and acceptance of the measures being advocated by the colonial government; and third, the chief's willingness to devote his energies to their implementation. In some areas, matters never got beyond the question of legitimacy and there was incessant bickering and ill-will concerning tribal leadership. Most of the complaints district officers made were lodged somewhere between the second and third impediments.[16]

Bureaucratic performance criteria were invariably used by officials and commentators for judging chiefs. The peasant's perspective was undoubtedly very different.[17] Chiefs had a strong identification with their people, precisely because their elite status was bound up in representing them to the colonial government. Such identification is a feature that is not always present in clientage relations and has implications for clientage practices, as will be argued later.

Native Authority clerks, unlike the chiefs, were all literate, mission-trained and generally fluent in Kiswahili. Like others on the payroll of the Native Authority, they often owed their jobs to the fact that they were relatives of the chief. Their record keeping and general clerical duties were central to the operations of the Native Authority and district officers worried about illiterate chiefs being dominated by their clerks.[18]

Clerical salaries were extremely low and incremental scales were avoided until the late 1940s because the remuneration was intended for men 'who continue to lead their own life in their own rural centre, occupying their own land and their own house'.[19] But minimal earnings and a parochial outlook were precisely the things that an educated man was trying to escape. Frequently, irregularities in tax collection, pilferage and embezzlement of Native Authority revenues were traced to clerks.[20] District officers used harsh words to describe the clerks: 'Repeatedly was I sickened by cases where an unsophisticated bush African had been fleeced and cheated by a literate clerk. . . . I often shuddered to think what might be going on close to my office, one could only make the best safeguards possible. The cunning of some of these educated types was unbelievable.'[21] 'It is usually the educated native who is a thief.'[22]

However rudimentary his education, it was his education, his literacy and numeracy, his knowledge of Kiswahili and perhaps English or German, that set him apart from the other villagers, and led him to identify more strongly with his former classmates, often in other parts of the country, than with the local chief and peasants. Almost before he arrived back in the village, the clerk yearned for a more cosmopolitan setting and hoped his clerical job in one way or another would provide him with the means of moving to the town.[23] He could far more readily abscond with Native Authority funds than the chief who forfeited his elitist position in so doing.

3 NATIVE AUTHORITY CLIENTAGE PRACTICES AND NETWORKS

Clientage has been defined as non-market personalised exchange in which the client assumes a dependent status that alleviates his material insecurity, while the monopolist patron assumes dominance which enhances his prestige and power. The monopolist seeks to maximise his prestige regardless of state laws or alternatively communal moral obligations.

Traditionally, chiefly prestige had been held in high esteem, being considered a reflection of the general prosperity of the community. But the chief's prestige aggrandisement through tribute collection, beyond the needs of tribal food security stocks and the consumption of the chiefly retinue and tribal old and infirm, had been restricted within affordable bounds by a number of subtle checks and balances imposed by the elders, clan heads, secret societies, young warriors and other authority figures. If chiefly excesses did exceed the consensual limit, threatening the well-being of the community, the chief could readily be replaced with a successor.

Colonial rule destroyed the internal power balance in tribal communities. Many of the authority figures that had imposed checks on the chief were not accorded legitimacy. Chiefly wealth took on a monetised form that was made personal and divorced from moral obligations to the people.[24] Tribute collection was outlawed, but tribute collection did not totally cease. The colonial state openly tolerated tribute of a ritualist nature and encouraged it to some degree by using the chiefs' traditional labour call-up powers for colonial economic purposes, notably for public works and porterage. In this way the tradition of tribute in labour and goods was perpetuated and chiefs continued to collect various traditional forms of tribute as well as adapting the tradition to new purposes.

Under British colonialism, the chief was accorded prestige through the payment of salaries vastly exceeding the earnings of other tribal members. He had three main sources of monopoly wealth: his official salary, his tribute-collecting potential and the extra-legal or non-bureaucratic exercise of his Native Authority office for prestige aggrandisement. The latter included: non-execution of formal duties, discretionary decision-making in public office, the appointment of relatives to Native Authority posts, and financial irregularities in the form of fraud, pilferage and embezzlement.[25] All these activities were considered to be abuses of office by the colonial state, but from the perspective of the chief they were part of a logical, often requisite, behavioural pattern. The non-execution of formal duties was usually with regard to measures that the chief knew would make him unpopular with his people. These were often labour-intensive projects such as soil conservation, or measures that required people's physical exertion but appeared to have no immediate benefits such as planting a new crop. Discretionary decision-making arose in innumerable instances, be it with regard to court orders and fines, illegal tax exemptions or allocation of tribal land and resources which were often hazy areas where customary law and colonial state policies were at odds. Whenever a chief was in a position to raise his prestige by helping or hindering someone, in contravention of colonial state laws and policy, he was likely to do so if the possible penalties to himself were not too great. The appointment of relatives to Native Authority office went back to the pre-colonial period when chiefs had surrounded themselves with their close kin to build up a viable political power base. Sometimes these appointments were made irrespective of Native Treasury revenue estimates. The irregular financial practices were quite new and related to the fact that pecuniary gain afforded conspicuous consumption or investment in social capital both of which ultimately led to prestige aggrandisement.

These practices posed an enormous dilemma for the colonial state which, on the one hand, did not wish to undermine the prestige of the chiefs but, on the other hand, wanted a modicum of bureaucratic accountability and wished to prevent chiefs' abuses of power and finance from reaching a level which would cause alienation or material detriment to the peasants concerned. The dilemma is reflected in the *Native Authority Ordinance*.

> chiefs are not salaried servants of the Government in the way that Liwalis are or Akidas were, provided therefore, that their work is generally satisfactory, their 'minor' delinquencies should be made the occasion for guarded rebuke rather than punishment . . . there is sometimes a temptation to look for too high a standard in the native chief. . . . As regards abuses, it must be remembered that abuses are inevitable, but the power of supervision exists and must be exercised, and we are using in this scheme of Native Administration an instrument which is being carefully and patiently fashioned for our purpose. . . . Administrative officers must, of course, at once step in to put a stop to abuses, and if no other course is possible the deposition of the delinquent chief may be necessary but it should be regarded as an extreme step only to be recommended when all other means have failed.[26]

Despite this expressed restraint, Native Authority depositions for financial misappropriation or inefficiency, sometimes a long consecutive string of them, were a common occurence. The clientage practices did not lessen overtime as Cameron's strategy intended. During World War II, Native Authority efficiency was described as 'as low as ever'.[27]

Chiefs were at the apex of the clientage network. The appointment of relatives and friends to the positions of headmen, clerks, messengers, tribal dressers or lorry drivers formed the second, broader layer of the network. Chiefs had large immediate and extended families. Polygamy was widely practised; some chiefs had dozens of wives. The chief rarely if ever suffered a shortage of people to appoint as his clients, who in turn could operate as 'sub-patrons' with their access to the monopoly of goods, services and monetary funds at the command of the Native Authority. Because their salaries were far lower than the chief's there was an element of need that a chief could not so readily claim. Clientage practices, particularly on the part of native clerks, were widespread. The chief's Native Authority appointees like the lesser headmen were unsalaried, but the title was a boost to personal prestige and possible pecuniary gain.[28]

At the bottom of the clientage network, the peasantry sought material security in a variety of forms from their immediate patrons and ultimately the chief. Peasants' primary concern was ensuring access to basic subsistence goods, precisely because these goods could not be taken for granted. The chief's famine prevention and relief duties contributed materially to the guarantee of peasants' subsistence, but apart from that, in the absence of a notable financial commitment to development on the part of the colonial government, chiefs for the most part were not, as later patrons under cooperative and parastatal clientage would be, intermediaries for the provisioning of 'modern' production and consumption goods to the peasantry. The chief's patronage to his people had a greater symbolic and spiritual content than patrons would have in subsequent cooperative and parastatal clientage networks.

The clientage practices, some which were clearly at the expense of peasants' material well-being, tended not to be of great concern or moral outrage for the average peasant and were not usually reported to colonial officers. In most cases peasants had a sufficient amount of respect and loyalty for their chief, tribal pride or fear, that kept them from informing the foreign district officer about the chiefs' clientage practices. A former district officer recalls an illustrative incident: 'In 1938 a retired Police Askari, accustomed to European procedure complained to me that the Mteni of Uyui had stolen his tax money. I camped at Uyui to investigate and, as complainants gained confidence, finished with over 70 separate complaints of a similar nature. To one complainant, whom I happened to know, I said: "We have often met, why have you never complained before?" To this day I remember his scandalized look, and his answer: "Complain against my chief?"'[29]

It was more likely that a peasant would feel the urge to lodge a complaint about a sub-patron such as a tax clerk, but in those cases the peasant feared that the chief and clerk would be cooperating with one another and he would face reprisals even if he won in court.

Complaints were more frequent in areas where chiefs had not traditionally ruled but were nonetheless imposed.[30]

Clientage practices rarely marred the good standing of a chief when he was known as an effective ritual leader. Peasants could get annoyed with the demands to intensify their labour effort issued by a zealous chief on behalf of the colonial state, but the ultimate criterion for judging a chief was his ability to intercede on their behalf with the ancestors to bring about favourable weather and soil conditions. The chief who failed in this role could meet with the wrath of his people. Despite the colonial government's removal of traditional checks and balances, peasants who were at odds with their chiefs always retained the traditional last resorts of escape or witchcraft. An irritating chief could be avoided by moving away or he could be confronted, indirectly but forcefully, through the retaliatory weapon of witchcraft.[31] A chief who was suspected of tampering with the spiritual forces that guaranteed the community's well-being or otherwise acting to create discord and harm could be poisoned or his household huts burnt down with magical forces to blame.[32] Some areas of the country were rife with witchcraft, often those areas where chiefs' official performance in all senses of the word was deficient.[33]

Finally, rivalries existed between chiefs and between chiefs and people who had just as much right to be appointed to chiefship but were not. They sometimes took the form of boundary disputes with the aim of acquiring jurisdiction over more population as a means of getting a higher salary and more prestige and contributed to a high degree of intra-tribal clan consciousness in some areas, much to the chagrin of colonial officials who were hoping for larger units of identification.[34]

4 OCCUPATIONAL MORALITY/ACCOUNTABILITY: FOOD AS A PERFORMANCE INDICATOR

Traditionally, tribute given to the chief in the form of grain was not a fixed amount; a poor harvest resulted in very little or nothing being demanded, whereas peasants gave in abundance when a good harvest occurred, believing that the chief was at least partially responsible.[35] Tribute contributions were usually millet and sorghum, bulrush millet being particularly well suited to long storage of up to three years.

These grain stores were at the disposal of the chief to distribute to the community on an individual basis to especially needy people or at a time of collective hardship in the aftermath of drought, locust attack or a raid and could justifiably be used to feed his own household, but not to trade away or otherwise enhance his personal wealth.

In his capacity as guardian of the community's food supply, the chief could issue famine prevention orders that his people were compelled to heed, such as the prohibition of beer-brewing, the threat of punishment for anyone caught stealing crops in the field during a famine, as well as instructions on how and what to plant.[36] Tribal discipline of this sort and tribute contributions were only possible when the people had faith in their chief. As stated before, social cohesion and moral order centering around the chief as the people's intermediary with the ancestors who controlled their fate was underpinned by a system of consensual politics; a chief could readily be ousted in the event of consecutive poor harvests and material deprivation of the community.

Although chiefs were still found feeding needy subjects in some places at the outset of British colonial rule,[37] this welfare system was soon undermined. Famine prevention and famine relief functions which had been integrated and controlled by the chief were separated and bureaucratically compartmentalised. Under the Native Authority Ordinance, the chief was given responsibility for famine prevention which included the power to issue orders prohibiting the manufacture and distribution of intoxicating liquor, requiring peasants to cultivate minimum acreages to ensure adequate food supplies or drought-resistance crops, and during famines he could prohibit the sale or removal of foodstuffs from the area, require peasants to move to a place where they could be conveniently fed and order able-bodied men to work on public works. No longer the custodian of communal grain stores and no longer operating with discretion over famine relief distribution, the chief's role was to facilitate the colonial authorities' famine relief operations; in the course of which he was heavily supervised. In effect, the tribal food security system pivoting around the chief was shortcircuited with the powers to punish, that is, famine prevention orders were still in the hands of the chief, whereas the powers to reward, that is, the distribution of free food, were replaced with bureaucratically administered famine relief controlled by the district officers that was withheld from certain categories of peasants,[38] and had to be paid for.[39]

Since the people could no longer remove chiefs at will, the chiefs' accountability to the people in famine prevention and rain magic was formally lost. On the other hand, a chief who did not have the respect of his people found it difficult to get their compliance on laborious famine-prevention measures and the colonial authorities were quick to fault chiefs whose people suffered frequent famine from what was referred to as 'indolence' and 'improvidence', which generally meant laxity in planting drought crops and excessive beer-brewing.[40]

Chiefs and headmen were accountable to the colonial government in this regard, and famine prevention negligence could be contributing causes to the removal of a chief for incompetence. In one case, a district officer tried to mete out a more immediate reprimand, by withholding half the salaries of four superior headmen and publicly whipping 25 village headmen. The salary measure was approved by the Chief Secretary but the corporal punishment caused the Governor to rebuke the District Officer.[41]

Regarding the immediate conflicts chiefs might have had between their official role in facilitating the distribution of famine relief to peasant households and on the other hand, ensuring their own households' food supplies, the temptation to take advantage of their position was probably not very strong compared with the costs of being discovered. Unlike colonial officers and Asian merchants, chiefs tended to have the same diet as the ordinary peasant, but in both the traditional and the colonial food security systems, chiefs and their families would be the last to starve. Strategic control over tribute contributions would have made this so in times gone by whereas during colonial rule chiefs were usually amongst the few in the rural community with cash to spare for buying food.[42]

Clientage practices on the part of the Native Authority personnel in the distribution of famine relief, i.e. favouritism in supply to specific clients or food pilferage, was restricted by colonial officers' heavy supervision of food allocation. Circular No. 33 of 1930 stipulated that 'European supervision at the work or place of food issue is essential' and additional colonial staff was to be made available where needed.[43]

The long-term interests of the chiefs in famine prevention and relief work were contradictory. To retain the sanction of the colonial state and stay in power, chiefs had to make some pretence if not actually exert themselves in exhorting peasants to undertake famine prevention measures.[44] Chiefs occupied an awkward position; to be too stringent in requiring peasants to follow laborious famine measures or plant upopular crops like cassava without being able to offer in return a guaranteed free food supply after a harvest failure made chiefs liable to falling into complete disfavour. Non-cooperation from their people could follow which placed the chiefs in a poor light *vis-à-vis* the colonial authorities. Thus, as in the pre-colonial period, food adequacy of the tribal community was an ultimate indicator of chiefly performance, but a particularly dodgy one.

Summary of Part III

In this section, the significance of context was stressed in delineating and defining Tanzania's main social institutions. Due to the unharnessed physical environment, the low level of commodity exchange, and the high degree of food insecurity experienced by the peasantry, the state and the market's institutional functions do not exhaust the peasants' extra-household organisational needs. Clientage networks constitute a third extra-household social institution that are epitomised by non-market personalised exchange between prestige-seeking monopolist patrons and people pursuing the alleviation of material insecurity. By subordinating themselves to a monopolist commanding allocative powers over scarce or valued resources, a client is in a position to make appeals to the monopolist in times of need. Between 1919 and 1950, clientage networks were most clearly manifest in the Native Authorities.

The content and structure of the state, market and Native Authority clientage networks are reviewed and their operations compared with respect to the problem of peasant food insecurity. It is argued that peasant commodity production was encouraged through Asian market penetration into up-country areas and through chiefs, but that the colonial state sought to avoid undermining the food production base of the peasantry by advocating a household and district food self-sufficiency policy. The colonial state assumed the chiefly function of ensuring peasant food security, but revamped famine relief to suit administrative procedures. Native Authorities, and to a much lesser extent Asian market agents, were drawn into the distribution of famine relief, both subjected to a great deal of supervision. Thus all three social institutions played a role, often ambiguous but primarily positive, in ensuring peasant food security between 1919 and 1950.

Certain conclusions can be drawn from this section. While it is commonly acknowledged that the colonial period was characterised by a racial division of labour, it is perhaps more significant to recognise that Tanganyika's extra-household social institutions were racially separated: a British state, an Asian market and African clientage networks, each with a different logic and occupational morality/accountability. The logics of bureaucratic accountability in the state, profit-maximisation in the market and face-to-face accountability of prestige-seeking patrons were not innate racial characteristics; they resulted from the objective positions of the state, market and clientage agents in the division of labour and in a subjective sense, their greater or lesser proximity to the material insecurity of the peasantry. It has been stressed that British colonial officers and Asian *dukawallahs* were materially as well as culturally isolated from peasants and were themselves distant from the threat of famine or serious food shortages. Clientage relations were foreign to them, not in the sense that they were incapable of being a part of them, but rather that they were removed from fundamental material insecurity, and therefore had no cause to be a part of them.

Native Authority clientage was not a pure form of clientage, because it was transitional, having many vestige elements of the pre-colonial consensual society with its communally-accepted moral obligations. There was a lack of 'modern' production and consumption goods for monopolist patrons to distribute to clients, because the external supply of these goods was minimal. Chiefs and other patrons often dealt in intangibles, namely rain rituals and symbols. The Native Authority patrons were far more integrated with the state than the market and their networks were composed of subdivided, non-overlapping branches under each district colonial administrative station. The clientage supply of goods and services was not transferred horizontally between patrons, only vertically from patron to client. The face-to-face accountability of the chief was fairly strong, partly because of his traditional obligations and perhaps, more importantly, because of the chief's strong local identity and lack of mobility associated with his hereditary position, unlike the Native Authority clerk, whose mobility was precursory to later forms of clientage relations. Finally, chiefs competed for prestige through conspicuous consumption. Generally their wealth was spent on consumption for themselves and their clients rather than being channeled productively into agriculture.

Overall, the colonial state, the Asian market and the Native Authorities' famine prevention and relief measures could be considered successful in protecting peasant households during the period between 1919 and 1950. The rural population did not decline over this period, but rather grew, with a likely decrease in famine deaths. However, this population growth belied chronic food inadequacy and could only be addressed by policies aimed at radically developing food production in the peasant household rather than merely maintaining peasant food production and consumption at survival levels.

Part IV
Wage-Labour Force Food Demand and Supply Arrangements, 1919–50

In this section the general configuration of the wage-labour force, the sources of food supply, and the types of food demand and supply arrangements are described for the interwar period. Changes in the nature of non-peasant household food demand and supply which occurred during and after World War II are then traced.

10 Food Supply for an African Wage-Labour Force, 1919–39

So far, analysis of African productive activity has been limited to that contained within the peasant household, almost all of which was family rather than wage-labour. There was, however, a considerable amount of hired African labour involved in European and Asian-owned sisal and coffee plantations and extractive industries, particularly gold and diamond mining, as well as in state infrastructural development, mainly communications, road building and railway construction and maintenance, and finally in domestic service work located primarily in the towns.

1 GOVERNMENT LABOUR POLICY AND THE MALE MIGRANT BACHELOR WAGE LABOUR SYSTEM

In 1926, Governor Cameron issued a policy statement regarding the division between peasant agriculture and wage-labour. Its contents were influenced by prevailing labour force patterns and practices, Mandate sanctions against 'forced labour' and the pressures of European planters for easier access to African labour.[1] It stressed the need for government to induce African peasants to produce a surplus, be it in the form of cashcrop or wage-labour, but not at the expense of household food production. In regions where there was no climatically suitable, marketable crop, peasants were encouraged to seek waged employment. On the other hand, district administrative and agricultural officers were to refrain from promoting cashcropping in areas long accustomed to wage-labour force participation. In remote areas it was surmised that migrant labour was the best course to follow.

Official opinion held that the divorce of Africans from usufruct land rights, 'de-tribalisation', and proletarianisation were to be avoided at all costs. Household provisioning of subsistence food needs was seen as the vital essence of African culture that had to be complementary to rather than undermined by African wage-labour.

'The creation of large industrial centres with workers completely divorced from food production would be an entire innovation of very doubtful desirability; it appears most unlikely to occur. The African man, and still more the woman, is firmly attached to the soil, and the whole fabric of social organization is based upon the right to cultivate; it thus seems probable that the native will always aim at having his own home among his own crops, whether in a distant village or as a "squatter" on an estate.'[2]

In practice, keeping the household and tribal units intact seemed a contradiction in terms. Theoretically, households were free to relocate proximate to the place of work, but Native Authorities were not keen on losing taxpayers and, while willing to let their men migrate, they exerted pressure on women to stay behind, as an incentive for the men's eventual return.[3] District officers noted difficulties in governing 'settler' communities, who were recalcitrant to rule by the local Native Authority and complained about the indiscipline of youth growing up in such communities. Plantation and mine management tended to encourage men of the same tribe to live together and elect an elders' council from amongst their numbers for governing their compounds, with ultimate appeals handled by the management.

Management's concern was primarily to obtain cheap labour. Local labour supplies were never enough to fill employers' needs. Sisal production, the main absorber of African labour, took place on the coast and along the Central line where local labour was not forthcoming in sufficient quantities. Wages were low but colonial theorists were of the belief that higher wages would not increase the supply of labour because labourers worked to reach a target rather than maximising income. Tanganyikan production of tropical export products such as coffee, tea and sisal had to compete with products produced under the cheap labour conditions of Asia. With the severe drop in world commodity prices during the depression, wages tended to decline by a third to a half.

The two main categories of labour, local and migrant wage-labour, can be further subdivided. Local labour was derived from adjacent indigenous, settler or squatter populations. Migrant labour was attested labour which was recruited and transported to the workplace by an intermediary agency or non-attested labour which arrived unassisted from distant places. In view of the unavailability of reliable labour statistics it is difficult to establish what the relative proportions of people falling into these categories were and how much they varied over time. It appears, however, that generally over half of the African wage-labour force were migrants and the bulk of migrants, as many as three-quarters of them, were unattested.[4]

All the categories were involved in the *kipande* system, whereby labourers were employed to work thirty-day stints that did not have to be on consecutive days. A day involved a specified work load which was marked on the labourer's *kipande*,[5] and at the completion of thirty days' work he was entitled to his full pay. Migrant labour was recorded as having between a 75 and 90 per cent daily turnout as opposed to local labour's 50–5 per cent.[6] On the other hand, migrant labour was generally only available for work for between six months and two years, and tended to do the more arduous tasks such as sisal cutting as opposed to clearing and hoeing. Local labour was continuously accessible. In either case, the labourer was being paid low, 'bachelor' wages. As much as half of the wage was spent on food costs while on the job, the remainder going towards the labourer's tax commitment, with little remaining for the purchase of consumer goods. The peasant household, nearby or distant, was the vital back-up to such an under-invested labour force.

It is difficult to construct an exact picture of the size and distribution of the wage labour force. Prior to the 1944 labour census conducted by the Labour Department, published statistics are based on estimates rather than actual counts. Table 10.1 lists the totals for African wage-labour force participation by sector and year. Its most noteworthy features are the decline in porterage evident in the transport category, the drop in total employment that occurred during the Depression and its sharp rise during World War II. In 1929, roughly 20 per cent of the African male adult population was in waged employment.

Apart from the sprinkling of labourers engaged in porterage and public works throughout Tanzania, the wage-labour force was geographically concentrated by commodity. The sisal industry, centred in Tanga and radiating southwards along the coast and along the Central Line to Morogoro and Kilosa, was the biggest employer. In 1949, 46 per cent of the territory's African labour force was working in Tanga and Eastern Provinces.

Between 1919 and 1950, only Dar es Salaam could be counted as an urban area numbering more than 20 000 people. Dar es Salaam represented a tiny proportion of the total territorial population. Even when the ten largest 'towns' are counted, only 1.2 per cent of the total population in 1931, rising to 1.9 per cent in 1951, lived outside

TABLE 10.1 *Numerical estimates of the African wage-labour force, 1926–50**

Year	*Agricultural workers*	*Trade, transport, industry*	*Mining*	*Public works dept*	*Railway*	*Domestic and Personal Service*	*Timber production*	*Misc.*	*TOTAL*
1926	140000	109000	7000	n.a.	n.a.	20000	n.a.	n.a.	276000
1927	150000	60000	7000	n.a.	n.a.	21000	n.a.	n.a.	238000
1928	170000	53200	7000	n.a.	n.a.	25000	n.a.	n.a.	255200
1929	185000	54200	7000	n.a.	n.a.	27000	n.a.	n.a.	273200
1930	140000	45100	4000	10321	10462	24000	n.a.	n.a.	233883
1931	110000	41100	4000	12223	8691	20000	n.a.	n.a.	196014
1932	110000	41000	4000	5139	6910	18000	n.a.	n.a.	185049
1933	110000	43000	16000	4693	6219	18000	n.a.	n.a.	197912
1934	110000	43000	24000	8640	6426	18000	n.a.	n.a.	210066
1935	112000	37000	24000	8546	6479	20000	n.a.	n.a.	208025
1936	124000	40000	32000	19034	7072	20000	n.a.	n.a.	242106
1937	125000	37500	32000	9151	7146	22000	n.a.	n.a.	232797
1938	125000	51000	n.a.	7250	7244	30000	n.a.	n.a.	220494

1939	125000	51000	n.a.	6228	7319	30000	n.a.	n.a.	219547
1940	125000	51000	n.a.	6228	7703	30000	n.a.	n.a.	219931
1941	125000	51000	n.a.	21848	7175	30000	n.a.	n.a.	235023
1942	133000	41100	24000	12649	9437	35000	n.a.	n.a.	255186
1943	133000	32000	18000	12236	16937	25000	n.a.	6100	243273
1944	170500	15000	21000	32540	11901	25000	11500	22000	309441
1945	197000	14000	17500	30400	11185	25000	15000	18500	328585
1946	175500	14500	17000	11000	12728	25500	10000	20000	286228
1947	185000	16500	16000	13000	13450	25500	8500	20000	297950
1948	211000	20000	16000	13000	n.a.	30000	7500	25000	322500
1949	n.a.	n.a.	n.a.	n.a.	n.a.	n.a.	n.a.	n.a.	349239
1950	196141	28049	18833	n.a.	11064	37173	10775	58208	360243

NOTES

1. No labour statistics are available before 1926. Labour censuses were conducted in 1944 and 1949.

2. The 1944 labour census yielded a much higher total number of labourers than anticipated and suggests that totals for previous years may have been underestimated by a considerable degree.

SOURCE

TT, Blue Books, 1926–48 and Department of Labour Annual Reports, 1949–50.

of a strictly rural setting.[7] In urban areas, Africans' employment opportunities were largely confined to manual labour in the Public Works Department, Tanganyikan Railways or domestic service.

2 SOURCES OF FOOD SUPPLY AND TRANSPORT

In the interwar period, as food demand of an expanding wage-labour force increased, ad hoc supply arrangements evolved that were structured on various combinations of household, clientage networks, market and state operations. These arrangements were accomodated to the specific magnitudes, frequencies and location of demand. Nonetheless, supply difficulties continued to arise from production and transport constraints. There were three sources of food supply: non-specialised territorial production, specialised territorial production and import. Given the difficulties of transport, food supply for the wage-labour force generally took the form of grains, notably maize. The bulkier and more perishable staples like plantains, cassava and sweet potatoes were consumed on a more incidental basis when and where they were readily at hand.

2.1 Non-specialised territorial production

Most African-supplied foodstuffs represented non-specialised primarily subsistence rather than cash-motivated production. Peasant-grown foodstuffs were sold in local markets in or around European or Asian-owned plantations. Often the African producer sold directly to the consumer. Generally the amount sold was restricted to the surplus over and above the peasant household's needs and constituted only a fraction of the household's total production. Peasants were neither willing nor able to sell food in bad harvest years and areas of frequent drought did not lend themselves to regular or abundant marketed food supply. Despite the active encouragement to peasants in Handeni district to supply adjacent plantations, the number of years of famine relief issue probably exceeded years when peasants supplied plantations.

The highland areas overlooking the sisal plantations and mines, notably Lushoto and Upare in Tanga, Kilimanjaro, Uluguru in Morogoro, Uhehe in Iringa and Unyakyusa in Mbeya, were the most frequent sources of supply. As the population in highland areas grew denser, and in the absence of frontier land to colonise, average acreages declined and saleable surpluses grew smaller. Thus the Sambaa of Lushoto, who were reported to be supplying all the local sisal estates in addition to exporting to Tanga town in 1928,[8] became progressively less important as a source of supply over the years. Sambaa maize cultivation was increasingly replaced with cassava, in an effort to keep up with their own food demand.

It was normal for all categories of wage labourers to produce some of their own food. This was most pronounced amongst local plantation labourers or squatters on farms where the male labourer lived with his family, as opposed to mine workers whose jobs were usually full-time occupations.[9] The migrant *kipande* labourer's cultivation practice came in between these two extremes. It appears that the non-attested labourer was more involved in food cultivation than the time-constrained attested labourer.

In some of the more densely populated sisal estate areas of Tanga, which already had a substantial settler population in addition to the indigenous one, it would not have been easy to obtain land and rivalry for land did at times cause friction. However, even in cramped Korogwe usufruct rights were granted to alien labourers by Sambaa Native Authorities.

Tanner criticised the standard of plant husbandry of the *kipande* labourer whose lack of time during the agricultural season and short-term horizons led them to cultivate convenient, but agriculturally marginal sites, failing to give enough attention to clearing and burning, to the extent of causing uncontrolled fires, and leaving the plot after one or two harvests long before it had been fully exploited.[10]

2.2 Specialised territorial production

Specialised territorial food production refers to the foodstuffs which were produced under a profit-maximisation logic, such that market prices crucially affected resource allocation within and between the food-producing enterprises. Specialised food production was primarily in the hands of Europeans planters, to a lesser extent Asian planters, and was only beginning to involve African producers in a few isolated areas.

African marketed food demand was mostly that of African labourers on European and Asian-owned agricultural enterprises. Little information exists for the 1920s, but it appears that when and where possible the non-African planters were producing some food themselves, as well as encouraging Asian *duka* supplies and local peasant food markets.

In areas suited to the production of high value export crops like tea, farmers often felt that diversifying production into food crops was a waste of land. They preferred to rely on peasant surplus production and complained bitterly about 'lazy peasants' in the years when peasant marketed surpluses failed to materialise. In view of the risks of relying on peasant production, European tea farmers in the Southern Highlands petitioned the state for land on the plateau between Mbeya and Iringa, where European specialised maize production could take place. The state under Cameron's governorship was extremely cautious about land alienation. Nonetheless, land for one farm was alienated in a sympathetic acknowledgement of the problem.[11]

It was the Northern Province where officialdom had from an early date been of the opinion that European commercial food production, along lines similar to those existing in the Kenyan White Highlands, could flourish. Two blocks of land in Moshi district were alienated to European farmers in 1929 specifically for maize production. In 1930, a Senior Agricultural Officer instituted a 'Buy Tanganyika Produce' campaign in conjunction with encouraging the expansion of maize production in a low-lying belt of European farms around Kilimanjaro. The intention was to curtail large imports of Kenyan maize. By 1934, 60 European families in Moshi alone were reported dependent on commercial maize production.[12]

European maize production was generally mechanised, as well as being dependent on African hired labour. The European maize producers of Northern Province pressurised the state for 'favoured producer' status vis-a-vis Kenyan producers and demanded government supports along lines similar to those granted Kenyan European farmers.[13] In 1934 they formed the Kilimanjaro Planters' Association (KPA) and then endeavoured to make use of the existing Kenyan marketing and storage infrastructure by affiliating with the Kenya Farmers' Association (KFA). In 1935, 95 per cent of the membership of the KFA, re-organised as the Maize Growers Association, were non-African.[14] There was increasing European concern about the way Chagga producers undersold them in good harvest years.

In 1936, Tanganyika Railways announced its intention to double rail rates. The rate increase made it far cheaper for Dar es Salaam to import maize from Kenya than rely on domestic supply and the state refused to restrict Kenyan imports.[15] European planters of Northern

Province as well as the small number of Asian irrigated maize and cotton producers of the Central Province immediately protested.[16] Specialised food production was failing to prove its commercial viability. Transport was clearly one of the most intractable constraints.

2.3 Transport

At the outset of British colonial rule, the transport network consisted of two rail-lines and the movements of porters. Pack animals were mostly precluded by the prevalence of tsetse and other serious parasitic diseases. The Tanga rail-line, which serviced the sisal-producing areas of the northeast and Eastern Province, bisected the country.

Although the British colonial government had inherited from the Germans two major rail-lines totalling over 1500 kms gratis, and its investments had been restricted to extending these lines by another 300 kms, the state-owned railways quickly fell into debt, resulting from debt charges and severe under-utilisation of the railways.[17]

Government transport policy of the inter-war period never aimed to develop an integrated domestic economy. Balancing the budget was the guiding principle and this generally had the effect of stifling internal trade. It was only during World War II, as commodity production increased in response to favourable world prices and wartime supply urgencies that rail tonnages could better support overhead costs and allow cheaper rates for long-distance domestic trade.

In the meantime, roads were proliferating. Between 1921 and 1929, total road length increased at a rate of 20 per cent per annum. During the Depression, the growth rate was reduced to 5 per cent per annum. After 1933 and until 1950, growth in total road length slowed to between one and two per cent while road upgrading took precedence.[18] The number of licensed lorries and buses trebled between 1935 and 1950, and petrol was declared the 'lifeblood' of the territory.[19]

2.4 Imports

Tanganyika vacillated between net grain import and export during the interwar period (see Table 3.1). Until 1925, it was a substantial net exporter, primarily of millet/sorghum, but in the late 1920s and the mid-1930s it was forced to import large amounts of maize, interspersed by years when modest net exports were possible.

Net rice exports of between 10 000 and 30 000 quintals prevailed in the 1920s and rose in the 1930s to 50 000, then 80 000. From 1924 onwards, net wheat imports were steady at between 20 000 and 40 000, reflecting an urban demand which could not be met by domestic production. Most wheat imports came from India and Kenya, with the former being subjected to a duty of Shs 3 per 100 lb.

Unlike the other grains, maize import/export presents a more erratic picture. From 1925 onwards, with the exception of 1932, there was a net import. Between 1925 and 1929, net imports ranged from 10 000 to 30 000 quintals per annum then fluctuate far more widely between 10 000 and 130 000. Maize was imported primarily from Kenya and occasionally South Africa. Prices for maize, as well as for the other grains, were extremely depressed during the 1930s. Kenyan settler maize farmers were unable to find markets for their produce in Europe, so they were as dependent on Tanganyika for demand as Tanganyika was on them for supply. Both maize and maize meal were free of import duties.

3 FOOD DEMAND TYPES AND SUPPLY ARRANGEMENTS

There were four main types of food demand: small, incidental rural demand; small to moderate, fluctuating rural demand; large, predictable rural demand; and large, predictable urban demand.

3.1 Small, Incidental Rural Demand and Supply

Small, incidental rural demand was associated primarily with porterage. African porters were hired to transport goods, carry supplies in survey work and accompany colonial officers in their district touring. Peasants in many areas of the country disdained porterage, retaining vivid memories of the horrors associated with it during the German East African campaign of World War I.

There is virtually no information about the hiring and working conditions of porters by private individuals, whereas government porterage has impressionistic statistical and descriptive coverage. Total man-days worked by porters for various government departments and district and native administrations ranged between 281 000 and 331 000 between 1928 and 1930.[20]

Although the days of the caravan were over, sizeable groups of travelling porters seemed to be the norm. Bagshawe's diary recording his numerous foot safaris as District Officer, Provincial Commissioner and later head of the Land Development Survey, suggests that he frequently travelled with 20 to 30 porters, and during the survey had as many as 148.[21] During any safari of more than a few days' duration the number of porters expanded and contracted as some finished their required days, absconded or were sent off on errands while new recruits joined.

In view of porterage's historical legacy and the state's sensitivity on the issue of forced labour, porters' conditions of government service were clearly stipulated. In the 1920s, voluntary and involuntary porters could not be made to work for more than 60 days in a year. This was later reduced to 30 days. Loads were not to exceed 50 lbs. The daily march was not supposed to last for more than eight hours which was equated with roughly 16 miles.[22] Distances covered in a day, however, varied with the terrain and purpose of the safari. Generally, the march began before dawn and continued until around mid-day.

The district officer or senior officer-in-charge was held responsible for adequate food supply to their porters in government porterage. They were expected to ensure before embarking on the journey that supplies could be obtained en route. If there was any doubt, they were required to arrange for the carrying of supplies with them. The difficulties of getting an accurate picture of the supply situation in the area to be visited in view of the lack of markets and poor communications, meant that certainty of adequate supply was very rare. On the other hand, arranging for the entourage's food supply to be carried involved the transport of over 2 lbs of food per person per day. A 30-day safari with 30 porters would have entailed approximately 20 additional porters carrying nothing but food, and raised the troublesome issue of who would carry their food. Obviously some risks had to be taken regarding the procurement of food on the way. A relay system was sometimes instituted with porters plying back and forth between the encampment site and district headquarters or a market centre to maintain a regular flow of food, but similar manpower and logistical tangles usually ensued.

In areas where market activity was widely developed, porters were paid in cash, and expected to buy their own food, sometimes with the warning that they must not buy more than a day's rations to avoid too much additional weight to their load. However, such areas were frequently where motorised transport rather than porterage could be expected to be found. In villages off the beaten track unaccustomed to producing foodstuffs for sale, or localities where harvests had failed and stocks were low, porters were expected to rely on supply arrangements organised by the officer-in-charge.

Officers' en route supply arrangements consisted where possible of bulk purchases through the Native Authorities as well as some degree of self-provisioning in the form of wild game. Many government officials travelled with rifles, ready to shoot a buck or other animal on site. More importantly, Native Authorities were expected to facilitate the safari by the sale of foodstuffs at a fixed price. Government policy was opposed to officials accepting gifts of food from chiefs on behalf of themselves or their porters, whether or not this was a traditional form of hospitality. So too, the government wished to avoid placing peasants in a position in which they had to present food to the chiefs in a tributary manner which the chief in turn sold to the strangers. It was clearly stipulated that chiefs were obliged to arrange to have their people sell food directly to the official at the fixed price. There were instances of chiefs' unwarranted non-cooperation in the sale of foodstuffs, but these were isolated cases.[23] A clause in the Native Authority Ordinance permitted District Officers or Provincial Commissioners to issue a Native Authority with orders to supply food in emergencies or when food was plentiful and the inhabitants refused sale.[24] This was to be used as an extreme last resort and applied only to basic foodstuffs rather than eggs, milk, chickens, etc. Non-government safaris were also required to pay the fixed prices for food.

Overall, supply arrangements were tedious. In a desparate situation a runner could be sent to district headquarters with instructions for additional porters to bring supplies. The officer's safari diaries were strewn with numerous housekeeping notes about who had gone off to procure food, and the payment for this or that consignment of a few bags of maize or beans from a particular Native Authority or trader, and concern that the cook did not abscond with supplies.[25] When one runs across diary entries, such as 'For once in our lives we have plenty of food!',[26] one realises that despite the organisational attempts of the officer-in-charge, food insecurity was a daily event for the safari porter.

3.2 Moderate, Fluctuating Rural Demand and Supply

Moderate, fluctuating rural demand was most commonly found in mining areas, lumbering sites and at en route labour camps. Labour camps had a seasonal occupancy pattern related to the agricultural year. Mining camps were often impermanent sites. In both cases, the unpredictability of demand and the remoteness of the locations made them difficult to supply.

Labourers migrating to the coastal sisal plantations usually took several days to reach their destinations, especially in the 1920s when most of the distance was covered by foot. Attested labourers were supposed to be fed by their recruiter, while the majority who were unattested took supplies of dry foodstuffs with them. Apart from the difficulty of carrying enough food for their needs during the journey, they frequently lacked adequate cooking utensils, and employers were constantly complaining about the poor nutritional state of newly arrived workers.

As the years passed and the migrant labour system became more entrenched, well-trodden migration routes emerged, which sometimes actually prompted some market response in the form of wayside taverns. However, this was uncommon. Migrating labourers had little or no money to spend on their way to the work site or for that matter on their way back. In many cases, they had to make their food packets from home last, or otherwise work for food during the journey.

The Labour Department was established in 1926, and one of its main functions was to operate en route labour camps at strategic places, ideally one day's walk apart from each other on the most frequently used labour routes. Kilosa camp, the earliest and most important camp for sisal workers, was catering for over 38 000 labourers in 1927.[27] By 1940 there were 201 840 travelling labourers accomodated in 26 labour camps.[28] But here again, there was a problem of payment for food. Workers who were accredited labourers of any well-known plantation or farm could have their meals charged against that workplace, whereas the others were expected to have the means to pay. Citrus fruit, a source of ascorbic acid which prevents scurvy, was the only free hand-out. It appears that there was little problem in keeping the labour camps stocked with sufficient foodstuffs, because monthly statistics were kept of labour camp occupants so that seasonal demand could be predicted. Furthermore, many of the labour camps were located on major roads and rail junctions and therefore easy to supply.

The main mining areas during the interwar period were the Lupa, Southwest Mwanza and the Musoma goldfields. Lupa was an arid, inaccessible plain of the Southern Highlands that was uninhabited in the mid-1920s, when the gold rush began. From a mere trickle of non-African 'diggers' and their African labour, the Lupa goldfield grew to a population of more than 20 000 by the mid-1930s. The alluvial deposits beckoned to amateur miners and adventurers as well as the professionals.

Food supply to the area was problematic owing to the lack of peasant habitation and agricultural potential in the immediate vicinity as well as to remoteness from the railway and the absence of roads. To boost labour productivity, employers tried to provide food rations to their labour. In the early days, diggers appointed buyers from amongst their hired labour and sent them off in the company of several porters to Tukuyu, some 80 kms away to purchase foodstuffs. The diary of Dickson, a young gold mining adventurer who roughed it for six months on the Lupa in 1925, reveals that he had between 10 to 30 workers with four to five additional men who served as buyers, assisted by anywhere between three and ten porters each, operating in relays.[29]

As small-time venture capitalists, the non-African diggers were frequently illiquid and could not pay their labour in money or food, let alone provide decent housing. Nor had they the means to buy foodstuffs in quantity, for storage, during the harvest when prices were low.

By the early 1930s, the Lupa had gained the reputation of being Tanganyika's inferno. Sanitation and food supplies were stretched far beyond the limits of public health. Scurvy was rife. Asian traders had appeared, purchasing maize, rice and beans from the Native Authorities in Mbeya, the closest being 60 kms away, and transporting most of the foodstuffs by porterage. Maize was selling at over two times the amount that was considered 'normal' in other parts of the country. The Indians were accused of forming a collusive ring to escalate food prices. To what degree high maize prices were due to Indian collusion as opposed to a genuine shortage of maize and a transport bottleneck is impossible to ascertain now, but it is unlikely that the sharp increase in food demand over such a short space of time could have elicited an immediate supply response.

A supply response was, however, developing. Nyakyusa peasant households were migrating from their densely populated home areas in Rungwe and Tukuyu to Mbeya, where they produced maize as a cash crop. Similarly, the shores of Lake Nyasa were being planted with paddy for the Lupa market, and in the process ploughs were increasingly being used. But colonial officials were impatient with the rate at which the Nyakyusa were managing to supply the market and encouraged Mbozi European coffee planters to produce maize, as well as considering alienating more land to European farmers.

The government was slow to take action amidst the Depression. In 1935, a road was built from Mbozi to the Lupa to facilitate supply. A medical inspector was appointed to the area the following year and in 1937 Kenyan hybrid seeds were distributed to farmers and special concessions were made to allow food imports from Nyasaland duty free. The latter measure came after the domestic supply of foodstuffs was virtually resolved. Food imports were anticipated to have disincentive effects on local production.

African labourers were generally dependent on their employers for their rations, and worked on a full-time daily basis rather than taking time off to procure food or grow it. However, most were reluctant to work for more than three or four months of the year and tended to return to their home areas to cultivate when the planting season arrived. The majority were Nyakyusa from the surrounding highlands.

Food supply to the Southwest Mwanza and Musoma goldfields posed less difficulties. These consisted of reef mines, usually involving working populations of over 50 people, and in one or two cases as many as 3000. They were in accessible areas, either proximate to densely populated settlements of peasants who were used to producing cotton and rice for the market, or in the case of Southwest Mwanza, more sparsely populated, but through employers' active encouragement peasant settlement and marketed food production had gradually developed. If the local peasants' harvest failed, the mines were relatively accessible to the railway for easy food importation from Dar es Salaam or by lake from Kenya. Mine labourers' demand for maize was instrumental in prompting the adoption of the plough in the Lake Province during the late 1930s.[30] Rations were usually provided by the employer, but the employers were more likely than on the Lupa to be professional miners, small syndicates or mining companies able to pay better wages and provide food regularly. In the large mining concerns food was cooked for the labourers. Geita mine, in particular, was officially viewed as a model workplace with respect to its provisioning of a balanced, daily diet of cooked food for the workers.

Diamonds were not discovered at Mwadui until 1940. The Mwadui diamond mine was financed by international capital, notably that of the South African, Oppenheimer. To prevent diamond thefts, workers lived in closed compounds, with their rations fully provided for them. After World War II, Mwadui became a model of social welfare measures for workers.

The fluctuating demand of rural labourers working on the railway and in the timber industry is evident but not well documented. Rural railway workers got higher than average pay because of the isolation of their work and the expectation that they would be working full-time on the job. Fairly detailed commentary exists on enclaves of railway platelayers at Itigi and Tengeni in 1946.[31] Railway workers were normally not provided with rations, but at that time they were given the option of receiving a food ration in lieu of a portion of their wage. 1946 was a year of widespread food shortages and all opted to take the rations. However, it was found that many were selling some of the more basic items in their rations like maize meal on the lucrative black market, while trying to make the remainder stretch to meet their families' needs. Railway men were not in the habit of cultivating the surrounding area, anticipating that crop loss through animal depravation would make it a waste of time. Instead, they were accustomed to returning to their home areas during the planting season. However, in so doing, they forfeited the chance of receiving a retirement gratuity which required 15 years of uninterrupted service, in spite of the fact that many had worked for the railways for decades on a regular basis.

In summary, employers tended to provide rations or pay relatively high wages to wage workers situated in remote areas for concentrated periods of time or doing very demanding work, rather than leaving it up to workers' food self-provisioning on the job. But there was no fixed pattern. Employers and workers resorted to all sorts of ad-hoc measures depending on the agricultural potential of the surrounding area, distance from worker's home area and the resources and concerns of the employer. In contrast to the small, incidental food demand discussed earlier, Asian traders came to play an active role in supplying mining and other fluctuating populations of wage labourers, since the extent and location of demand, could be anticipated within a reasonable range of accuracy.

3.3 Large, predictable rural demand and supply

Large, predictable rural demand emanated from the plantations and farms of the sisal corridors and European farm clusters of the country. These enterprises constituted the bulk of non-peasant household food demand in the country and exerted the greatest pressure on the country's restricted food-producing capacity. Generally, with the exception of some of the Southern Highland farms, they were accessible to the railway or a high-grade road. Reliance on imported food was quite pronounced.

The government held employers responsible for the adequacy of their workers' diet. The government-recommended diet for labourers consisted of a daily ration of 24 oz. of maize meal, 4 oz. of beans, 2 oz. of groundnuts and a weekly allocation of 2 lbs of meat, 1 lb of fresh vegetables and 2 oz. of salt.[32] The state declined to make this diet statutory, arguing that owing to the difficult food supply conditions in so many parts of the country, employers had to be left with room to adapt to the local availability of foodstuffs and transport circumstances. Labour inspectors, with the powers of second-class magistrates, visited plantations and checked workers' complaints about diet. Despite the very dedicated work of labour inspectors like R.C. Jerrard, the small staffing of the Labour Department never allowed for comprehensive enforcement. Instead, the state tried to propagandise the advantages accruing to the employer who paid sufficient attention to workers' nutritional needs.

The Masters and Native Servants Ordinance of 1924 placed responsibility on employers to provide food for their non-local labourers only in the event that foodstuffs were not reasonably and readily available in the vicinity of the workplace. Those workers who were rationed by their employers, the so-called 'fed labour', were few in number on sisal estates. Attested labour often had a food ration clause in their contract, but they could opt out of this arrangement.

An employer's main task, therefore, was to ensure the adequate supply of purchasable foodstuffs for his labour force. A sisal estate labour force usually numbered between 200 and 1000 workers. The supply arrangements involved one or a combination of the following: first, encouraging local peasants regularly to sell their surpluses to the labourers; second, opening up a shop on the estate which they supplied through bulk orders for maize from Kenya or from nearby settler farmers who specialised in maize production; and third, allowing an Asian *dukawallah* to establish a shop on the estate to cater for the workers' food requirements. The first option rarely if ever provided a regular, inexhaustible source of supply. So it was the latter two, particularly the third, that became common features of the estate landscape.

The government was alert to profiteering at the expense of workers' diet. Frequently, labourers were given small weekly or daily advances by their employer to buy food and other essentials before the completion of their *kipande*. The advance was often barely enough to cover the workers' essential food needs. The government was critical of the prolonging effects this could have on workers finishing their *kipande*. On the other hand, prior to remuneration labourers rarely had cash for purchasing food. Employers who engaged in the 'truck system' or had 'tommy shops' faced legal penalties. In the truck system, an employer unilaterally issued food claim chits in lieu of a portion of a worker's wage. This, in effect, was a barter transaction, labour for food with the labourer unable to judge how much he was getting in the exchange. Tommy shops were complementary to the truck system. The employer or his relations usually managed the tommy shop which they supplied with foodstuffs and other consumer goods that were either purchased in large bulk amounts at discount prices or alternatively were inferior quality goods purchased at cheap prices. The labourer was a captive customer who exchanged his claim chits for the goods, having no way of avoiding the inferior goods nor being availed of any discount.

Another employers' practice that jeopardised workers' nutritional well-being was that of withholding wages. Employers withheld wages as a disciplinary measure or because they were illiquid. Amongst the employers of fed labour there was the widespread practice of issuing rations at the end of the day but linking the more desired items like meat to work output or the completion of five or six consecutive days of work. In addition, food rations were frequently underweighed, or an undue proportion of maize meal was issued in place of protein dietary components. Absentee or sick labourers were not always given their full daily ration.

Similarly, the state had its reservations about Asian *dukawallahs*' practice of extending credit to African labourers to buy foodstuffs and consumer durables. It was a well-entrenched system that the state voiced disapproval of, but did not act to dismantle. The consumer durables were kept in locked tin boxes in the *duka* until the completion of the workers' *kipande* when accounts between the *dukawallah* and labourer could be settled. Sometimes a *dukawallah* had hundreds of these boxes in his shop. In the event of bankruptcy, these boxes could not be claimed by the creditor owing to the Restrictions of Credit to Natives Ordinance.

As for labourers' self-provisioning of food under the *kipande* system, in some cases, employers directly facilitated the practice by allocating a section of the estate for food cultivation. In the Southern Province, where food rationing was exceedingly rare, workers were encouraged to plant food crops between the rows of sisal on many estates. In isolated instances, there is evidence that some employers were openly antagonistic to workers' food cultivation; for example, one employer uprooted his labourers' food crops in protest against their low labour productivity and was fined by a labour inspector for doing so.[33] It is difficult to surmise from the existing literature the proportion of self-provisioned as opposed to purchased food that workers consumed, but it seems likely that the bulk of food consumed on sisal estates was purchased, because of the constraints on the worker's time. Farms were different. Farm labourers and their families generally squatted on the farm and grew most of their own food.

A good deal of the early official concern centered on dietary standardisation rather than dietary improvement. Labourers coming from a variety of geographical areas with different basic food staples had to be made accustomed to a maize-based diet to facilitate lower labour costs. Those coming from plantain and milk diets were considered especially vulnerable.[34] De-worming and a special feeding programme for those workers who arrived at plantations in obvious states of malnutrition were recommended. Dietary considerations were constantly linked with the issue of labour productivity. Estate managers and state officials alike claimed that labourers tended to leave the plantation in a better state of nourishment than they entered.[35]

During the 1930s the state became increasingly sensitive to the nutritional deficiencies experienced by the Tanganyikan wage labour force, particularly on sisal plantations. Labour inspectors were highly conscious of the variation in estates' food policies and the detrimental effect of managements that tried to cut costs by inadequate provisioning of food to workers. The 1938 committee report on the supply and welfare of native labour reflected the growing international recognition of nutritional problems in the colonies.[36] It took the view that the widespread nutritional inadequacies were systemic rather than being due solely to negligent employers. Against the background of a growing labour shortage and the belief that there were no untapped labour reserves to be drawn upon (hence the need for making the existing labour force more productive), it associated nutritional inadequacies with the lack of fed labour and aspects of the bachelor wage system. They argued that those labourers who did not receive rations from their employers tended to skimp on food purchases, and were too tired at the end of a day's work in the field to collect firewood and cook, let alone engage in food cultivation. Thus the report recommended that employers provide their labour with cooked meals, or alternatively encourage the settlement of entire families, so that labourers' wives could attend to the food production, firewood collection and cooking.

Soon after this report was published the state commissioned a committee to advise on nutrition.[37] The war underlined the need for nutrition reform. One-third of the African men who were conscripted for military service during World War II did not pass their medical examination.[38] In 1944, a standardised diet became compulsory for fed labour. After World War II, the incidence of fed labour increased, a prelude to the overhaul of the bachelor wage system that was to follow in the decades to come. Furthermore, there was a growing concern on the part of nutritionists that a 'fed' labourer living with his family needed additional rations to feed his wife and children, to ensure that the labourer consumed the entirety of his ration rather than sharing it.

3.4 Large, predictable urban demand and supply

During the interwar period, Dar es Salaam was the only population settlement numbering over 20 000 people. Between 1921 and 1939, its population rose from 24 600 to approximately 41 000. In 1939, roughly a quarter were Asians, and Europeans comprised between 2 and 3 per cent.

The marketed food demand of Dar es Salaam contrasted quite strikingly with that of the rest of the country. Three cultural food traditions intersected: the diverse African staple food tradition of sorghum, millet, maize, plantains, rice and cassava; the Asian predilection to rice and, to a lesser extent, wheat; and the European one to wheat and Irish potatoes. Interestingly, rice was the city's preferred staple food, and had been so already in German times when African migrants from up-country areas eager to adopt an urban image embraced the Swahili coastal culture with its rice-based cuisine. In 1931, amidst the reduced purchasing power of the Depression and the imposition of a duty on imported rice in conjunction with incentives to increase domestic rice exports, the African population was forced to turn to maize as their staple. However, they continued to disdain *posho*,[39] and insisted on the more refined but less nutritious *unga wa kutwanga*.[40] Asians preferred particular rice varieties imported from India to Tanganyikan rice and were thus more affected by the 1931 duty than any other group. However, their higher incomes allowed them to maintain their consumption pattern.

Dar es Salaam was served by numerous *dukas*, usually owned by Asians or Arabs, which carried basic staple food items which were often sold on credit. With the exception of domestic servants, most employed Africans did not receive food rations from their employers and had to make their wages stretch to meet food and non-food requirements. African wages in Dar es Salaam for skilled and unskilled labour were considerably higher than in the rest of the country, but prices were also higher, and living in close proximity to brown and white populations that were receiving salaries in vast excess to their own made African Dar es Salaamites acutely aware of the discomforts of a low wage.

In Dar es Salaam, as elsewhere, African employees were subjected to a bachelor wage system but they were more likely to have dependants living with them, in contrast to the bachelor compound existence of plantation labourers. In 1942, a state enquiry revealed that 90 per cent of the African government unskilled employees sampled were living with women. The average family consisted of a man and woman and 1.23 children. Earning less than 60 Shs. a month, they were found to be 'in receipt of a wage on which they cannot possibly subsist without getting into debt and remaining in debt'.[41] These findings confirmed the observations of previous commentators and inferred grave difficulties for unskilled non-government employees, whose wage rates tended to be less than half of those of the government. There were no great voices of reform calling for an increase in African wages, Orde-Browne, alert to the possibility of any appearing, had written more than a decade before: 'An increase in wages will . . . prove the merest temporary palliative; the higher the wage the greater the extraction of the magnet and the larger the flow of deluded victims towards the mecca of the town harpy, and the worse the eventual result. The town native will be eventually no better off and the cost of living will have increased for all concerned.'[42]

Without waged employment, it was difficult to survive. Legislation restricting itinerant trading acted against the development of a large informal sector.[43] African unemployment in Dar es Salaam had been a policy concern from the outset of British colonial rule. Following the war in 1920 and 1921, destitute Africans were repatriated to the rural areas. During the Depression unemployment mounted. By 1939, an estimated 4300 men, approximately 33 per cent of all adult men, had no visible form of income.[44] The state's reflex response, as always, was to get the African back on the land.

Cultivation on the outskirts of Dar es Salaam was primarily to meet subsistence needs and, along with direct farm supply from the up-country homestead, was a vital part of African urban household food supply. However, whether the foodstuffs consumed in Dar es Salaam were bought in the market or came directly from farms, the bulk of the city's staple food supply did not originate in the immediate environs of the city or Uzaramo. Rice came from Rufiji and Mwanza; maize from Northern and Central Provinces; cassava from the surrounding districts of Kisarawe, and Bagamoyo; sorghum and millet from Lindi. The railways and roads all led to Dar es Salaam, so sources of domestic supply were diverse. As the country's major port, Dar es Salaam was in the most accessible position for receipt of food imports. In comparison with other places, Dar es Salaam was easy to supply. It had the largest number of consumers dependent on purchased supplies and the heaviest concentration of Asian traders to facilitate distribution. The market in food was well-developed. Nevertheless, food provisioning direct from peasant household farms was a significant feature of Dar es Salaam's urbanised setting.

11 The Systematisation of Territorial Food Supply: 1939–50

State food marketing policy during the interwar period was non-interventionist. With the exception of rice which was an important export crop, marketing of foodstuffs was not subject to state controls. Sources of food supply for the wage-labour force, produce marketing arrangements and food distribution to workers were left to develop on an ad hoc basis. Patterns were identifiable as described in the preceding chapter; but there was great spatial variation. During the 1940s, this was to change. Under increasing state intervention in the spheres of distribution, production and consumption, a more uniform, territorial pattern of supply evolved.

1 THE WORLD WAR II ECONOMIC ENVIRONMENT

World War II was a tremendous boom to the Tanganyikan economy. Sisal, coffee, cotton and tea were in short supply in the allied world and their prices rose accordingly. Pyrethrum, a fairly new crop, and rubber, which Tanganyika had relinquished to East Asian competition some decades back, became important export crops. Increased tonnages of export crops removed the railway under-capacity and debt problem. The country's balance of payments became very strong and the territorial budget was continually in surplus.

Labour demand reached an all-time high. Employers' ability to attract labour was hampered by the acute shortages of imported consumer incentive goods which afflicted the country as well as the higher earnings peasants made through the sale of food crops. To optimise labour usage the state made it mandatory for a labourer to complete a *kipande* in 42 days in prescribed areas, and the Tanganyika Sisal Growers' Association agreed to pay a bonus of three shillings for its completion in that time.

Immediately upon the outbreak of hostilities in September 1939, the Tanganyikan state instituted price and commodity controls on lines similar to those of Britain. The intention was to retain the prewar cost of living and ensure consumer supplies of vital goods. This involved setting retail price levels for a number of basic commodities. Under the Defence Regulations, an Economic Control Board was set up whose main functions were to select the commodities to control and authorise approved traders for them. Organisationally, it was divided into an East African War Supplies Board (1940) which provisioned military foodstuff requirements and the East African Civil Supplies Board (1941) that facilitated close cooperation between the three East African territories in import, export and commodity control of foodstuffs and other categories of goods. These agencies increasingly intervened in Asian trading channels, at first merely at the extreme ends, i.e. retailing and import/export, but, as wartime exigencies mounted, their monitoring and supervisory activities encroached on the whole gamut of trade.

2 BURGEONING FOOD DEMAND AMIDST DOMESTIC PRODUCTION CONSTRAINTS, 1939–45

During World War II, Tanganyika's economy was kindled by better export crop prices and imperial demands for strategic raw materials. Tens of thousands of young men were recruited into the military. Tanganyika's plantations and mines were faced by a severe shortage of African wage labour. Labour conscription and measures to spur workers to finish their 30-day *kipandes* more quickly were intended to rationalise African wage labour usage. The *kipande* restriction was the first step in a long process of stabilising the labour force and removing the food self-provisioning element of African wage labour. The expansion of the rural labour force was accompanied by a deluge of migrants into the city of Dar es Salaam and the smaller towns.

The number of people dependent on purchased food catapulted. The additional people included several thousand refugees and prisoners of war, most of whom were European, and tens of thousands of African labourers, military recruits and urban migrants.[1] The former lived in camps and were fed a wheat-based diet, while the Africans were usually consuming the standard maize *posho* diet. In addition, Tanganyika was expected to export food to the Middle East as part of its war contribution.

In 1943 drought struck much of the country, causing severe famine in Central Province. The drought affected Kenya as well and eliminated her maize export capacity, leaving Tanganyika without a cheap source of imports. The Colonial Office engaged in a worldwide search for grain and shipping space to rescue East Africa. Failing to procure Argentinian maize, Tanganyika eventually had to make do with large imports of expensive Australian wheat.

Crisis conditions led the state to pursue four main policies to boost domestic production: exhortation of peasants, plantation self-sufficiency, non-African production support and state farms. Towards the close of 1942, when the certainty of food shortages in the following year loomed large, the state stressed the need for the stimulation of peasant production by propaganda, fair prices and, if need be, planting orders issued through the Native Authorities.

Food self-sufficiency was already an aspect of Tanganyikan colonial agricultural policy with respect to the peasant household and district administrative units. Its appearance in 1943 in the form of plantation self-sufficiency is noteworthy. Up until that time, the Tanganyikan state had encouraged maximum production of the strategic exports such as sisal, rubber and pyrethrum, with a clear division of labour between food-producing and export crop-producing non-African farm units. In 1943, the Governor was forced to acknowledge that food production was 'the first essential in the maintenance of the whole war programme' in Tanganyika.[2] Plantations were served with planting orders, with the general intent of making them produce food for their own labourers as far as possible. Plantation managers frequently protested, complaining of the unsuitability of their soils, but agricultural officers made periodic checks to ensure their compliance with the policy.

Having been organised into District Production Committees, European farmers were ready to pressurise for all sorts of perks to boost their commercial food production. They were availed grants and loans for the breaking of new ground and the purchase of machinery.[3] By the end of 1944, approved agricultural loans totalled £55 000.[4] Non-African maize and cereal acreage increased by 10 000 acres between 1939 and the end of 1944.[5]

As the war progressed, non-African producers, particularly food producers, found it increasingly more difficult to procure adequate amounts of waged labour. The state came to their assistance by conscripting labour under the Defence Regulations. During 1941 and 1942, labour conscripts numbered 3 255, then shot up to 13 594 in 1943, 30 647 in 1944 and 26 256 in 1945. Almost one-third of all conscripts over the years were engaged in food production, mostly on farms in Northern Province.[6]

Europeans and Asians persistently pressured the state for land alienation during the war. The state maintained its mandate stance, but compromised by demarcating blocks of land in Iringa, Moshi, Arusha and Mbulu where they were willing to give short-term land leases, usually of three years on the approval of the Governor. By the end of 1944, over 50 000 acres of agricultural and pastoral land had been leased.[7]

The initiation of state farming was prompted by the desire for wheat import substitution. Using US Lend Lease equipment and Masai grazing land, the state launched the Northern Province Wheat Scheme. The Scheme lasted four years, ending with the 1947 wheat crop. Average yields over the period of four years amounted to a disappointing 2.35 bags per acre, which was attributed to a sequence of alternating extremely heavy and light rain, army worm attack, and lack of trained mechanics.[8] However, the scheme had succeeded in its original purpose of import substitution to save shipping space. The equivalent of two shiploads was produced over the four-year period.

During the 1943 food shortage, the state reduced the recommended ration of fed labour from 28–30 oz to 20 oz maize meal and on the Tanga line it was further cut to 12 oz.[9] The onus was on employers to substitute other foodstuffs. It is remarkable that while measures were being taken to reduce labourers' grain intake, the state was on the other hand making special efforts to ensure the supply of food to government employees, and a free ration was instituted for African government employees in Dar es Salaam and Tanga in June 1942. At the beginning of 1943, a Cost of Living Relief Committee was appointed to consider the nature and level of cost of living allowances to be awarded to African, Asian and European civil servants, aimed at maintaining their standard of living at prewar levels. It was estimated that the European cost of living had increased by 30 per cent between 1939 and 1943, whereas Africans in Dar es Salaam and Tanga had experienced not less than a 50 per cent increase.[10]

European and Asian allowances depended on the officer's salary level and family size and could not exceed 25 per cent of the officer's salary.[11] They were applicable to Europeans earning less than £644 and Asians earning less than £252. Africans earning less than 60s per month were given a monthly allowance of 2.50s plus a food ration. Those with earnings over 60s received an allowance of up to 12s without a ration. Africans complained about the mixed cash and food form of their allowance and stated they preferred receiving all cash, which the government ruled was nutritionally inadvisable. The cost of living allowances were reviewed and upgraded on an annual basis.

Asian traders were increasingly squeezed out of grain trading. In 1943, produce control was introduced which entailed grains like maize and sorghum being bought and sold at appointed selling places under the Economic Control Board. Only persons holding permits could purchase and move the grain from one district to another. At the retail level, public food rationing at controlled prices was instituted in Dar es Salaam and Tanga. A retailer was only allowed to sell to those presenting coupons from his area and not all retailers were given rations to distribute. The consumer endured long queues and tiresome inconvenience, which Economic Control Board officials hoped would serve as a deterrent to further urban migration.

Public food rationing was racially differentiated: Europeans received 4 oz Straightrun wheat flour per day, 8 oz rice per month and 16 oz sugar per week; Asians, 18 oz of rice per week, 12 oz of Atta flour per day, 16 oz sugar per week, 8 oz ghee per week, and Africans, a maize/millet/sorghum/cassava mixed flour ration varying between 18 and 28 oz depending on the area, 8 oz sugar per week and cooking oil.[12] Rationing was a means of controlling urban influx. Migrants were refused ration cards, unless they had been instructed to come to Dar es Salaam by an employer. Nonetheless, the consumption of African foodstuffs by registered ration card holders exceeded all estimates. The growth of Dar es Salaam was likened to 'a volcano which may erupt at any moment'.[13]

3 POST-WORLD WAR II ECONOMIC HARDSHIPS AND HORIZONS, 1946–50

The cessation of the war did not bring a removal of state concern over the territory's food supply. A world wide grain shortage led to exceptionally high international grain prices and reversed Tanganyika's historical position as a relatively high-cost producer. It became beneficial to rely on domestic production rather than expensive grain imports.

It was apparent that the increased number of purchased food consumers of the war period was going to be a permanent, if not continuously expanding, feature of the economy. Returning military servicemen were considered unlikely to quietly slip back into the peasantry. Many would desire town life. After six years of war, it was impossible to expect a siege economy to be acceptable to the populace. The food demand of the urban and rural wage labour force was going to have to be met in some other way. The 'era of development' began, with hope vested in economic planning, agricultural experts and mechanisation.

3.1 The cost of living and incomes

Everyone had an acute awareness of the cost of living. Racially-distinct standards of living based on markedly different income levels starkly manifested the three-tiered racial structure of the society.[14] Rationing further enforced the day-to-day consciousness of a world in which race was fate and fate was niggardly. In 1946, cereal rations were cut by 2 oz per day for Africans, with the warning that no further Africans arriving in Dar es Salaam after May 5, except civil servants and military staff, would be issued with rations. In September, there was a mass demonstration by Africans in Dar es Salaam protesting not so much at the quantity of the ration, as at its quality; the mixed meal contained mostly cassava and sorghum. African resentment remained at a high pitch in the years that followed, receiving additional punch from the political combativeness of African nationalists.

Despite efforts to hold down food prices, the price of a kilo of maize meal in Dar es Salaam rose from 9 cents in September 1939 to 23 cents in September 1948, then to 39 cents in November 1949, and 44 cents in 1950.[15] African urban workers, rather than plantation labourers, were the hardest hit by escalating prices, since very few had employers providing them with food. A sample of 100 Dar es Salaam African households earning 75s a month revealed that actual calories and protein consumed were approximately half of the amount contained in the government's recommended diet.[16] Plantation labourers however had their share of problems as well. During the 1946 food shortages, bulk allocations of maize at provincial and district levels destined for employers' distribution to their workers did not always cover the needs of labourers' resident wives and children.

Racial differences in salaries were being challenged. Two Africans were appointed to the Legislative Council and started registering their dissatisfaction. Labour unrest and strikes were on the increase. The 1947 dockers' strike became a general strike that spread along the rail-lines to Morogoro, Dodoma, Tabora, Kigoma, Mwanza and Mpanda, involving railway workers first and foremost, but in various places plantation labourers, teachers and civil servants also participated. The strike resulted in pay rises of 33 per cent on average for harbour workers.

The Railway African Association and the Dockworkers' and Stevedores' Union were both formed in 1947. In 1950 a dockers' strike sparked off rioting that resulted in violent confrontations and the deaths of two Africans. The state arrested the strike's leaders, confiscated the union's property and caused many of the dockers on permanent employment to flee. Iliffe notes that this effectively destroyed the traditions and dispersed the experienced personnel of the African labour movement which had been built up over the preceding decade.[17]

Meanwhile the state had made some efforts to improve conditions for the rural wage labour force. With the increase of sisal prices by £18, l0s per ton, the Ministry of Supply stipulated that £2, l0s per ton must be devoted to workers' welfare measures in the industry and the Labour Commissioner could sanction the withholding of this amount if a plantation did not comply. But this measure was a reforming gesture that begged the larger issue of eliminating the need for recruitment altogether and stabilising the wage labour force. Many sisal plantation employers were favourably inclined to such a development, seeing 'permanent settled labour on the basis of family life . . . the most satisfactory form of labour'.[18] Orde-Browne put his rubber stamp on the need for it:

> there appears to be little doubt that there must gradually be a readjustment of population to bring the workers nearer their place of employment, and thus to eradicate the existing constant waste of time and energy represented by the journey to and from the industrial centres. This will of course entail heavier charges on industry for the social services at present lacking or superfluous; but the great economy effected, and the resultant increase in efficiency should counterbalance this expense.[19]

In the same vein, there was a general feeling in the government that bachelor wages were not suitable for urban African workers. A Minimum Wage Ordinance had been passed in 1939 which remained a mere formality in the absence of any machinery for wage fixing. In

1947 and 1950, bills were passed to set up a Minimum Wages Board and Wages Council as a first step towards establishing a minimum wage for urban areas.

3.2 Planning production and distribution

During the interwar period, the territorial economy was only nominally integrated. Perennial labour shortages led to state efforts to rationalise labour usage geographically and temporally. Outside inter-provincial transport of labour, there was little official concern with or promotion of inter-regional commodity flows. Export and food commodities travelled by road and rail to Dar es Salaam or Tanga to be exported or consumed there. Imported food and consumer goods in turn were transported up-country.

After World War II, this began to change when it was realised that cheap food imports from Kenya and the outside world could not be used to balance supply and demand to the same extent as before. Suddenly basic foodstuffs, their domestic production and transport, became pivotal. Food pricing was at the heart of a conscious process of territorial economic integration. Government fixing of producer prices for food relative to export crops and geographical differentiation of producer and consumer food prices were aimed at balancing the economy and promoting economic expansion rather than mere maintenance and survival.

The alleviation of food insecurity remained an underlying premise of policy. Grave concern over the territory's food supplies instigated the launching of a 'four-year food plan' implemented between 1946 and 1950 with the intent of making Tanganyika self-supporting; the theme of self-sufficiency had at last reached the territorial level. African wage labourers' food requirements strongly motivated the plan. Miller, the Director of Agriculture, calculated that feeding the 350 000-strong wage labour force would require the utilisation of 407 050 acres of arable land and 1 750 000 acres of pasture and would demand 10 per cent of all African peasants' farming efforts, which they could spare in a good agricultural year, but not in a poor season.[20] The solution to this dilemma was seen to be agricultural intensification and storage. Mechanisation was both a means and an end. On a more modest scale, the four-year food plan mirrored the Groundnut Scheme's belief in the machine.

Settler farming rather than peasant farming was the *modus operandi* of the plan. Peasant agriculture was regarded as too erratic and lacking in policy responsiveness: 'It is essential to maintain, and as far as possible to increase the European production of wheat and maize which has proved the most dependable source of supply. Unless this is done there is grave danger of a deficiency.'[21] Subsidies to non-African farmers averaged over £60 000 per annum between 1946 and 1948.[22] Planting orders and guaranteed minimum return acreage payments were primarily for maize. The Land Bank was established in 1947 to facilitate agricultural loans to non-Africans. Furthermore, the short-term land leases of the war were renewed for another four years.[23] Over the same period the ex-German properties, totalling 278 000 acres, were allocated to settlers, in addition to 95 farms on newly alienated land covering 73 000 acres.[24]

Peasant agriculture was not totally overlooked. Peasants were encouraged to intensify their production by adopting better farming methods, rather than being expected to increase their acreages. An Agricultural Development Fund was established that dispensed approximately £45 000 by 1950, mostly in small amounts of £50–£100.[25] Seven Native Administration ploughing schemes for the cultivation of rice were introduced in the river valleys of the Ruvuma, Kilombero, Rufiji and Luengera, as well as at Same, Kilosa and Bagamoyo.

Since 1943, the state had hankered for a food marketing organisational structure with storage capacity that could iron out the wide fluctuations in year-to-year production. In 1949, state aspirations came to fruition with the founding of the Grain Storage Department (GSD), headquartered at Moshi. The GSD took over the marketing and storage of African staples from the Economic Control Board and was the agency through which Tanganyika continued its membership of the East African Cereals Pool. The GSD was set up to operate as a self-financing parastatal with an ultimate planned storage capacity of 52 600 tons. Managing its stocks in relation to the booms and busts of Tanganyikan harvests was to prove its biggest headache, but stock losses were very minimal. In 1949/50, only 1.7 per cent of its stock disappeared in transit from source of supply in Kenya through the docks and by rail to ultimate retail destination and 0.4 per cent was lost due to pest infestation.[26]

In the GSD's founding year, a drought occurred which was described as the worst drought in 50 years. The GSD was plunged into the necessity of importing huge amounts of grain to bridge the gap between territorial purchases of 15 831 tons versus sales of 111 050 (see Table 14.2). Dar es Salaam, where food import was the mainstay, was in a particularly vulnerable position.

The late 1940s had been a period of oscillating food insecurity. 1946 and 1949 were exceedingly bad years for domestic food production. 1945 net food imports, at over 1500 tons, was the highest to date, but 1946 imports more than doubled that figure and 1950 imports in the wake of the 1949 drought quadrupled it (see Table 1.1). Thus although it was the conscious policy of the country to avoid food imports they were more than ever dependent on them. However, it was a period of budgetary surpluses, making food imports not as serious a drain on the economy as might have otherwise been.

Amidst the drought of 1949, the newly appointed Governor Twining re-iterated the call for self-sufficiency in food, but in so doing he added a new twist. For the first time, there was a call for regional specialisation and an implicit rejection of district and household food self-sufficiency, the cornerstone of peasant agricultural policy for over 30 years:

> much effort is wasted in endeavouring to grow foodstuffs in unsuitable soil and climatic conditions . . . it may . . . be necessary for us to make some fundamental changes in our internal economy and to concentrate on the production of foodstuffs in those areas where soil and climatic conditions are favourable and to encourage the breeding of livestock and the cultivation of cash crops in the areas where staple foodstuffs are difficult to grow.[27]

If implemented, the implications of such a policy for the country's social division of labour would be profound.

Summary of Part IV

Between 1919 and 1950, the size of the African wage labour force expanded with only a temporary setback during the Depression. The interwar years were characterised by four different types of food demand met by assorted supply arrangements involving marketed supply from peasant households, European farms and imports, as well as direct farm supply from peasant households or through clientage. Under the influence of bachelor wages and the *kipande* system, workers divided their time between wage labour and their own food production, the latter being either interspersed with day-to-day work on the plantation or pursued in their home areas after spending short intervals in paid employment. Over time, the *kipande* system came under increasing criticism for the low level of labour productivity that was achieved under its sway.

During the war, the increased numbers of people removed from their rural households and the presence of thousands of refugees sojourned in Tanganyika for the duration of the war caused an extremely rapid rise in purchased food demand. Food supply arrangements of the previous decades had to be revised. From the outset of the war, state supervisory agencies were established to monitor the food trade. During the drought and food crisis of 1943, the state assumed more and more market supervision functions, and over the remaining years of the decade state price controls led gradually to the evolution of a territorially-integrated food market. Trying to avert heavy reliance on food imports, the state-subsidised European commercial food production, but the policy failed to achieve its ends; imports oscillated reaching higher and higher peaks on the upswing.

Despite the differences in food supply arrangements during the interwar years and during World War II, the two periods can nonetheless be regarded as part of the same food supply regime. From an institutional perspective, the persistence of bachelor wages resulted in the peasant household serving as the material fallback for workers' needs. Workers continuously drew on their peasant farming skills. The assumption underlying both rural and urban wage employment was that the worker would sooner or later return to his upcountry home.

The state, the market and clientage remained quite distinct and separate institutions identifiable with European, Asian and African agents respectively. State supervision of the Asian market during the 1940s led to some displacement and a hierarchical ordering of power relationships but not institutional mixing. Clientage seems not to have played a very central role in workers' food supply. Clientage networks were operating primarily within Native Authorities, with networking beyond the geographical boundaries of the Native Authority restricted by limited access to transport and communications. Neither state nor market agents were able or found it necessary to merge their activities with clientage activities. European state agents and Asian market agents were not exposed to the material circumstances that would have made them amenable to clientage practices. They acted on logics that were in many respects antithetical to those of clientage. On the other hand, African employees in the state and market were heavily supervised, to prevent them from engaging in clientage practices. And in the 1940s when they were exposed to serious deprivation, African state employees were cushioned against extreme hardship with the award of cost of living allowances.

Between 1919 and 1950, increasing food importation asserted itself as a long-term tendency (see Figure 5.1). During the interwar years the state saw food imports as a natural outcome of Tanganyika's poor harvest years as well as its lack of comparative advantage in producing maize and wheat. In the 1940s, the rise in international grain prices gave Tanganyika a relative advantage in grain production. But poor, and in 1943 and 1949 devastating, harvests, in addition to the strains of rapidly expanding food demand, and the even greater comparative advantage that Tanganyika had in some of its export crops made imports not just a continuing feature, but a deepening one. At the macro level, under the direction of the Colonial Office, the Tanganyikan state was following a classic Ricardian comparative advantage approach with respect to staple food production and import policies.

One of the central arguments of this book is that there is a tendency for the institutional influence of the state and the market to decline under conditions of increasing food insecurity. At first glance, the evidence of this section would appear to contradict this argument. After all, during the food insecurity of the 1940s, the state assumed a more dominating, supervisory role and there is no indication that the market contracted.

In defence of the argument, it is necessary to differentiate the experience of food insecurity in the population. The state took action to ensure the relative food security of its agents. Market agents as distributors probably had the most reliable food access in the economy. As long as market and state agents were not directly exposed to food insecurity, it was possible for the state and the market to remain coherent.

Going on to another central tenet of the book, did occupational specialisation undergo a process of involution under the food insecure conditions of the 1940s? This was the era when commercialised food farming was getting a big impetus from state subsidies, and agricultural mechanisation was given generous support, which might suggest that the answer is no. However, it must be remembered that the commercialised farming which was expanding was European and thus pertained to a minute portion of the rural population.

The development of European commercial farming represented the intensification rather than the expansion of the social division of labour. The intensification of the division of labour on the basis of race in the economy at large was analogous to the deepening of the sexual division of labour in the peasant household. Both represented the involution rather than enhancement of the social division of labour. Even though the African wage labour force was growing during this period, it consisted almost entirely of unskilled agricultural labourers, with virtually no occupational differentiation.

The policy of subsidising European food farming was in effect a 'peasant bypass', postponing the urgent need to transform peasant agriculture technologically and socially. The policy was contrary to the spirit of the Mandate and was folly in terms of what it set out to do. Short of the achievement of miraculous yields, there were not enough European agriculturalists in the country to grow the requisite food crops. Peasant household production units, meanwhile, were not just bypassed, they were mined for labour. Tens of thousands of young men were siphoned off through military and labour conscription, which undoubtedly served to reinforce the sexual division of labour in the peasant household.

In conclusion, it is apparent that amidst the food crises of the 1940s, the colonial state's inability to mount a policy package that would confront the underlying causes of food insecurity directly led to policies that rigidified the social division of labour on the basis of race. The state and the market remained intact during the period, somewhat self-absorbed perhaps, while the peasant household and its many internal and environmental problems were for the most part shelved. Clientage, on the other hand, was waiting in the wings, preparing to make its big debut on the territorial stage.

Part V Structural Social Change and Urban Food Supply, 1950–73

In this section, the restructuring of the extra-household social division is described through an examination of the elimination of the migrant wage-labour force, the decolonisation and Africanisation of the state, the erosion of the Asian market and the changing nature of clientage relations in the proliferation of African social organisations that surfaced during the 1950s. The cooperatives' clientage relations are singled out for closer examination. Against the backdrop of these social changes, food demand and supply are traced and related to the growth of urbanisation.

12 The Re-ordering of the State and the Market

The years between 1950 and 1973 saw an African challenge to the three-tier racial structure of the colonial society. European and Asian personnel were replaced by Africans in the state and the market and the nature of these institutions changed in the process. The stark racial division of labour gave way to more subtle African cleavages, those of region, town and country and muted economic differentiation of the peasantry.

Perhaps the theme of 'nation-building' most aptly embraces the many developmental strands of the period. Nationalist consciousness prompted the dismantling of the racial division of labour and the harnessing of rural peasant household production to the national integrative forces of the state and market. Clientage networks served as the adhesive that often acted corrosively on state and particularly market functions. But before considering the interaction of the state, the market and clientage networks, it is necessary to examine the transformation of the African wage-labour force.

1 STABILISING THE WAGE-LABOUR FORCE

In the early 1950s, the African wage-labour force was largely agricultural, unspecialised and impermanent; it was made up of unskilled male migrants receiving bachelor wages (see Tables 12.1 and 12.2). Despite the state's prodding and employers' declared interests in promoting a more productive, permanent wage-labour force, it was the political pressure of African nationalists that finally brought about an end to the migrant labour system.

Formal labour organisation took shape during the 1950s. In 1955, two activists of the African Commercial Employees Association in close contact with the Tanganyika African National Union (TANU) founded the Tanganyikan Federation of Labour, which served as an umbrella organisation for the labour movement for the next nine years. An avalanche of trade union registrations followed. In 1957 labour unrest became very pronounced and did not abate until the establishment of a territorial minimum wage in 1963.

TABLE 12.1 *The African wage-labour force, 1950–60*

Year	*Estate agriculture*	*Mining*	*Manuf'g**	*Building and Const.*	*Commerce*	*Transport*	*Public services*	*Other services*	*Domestic service*	*Others*	*TOTAL*	*Non-African labour Force*
1950^{+}	206916	18833	9875	n.a.	29238		41383	n.a.	37173	16825	360243	
1951	239248	18329	25996	45667	19350	23905	31427§	26946	15342	9188	455398	
1952	234317	16529	22539	21253	14627	6951	89519^{xx}	16874	20430	558	443597	39868^{++}
1953	226601	17730	17691	14265	11743	6892	103037	12674	30000	7638	448271	
1954	218094	15453	19669	16373	11428	6535	100596	12565	30000	8381	439094	
1955	201350	14346	19014	12161	11267	6204	99368	11261	30000	8129	413100	
1956	207112	14596	18988	12977	9341	7416	102343	14054	40000	7382	434209	
1957	211351	12975	19839	11377	9675	8157	94284	12777	40000	10035	430470	38616§§
1958	213092	12182	21326	10438	11800	7891	97170	15559	40000	1089	430547	
1959	220199	9560	19737	11148	12572	8940	94350	16562	35000	200	428268	
1960	199021	11060	18349	9093	12835	6076	86237	14804	30000	n.a.	397475	
1961											383117	
1962											368816	

NOTES

* Includes electricity and water supply from 1951 to 1960.

+ Does not include an estimated 22000 women and children labourers and 38000 male casual labourers.

§ Government services and Native Authorities.

xx Includes all public servants – no allocation having been made to other industrial groups.

++ Taken from the 1952 Non-African Population Census.

§§ Taken from the 1957 Non-African Population Census.

SOURCES

Compiled from:

1. Tanganyika, Department of Labour Annual Report, 1950.
2. East African Statistical Department, *Statistical Abstract*, 1951–63.

The 30–day *kipande* system was abolished when minimum wages were granted in 1963. The imposition of the minimum wage had a more drastic effect on real wages in the agricultural sector than the non-agricultural sector. The bachelor wage system and all its trappings became a thing of the past. In wage negotiations, trade unions favoured the transmutation of food rations into cash.

The territorial minimum wage had far-reaching effects. An immediate dip in total employment occurred as many employers sought to rationalise labour usage (see Table 12.2). Agricultural employers made the most drastic cutbacks, which in the case of sisal were compounded by the severe drop in sisal prices on the world market.

The territorial minimum wage engendered substantial African income differentials. As a result of the minimum wage order, average real wages rose by 32 per cent between 1962 and 1963 (see Table 12.3). Not only did the wage permit labourers to bring their families with them to their work location, but many more men and women were attracted to wage employment and gravitated to the urban areas. Seemingly overnight Tanganyika's perennial labour shortage became a labour surplus and urban unemployment was identified as a social problem (see Tables 12.1 and 12.2).

In 1967, in conjunction with the Arusha Declaration which asserted Tanzania's intention to build a socialist society, the state's wage policy changed to one of concern over the increasing level of average wages for regular employees and the non-expansion of wage employment. Efforts were made to reduce income differentials, to limit overall annual wage increases to 5 per cent and to make them conditional on performance.

Labour specialisation amongst African wage earners progressed throughout the entire period. Unfortunately, it is difficult to give precise figures for this since labour statistics were collected on the basis of citizenship rather than race beginning in 1961. The increasing diversification of the African wage labour force is, however, implicit in the shrinking proportion of agricultural estate labourers (see Table 12.2).[1] The public sector, which was highly responsive to Africanisation pressures, was expanding relative to the private sector.

2 DECOLONISING AND AFRICANISING THE STATE

During the early 1950s, a growing nationalist consciousness was evident in towns around the country with its epicentre in Dar es

TABLE 12.2 *Total wage employment by industry and sector, 1961–82**

Year	*Estate agric.*	*Mining*	*Manuf'g*	*Public utilities*	*Building and Const.*	*Commerce*	*Transport*	*Services*	*Finance*	*TOTAL*
1961	204958	11875	26363	6910	41775	17700	21412	70853	–	401846
1962	203845	8674	23397	5277	41173	16943	23344	68496	–	391149
1963	165532	7596	22212	3880	28290	16477	24409	71948	–	340344
1964	163589	8035	23583	4637	33740	17341	25670	74662	–	351257
1965	139162	7418	25729	4752	31457	17843	26426	80968	–	333755
1966	126223	6191	29890	5303	37460	20935	27560	82935	–	336497
1967	123887	6493	31186	7093	41929	20077	29725	86351	–	346741
1968	109213	6121	35359	9601	47305	21415	31764	90933	–	351711
1969	112888	5919	40323	9755	52767	19072	32389	90556	4257	367926
1970	107368	6096	43746	11296	54569	20617	33813	93295	4835	375635
1971	108971	5753	55158	10603	50931	23353	37404	94929	5668	392770
1972	113843	5558	55389	12304	51842	24777	37049	98575	6356	405713
1973	109047	5013	59336	18904	104777	26713	38115	104083	6515	472503

1974	123973	4762	64921	16074	72810	25322	45166	123659	7399	484086
1975	121831	5143	74133	14872	61625	34982	45847	103008	9355	470796
1976	132343	5281	75003	15001	43044	37981	52206	110785	9080	480724
1977	126722	4984	79318	18145	35028	32338	52296	127283	7560	483674
1978	123374	4935	100072	21886	42311	34290	59189	140954	8934	535945
1979	127970	5859	107097	19786	50555	40047	55476	177667	12311	596768
1980	130979	5900	105803	19542	48650	38096	58319	181984	13920	603193
1981	129550	7020	114234	21060	49778	37653	59350	204217	15316	638178
1982	137449	7231	118234	21460	51377	38030	60166	229170	16900	676017

NOTE
* Includes Africans and non-Africans.

SOURCES
Compiled from:
1. Tanganyika, Central Statistical Bureau, *Statistical Abstract* (DSM: Government Printer) various years.
2. Tanzania, *Survey of Employment and Earnings* (DSM: Government Printer, 1962–78).
3. Tanzania, *The Economic Survey, 1982* (DSM: Government Printer, 1983) p. 63.

TABLE 12.3 *Minimum wage index, 1939–84*

Year	*Government unskilled wage rate (1939 = 100)*[1]	*Government unskilled wage rate (1950 = 100)*[2]	*Territorial minimum wage (1963 = 100)*[3]	*Nominal wage index (1963 = 100)*[4]	*Real wage index (1963 = 100)*[5]
1939	100			8	33
1940	160			13	n.a.
1943	200			16	43
1944	220			18	45
1945	260			21	50
1946	260			21	48
1947	320			26	58
1950	350	100		28	39
1951	430	114		32	38
1952	430	123		35	40
1953	510	137		39	39
1954	510	146		42	43
1955	600	171		49	51
1956		171		49	52
1957		192		55	56
1958		192		55	53
1959		229		65	64
1960		229		65	63
1961		229		65	63
1962		229		65	63
1963		351	100	100	100
1964			100	100	97
1965			100	100	92
1966			100	100	87
1967			100	100	85
1968			100	100	82
1969			113	113	91
1970			113	113	88
1971			113	113	86
1972			160	160	110
1973			160	160	101
1974			220	227	109
1975			253	253	81
1976			253	253	67
1977			253	253	57
1978			253	253	49
1979			253	253	46
1980			320	320	50
1981			320	320	39
1982			400	400	39
1983			400	400	32
1984			540	540	n.a.

SOURCES

Compiled from:

1. Tanganyika, *Labour Department Annual Report 1951*, p. 39; Iliffe, J., 'A History of Dockworkers of Dar es Salaam', *TNR* 71 (1970) p. 123.

2. Compiled from Tanganyika, *Labour Department Annual Reports*, 1950–63.
3. Compiled from Jackson, D., 'The Disappearance of Strikes in Tanzania: Incomes Policy and Industrial Democracy', *Journal of Modern African Studies* 17(2) (1979) p. 248; Jamal, V., 'The Political Economy of Devaluation in Tanzania', International Labour Office, Addis Ababa (1984) p. 32; *Daily News*, 15/6/84.
4. Compiled from references listed above.
5. Compiled from references listed above divided by the Retail Amalgamated Consumer Price Index 1939–83, which is calculated from Tanganyika, *Labour Department Annual Report 1951*, p. 39; Tanganyika, *Labour Department Annual Reports*, 1951–63, annual average calculated from monthly values; Bank of Tanzania, *Economic and Operations Report* (June 1975) p. 86; Bank of Tanzania, *Economic and Operations Report* (June 1984) p. 90.

Salaam. The Tanganyika African National Union party was founded in 1954. The early nationalists tended to have one thing in common. Almost all had travelled away from home, either through military service during World War II or wage employment. Most had had some formal education and were often employed in white-collar jobs in the civil service or teaching profession.

Julius Nyerere, the Makerere graduate and Dar es Salaam school teacher who became president of TANU, had a creative genius for adopting nationalist models to the Tanganyikan context and communicating them in a lively, convincing way. Under his leadership TANU was constituted as a mass party. Politicising throughout the country, TANU took up local peasants' disgruntlement over land issues and agricultural extension enforcement measures as a means of opposing the colonial state.

The colonial state tried to contain TANU's influence while hurriedly implementing reforms aimed at building up more productive and social service infrastructure as well as giving Africans some say in colonial government. The territorial budget expanded, assisted by the Colonial and Welfare Development Fund. Democratisation took the form of trying to establish a local government system based on elected representatives which would exist side by side with the Native Authorities. The first local governments were set up in Lake Province but were not successful due to interference from the chiefs' and TANU's disapproval. Nonetheless, after independence, the local government system was adopted by the post-colonial state in preference to Native Authorities.

The colonial state made an effort to train African administrators from the early 1950s. The education vote increased from 4 per cent to 15 per cent of the annual budget between 1950 and 1960/1. Numerous commissions deliberated on the issue of civil servants' remuneration which was controversial in view of the extreme racial differentiation of salaries. A compromise strategy resulted. African civil servants received substantial increases in salary particularly at subordinate and junior levels, but were not eligible for the various allowances that European civil servants enjoyed. Nyerere was the foremost proponent of limiting African salaries to what was affordable. Nevertheless, passage of the Tanganyikan Salaries Commission's recommendations placed the Tanganyikan civil service firmly in the mould of a meritocratic public administration with civil servants enjoying a considerably higher standard of living than their rural relations, thus removed from the fluctuations of the agricultural production base.

Between 1954 and 1960, the number of Africans holding senior positions in government rose from 5 to 346, even though only 70 Africans held university degrees in 1960.[2] In the late 1950s, colonial officialdom hurriedly revamped the territorial administration into a ministerial government. The power of the district commissioner was reduced and district administration became more plural and formalised. The numerous functions that the colonial district commissioner performed were parcelled out to different officers, the idea being that the Africans who assumed these new positions would have less education, less experience and would receive less pay than the colonial district officer. This expanded the available civil service jobs for Africans, but was criticised for causing disjointed administration.

The post-colonial state was a visionary government facing the abysmally low level of technology, harsh physical conditions and scanty productive and social service infrastructure of Tanganyika. The state's main constituency and developmental challenge was the multitude of peasant cultivators subjected to periodic famine, a low life expectancy and widespread illiteracy. A war on 'ignorance, poverty and disease' was proclaimed. The transformation of peasant agriculture from the land-extensive shifting cultivation by hoe to more intensive, permanent agriculture was seen as a development imperative. Industrialisation was a subsidiary theme.

These goals were couched in a humanistic philosophy which was palatable to peasants and liberal-minded Westerners alike. Nyerere's formulation of African socialism was a pragmatic blend of the traditional moral ethic of mutual support in peasant subsistence societies and Fabian socialism with policy elaborations frequently inspired by development experiences in other non-industrialised societies aspiring towards socialism. Its aim was participatory nation-building. It offered peasants a more intimate frame of reference than the anonymous nation-state. The term *ujamaa*[3] projected one's identification with immediate kin onto the country's citizenry, conjuring the need for collective effort throughout the nation for the nation in defiance of the extreme tribal heterogenity and regional variation of Tanganyika. African socialism was indeed an 'attitude of mind'.[4]

In 1967 Nyerere announced the Arusha Declaration marking Tanzania's intention to build a 'socialist' nation on the basis of the *ujamaa* philosophy. The Arusha Declaration urged rural development through collective endeavour in *ujamaa* villages, with the promise of government assistance to the *wajamaa*.[5] The importance of good leadership on the part of the government bureaucracy and party was emphasised and certain industries were nationalised. The Arusha Declaration heightened stress on state planning. The second five-year plan beginning in 1969 reaffirmed the country's concentration on agricultural development with industrial expansion as a secondary aim. The 1971 TANU Guidelines asserted Tanzania's socialist path more emphatically, urging people to scrutinise leaders who exhibit 'arrogant, extravagant, contemptuous and oppressive' behaviour.[6]

State-led nation building was the responsibility of the party and government bureaucracy. The party was seen as the organ of the common man, with a neighbourhood ten-house cell system and people's militia as the channels for mass participation. The government bureaucracy was the executor of government programmes and encompassed the more technocratic view of the newly-trained Tanzanian experts. Africanisation of the civil service proceeded rapidly; between 1961 and 1969 the percentage of Tanzanians in the middle and senior rank civil service rose from 26 per cent to 80 per cent.[7] Although their numbers were dwindling, expatriate officials were highly influential. As pensioned officers left, the government resorted to employing short-term consultants whose decision-making power was often considerable.

The high salary status of the bureaucracy became a source of tension. In 1966 Nyerere took a 20 per cent cut in pay in response to university students' complaints that ministerial salaries were too high. Heads of government and party followed suit with cuts in pay of 15 per cent and 10 per cent. The Arusha Declaration pared many of their fringe benefits, but bureaucrats remained economically privileged relative to other wage earners.

From 1964, there was no strict separation between the party and government. Civil servants were encouraged to become party members and could be promoted to party positions. Some positions, notably Regional and Area Commissioners, combined party and government functions.[8] Lack of government staff led party officials to take on governmental functions, even tax collection. Furthermore, party and government-appointed officials tended to be transferred frequently from place to place to counteract the possibility of an official developing a local power base, thus keeping him dependent on the powers that be in Dar es Salaam and reinforcing a national orientation to the job. Both government and party-appointed officials worked with a national schema in mind, however vague its policies might be.

The state bureaucracy was based on the principles of meritocracy, but overly selective recruitment was not possible nor desired in the face of a shortage of suitably trained Africans, political pressure for rapid Africanisation, and the increasing role of state-led nation-building programmes.[9] Civil servants were to be guaranteed not just a family wage, but one that insulated them from the material uncertainty experienced by the peasant population. Their salaries were to serve as their only source of income, so that they would not be tempted either to engage in ancillary income-generating employment that would detract from their official job, or to accept bribes in their line of duty. Bureaucrats were known to acquire commercial interests, notably real estate and transport businesses. But on the whole their salaries were not usually sufficient to provide the initial capital for a sizeable business, and use of office for private accumulation was, in the main, severely constrained by the Arusha Declaration and TANU Guidelines. Despite the lower educational qualifications of the African bureaucracy compared to their elitist Oxbridge-trained predecessors, the job performance standards were largely upheld during the first decade of independence. The monetary incentives of relatively well-paid employment and the nationalist fervour of the bureaucratic agents combined to stimulate professional performance.

3 ERODING THE ASIAN MARKET

Whereas peasants rarely came into contact with colonial officialdom, the Asian *dukawallah* was usually a familiar, but unpopular personage. African nationalists fanned these feelings to bring about an avalanche of mass support for the independence struggle and the cooperative movement.

3.1 Barriers to the emergence of the African trader

The colonial state actively encouraged the cooperative movement during the 1950s, particularly in the areas of high value cash crops. When the government Department of Cooperative Development was established in 1946, cooperative societies had already been operating for many years amongst tobacco growers in Songea and coffee producers in Bugufi and Kilimanjaro. The Kilimanjaro Native Cooperative Union was by far the most successful. The Cooperative Department was headquartered in Moshi and actively sought to register new cooperative societies and to ensure that each society had suitably trained personnel and facilities for produce-buying.

Simultaneously African cotton growers were taking steps against Asian traders. In 1947, independent weighing stations were established close to Asian buying posts on Ukerewe Island. They spread throughout the Lake Province and provided the nucleus for the formation of cooperative societies. In 1955 a three-tiered organisational structure was adopted; cooperative unions were formed to oversee the societies on a ginnery zone basis and the Victoria Federation of Cooperative Unions (VFCU) served as the umbrella organisation for Sukumaland as a whole.

The state's philosophy was that through 'cooperation' African peasants could circumvent the Asian produce market and gain economic benefit on the basis of principles of 'traditional' egalitarianism and mutual support. Economic uplifting of the community, rather than individual profit, was the theme. This policy begged the question of the emergence of the African entrepreneur.

African entrepreneurs were generally ignored by the colonial state and the nationalists. There were numerous farmer/traders, but very few rose to the level of operations of an average Asian *dukawallah*.[10] Their businesses tended to be very small and short-lived. The vast majority kept agriculture as their main preoccupation.

The Credit to Natives Restriction Act, which was not repealed until almost the eve of independence in 1961, made it difficult for Africans to obtain sufficient starting capital. In response to the East African Royal Commission's recommendation a credit scheme was initiated to promote African traders, but it was very low-key and seemed to have little impact. It was generally felt that African traders showed little talent for capital accumulation in comparison with their excessively thrifty Asian counterparts. Nyerere remarked:

> in my going round I have told the African this example. I say – there is this striking difference between the African and, say, the Asian. I have repeated this over and over again to drive the point: if you give an African Shs. 2000 his first idea is 'what do I buy?' and he rushes to the shop and buys this, that and the other thing. If you give an Asian Shs. 2000 his first idea is, 'what do I do to make this Shs. 2000 Shs. 4000?' That is what he thinks first. And he will do it. He will be busy and after a year or two or three he will tell you, 'That house is a result of the Shs. 2000 I have received.' The African will have squandered that in two days and get finished with it.[11]

The Africanisation of the market was infinitely more difficult than the Africanisation of the state. The Asian market was a 'closed shop'. The Asian family firm could not train young African merchants as the colonial service had trained civil servants; the family firm environment was too intimate and African/Asian relations too estranged.

Kilimanjaro was the only place where Asian traders were successfully challenged by African entrepreneurs. Significantly, this was made possible by the organisational strength of the Kilimanjaro Native Cooperative Union (KNCU) as well as the talent of the entrepreneurs themselves. During the 1950s the Chagga Traders' Cooperative, an offshoot of the KNCU, purchased consumer goods in bulk for African retailers. The KNCU tended to open up an area for African traders and then retreat when it was evident that they were able to withstand Asian competition.[12] Over the years, increasing rural population density and earnings from coffee had led to more and more off-farm cash-earning activities. Population pressure had generated a land market and a market mentality was generally more pervasive. Even though most traders retained one foot in agriculture, the success of their businesses was probably more vital to livelihood than in most other places in Tanzania.

3.2 The State trading option

After independence, despite the successes of the cooperatives in seizing control over coffee and cotton produce-buying, the Asian market was largely unconquered terrain as far as African nationalists were concerned. Post-colonial officialdom was made up primarily of men with peasant origins and civil service and academic training. They had little faith in African entrepreneurial abilities nor did they favour the growth of an African merchant class. Traders tended to be seen as synonymous with exploitation of the peasant. State trading was the logical policy solution to rid the territory of Asian merchant capital.

State trading expanded in four directions. First, the cotton and coffee marketing boards received further staffing and facilities, and other crop marketing boards were established which plugged into the cooperative marketing network. Second, the state-owned trading company, Intrata, a joint venture between a Netherlands firm and the Tanganyikan government, was launched. Third, in 1962, state wholesaling and retailing of consumer goods was vested in the Cooperative Supply Association of Tanganyika (Cosata), an apex cooperative commercial unit, managed by Israelis. Acting as an import-export-wholesale firm for the African retail cooperatives, it quickly proved not to be viable. Fourth, in 1965 the Tanganyika National Transport Cooperative Ltd (TNT) was formed, taking over vehicles from local debt-ridden transport cooperatives. Many of the vehicles were still subject to hire-purchase agreements which caused continual financial confusion. The TNT rapidly edged towards bankruptcy and the government had to step in with a guarantee.

In 1967, the Arusha Declaration nationalisations led to more of the import-export trade coming into state control. These firms were amalgamated with Intrata and Cosata to form the State Trading Corporation (STC). Just five years later, the STC had to be bailed out by the Bank of Tanzania and the Treasury and broken down into smaller regional trading companies. It was evident that poor management was the root problem. The hope was that smaller regional state trading firms would be easier to manage.

By the early 1970s, the foundation of the Asian market had been removed, produce marketing was completely in the hands of cooperatives and state marketing boards. State control of the import-export and wholesaling of consumer goods was extensive. The 'finishing touch' for African nationalists or 'final straw' for Asians was the Buildings Acquisition Act of 1971 which nationalised all individually-owned buildings, with the exception of owner-occupied buildings. Much of Asian capital accumulation had gone into urban rental property and buildings.

African state trading firms' weaknesses were most clearly evidenced in their handling of retail trade, so Asian merchants with their far more varied stocks were allowed to remain in urban retailing, although their stocks dwindled over time as wholesale supply became more erratic.

Since Asians were a small minority of the population and their colonial legacy was one of political powerlessness, Asians' most common response to nationalist policies was demoralisation, the running down of their businesses, capital flight and ultimately emigration. While the Asian population grew by 5.7 per cent per annum between 1948 and 1957, during the next ten years it declined by 0.2 per cent.[13]

In the dismantling of the Asian market, the form but not the content of Asian marketing activities was adopted by African market agents and state trading concerns. The consequence might best be described as a phantom market; there in name but not in substance. Entrepreneurial skills were lacking and market rationality was subverted by the logic of clientage.

13 Cooperatives and Neighbourhood Clientage Exchange

During the 1950s Native Authorities' budgets expanded in line with the economic development of the territory as a whole. Native Authority clientage practices were reportedly flourishing. But amidst the boom, the colonial state was experimenting with various alternative forms of local government, based on the English model. This experimentation precipitated the Native Authorities' decline, although at the time colonial officialdom denied that this was their objective. TANU, never overtly anti-chief during the independence struggle, nonetheless unsentimentally did away with the Native Authorities in 1963. Chiefs retained ritual functions in many areas. Some were wealthy or educated men who could find status and material rewards elsewhere, but the chiefs as a group and the Native Authorities as an identifiable social force vanished. It is questionable if Native Authorities would have lasted even if officialdom had been more supportive of them.

During the 1950s, chiefly authority and tribal solidarity were steadily being undermined by peasants' growing participation in commodity markets. Pressures on land and labour resources began to appear that challenged the harmony of local interests that chiefs were supposedly presiding over.

1 THE PROLIFERATION OF CLIENTAGE NETWORKS

As the colonial state made more investments in education, a growing number of young men with primary school education were beginning to populate the rural areas. The Native Authority gerontocracy made them restless. State initiatives to devise a local government system was largely in response to the Native Authorities' anticipated loss of legitimacy in the eyes of these young men, whose personal abilities and ambitions were being thwarted by uneducated, traditional chiefs. The energies of educated men were channelled into a variety of new social organisations with Western constitutional forms, based on democratic election rather than hereditary leadership. In addition to the new local governments, these included the party, the trade unions and the cooperatives.

It would be a mistake to assume that these Western-modelled organisations, transferred to Tanganyika, would or could operate with the same internal checks and balances on the exercise of power as operated in their exemplars. Their functions were also likely to differ from that in Western industrial societies because Tanganyika lacked occupational plurality and well-defined interest group politics. Political traditions were consensual rather than oppositional. Thus in Tanganyika's radically different material context, the content of these social organisations was bound to diverge from the model. New forms of clientage emerged in these organisations. Far from disappearing with the Native Authorities, clientage was penetrating new spheres of the economy and polity.

1.1 The context and content of neighbourhood clientage

In the 1950s and 1960s better than average weather conditions and producer prices offered peasants the possibility and indeed the expectation of an enhanced standard of living. The magnitude of improvement varied widely depending on regional differences in natural endowments. Furthermore, food insecurity was too fresh in peasants' memories and too likely to re-occur for market participation to become the dominant strategy for peasants, with the exception of a tiny minority. Nonetheless in most areas peasants had at their disposal either more monetary income or more state-provisioned social and productive infrastructure or both. The allocation of these 'improved means of production and consumption' was, to an increasing extent, mediated by young semi-educated African men who found their way into one or more of the new Western-styled social organisations.

In their allocative functions, these agents had two counterposing identities. On one hand, they usually had some education and were identified with Western occupational specialisations. Their technical skills were to be applied to the competent handling of organisational matters connected with the state and market. On the other hand, they were subject to the clientage demands of the people they served. These demands were modifications of those that had been previously placed on Native Authority personnel. They embodied the old need for insurance in times of material need as well as the people's expectations for a gradually improving standard of living. Thus, even though their appointment or election was usually posited on their Western qualifications, their performance was frequently judged on clientage criteria.

There was a new democratic element to the clientage equation when patron selection was based on elections rather than hereditary rule. With no legitimate claims to magico-religious powers, patrons were forced into a more egalitarian relationship with their clients. In the absence of ritual decorum and prescribed chiefly hierarchy, clientage was structured by the social etiquette of good neighbourliness and mutual benefit. The patron's prestige was still exchanged for the alleviation of the client's material insecurity, but the client was in a position to demand wider and more direct accountability than was ever possible with Native Authority chiefs who had been primarily subject to the colonial state's approval. Neighbourhood patrons could be held accountable through elections or by their clients' perhaps disingenuous appeal for professional standards of performance.

Yet the democratic element of neighbourhood clientage bore more resemblance to some features of the traditional agrarian society than to Western social organisation. There were at least two pre-colonial legacies of good neighbourliness that could be drawn upon. The first and very pervasive one was that of the moral claim to assistance from kin-neighbours in shifting cultivation societies. Gulliver describes it for the Ndendeuli:

> the rule that (1) 'You must help a man because he is your kinsman' had the same imperative quality as (2) 'You must cultivate because you must provide food for your family.' Both were accepted as axiomatic, and as having the same constraining quality as (3) 'You must cultivate because you need food to live': that is, all three statements had an inescapable, natural and practical quality. . . . They were part of the natural order of things, inherent in the process of living.[1]

Utani, the inter-tribal joking relationship that evolved between specific tribes during the long-distance trading of the nineteenth century, was a second tradition to draw upon. *Utani* involved members of one tribe considering any members of another tribe as relatives upon which they could make demands for food or other consumable goods en route, even though they may have had no means of immediate repayment. The relationship was accompanied by good-natured jesting which served as a means of identification of the stranger as well as helping to alleviate the strain associated with such demands. *Utani* was an inter-personal relationship that involved some risk to the individual participant but was of undisputed benefit to the tribal collectivity interested in maintaining peace. An *mtani* had to give a fellow *mtani* a proper burial if he should die away from his home and kinsmen; a practice that reflected the survival ethic that underlined social relationships.

Neighbourhood clientage had the features of a survival-based, welfare-enhancing exchange relationship based on reciprocity between individuals, one of whom enjoyed better access to 'modern' goods and services that he then shared with his client in return for prestige and political support. Neighbourhood clientage relations depended on locational proximity and frequent face-to-face encounters. Patrons, as deliverers of improved means of production and consumption were usually fairly geographically-mobile. They travelled between the source of supply of these goods, usually Dar es Salaam or some smaller regional town centre, and their clientele. Thus they were frequently out of the direct scrutiny of their clients and their social identity was not strictly local. Patrons often trod a very thin line between being an insider and an outsider in their neighbourhoods. When their clients deemed they had stepped too far out, they could be disposed of through elections or more traditional forms of non-cooperation. In this way, neighbourhood clientage engendered a much more fluid social situation than that of Native Authority clientage. There was more temporal and spatial instability of patrons. Nonetheless, patrons had a local identity and in some respects were more directly accountable to their clients than the Native Authority chiefs. Patrons frequently put the interests of their locality above the national policies and plans, in defiance of the duties of their official position. They often resorted to extra-legal means of marshalling resources to benefit their local clients. Furthermore, as under Native Authority clientage, resources and funds were sometimes siphoned off for personal use.

In the towns, a neighbourhood identity was sustained by tribal affiliation and *utani* association. One could expect special favours and loans from one's loosely defined kin, but in the wider arena of social interaction, cash rather than affective ties characterised the interpersonal clientage exchange relationship. This was the other side of the survival ethic. Encounters between unrelated Africans amounted to personal power plays. Just as the African peasant farmer faced a hostile physical environment that he exerted little or no control over, so too the urban migrant faced a hostile social environment, the *pori*[2] between the neighbourhood enclaves, which he had to resign himself to, getting by with help from his kin-neighbourhood wherever possible. Describing Dar es Salaam's economy in 1956, Leslie observes:

> one pays here to get a job, unless one is lucky enough to meet the Indian or European employer face to face; one pays to get favourable attention, or attention at all, for an official application; one pays to get to the top of a queue for rented housing, or a plot to build one's own; one pays to avoid arrest or to gain a further respite from the payment of tax; wherever there is a slice of power in a man's hands, to give or withhold, it has a price, and the price is exacted. This is not resented; or let us say it is resented in the same way and to much the same degree as one resents the income tax or a licence fee. It is unpopular (with the payer) but is recognized by Africans as the normal course of life . . . In general its effect is to strengthen the ties of kin which already hold a man's life together in town as in the country, by increasing the importance to a man of the help of his relatives, who alone may give what he wants free.[3]

1.2 Contradictory tendencies of neighbourhood clientage and nation-state

The party, trade unions, local government and cooperatives were Western social organisations that were adopted in step with changing attitudes and a new nationalist outlook, yet they provided the framework for neighbourhood clientage.

This development was not directly at odds with Tanganyikan nationalism and the policies of the state. TANU had won state power largely on the basis of rural populist sentiment. Populism continued to be a prominent feature of post-colonial party and government policies. The philosophy of *ujamaa* was couched in terms of kin loyalties. On the other hand, the state had set itself the task of spearheading technical and social development which involved mobilising people and resources to increase productivity. Economic investment requiring fairly long gestation periods and considerable material sacrifice was the order of the day. In this respect neighbourhood clientage practices were a distraction from the task at hand, if not a total derailment.

Althought TANU was a nationwide organisation it suffered from problems of integration and lack of control from central headquarters. The incidence of clientage practices in TANU's early days is largely open to conjecture. Leslie refers to repeated embezzlements in the main political parties at the time he was writing (1956), but other commentators reviewing the history of TANU do not mention this.[4] They emphasise problems of financial accountability, especially in the collection of dues with frequent failure to remit funds to TANU headquarters in Dar es Salaam, interpreting this as a matter of poor administration rather than suspected pilferage, even though TANU officials at that time worked voluntarily or received very low salaries.[5] The fervour of the nationalist vision and the self-sacrifice required from the early party activitists seems to have kept a check on clientage.[6]

1965 marked the beginning of the Tanzanian 'one-party' state. Stress was placed on bureaucratising the party's internal structure to increase administrative efficiency. Party cadres continued to be imbued with a strong nationalist outlook that was reinforced by frequent postings around the country. The party's expanding budget rested heavily on subventions from central government rather than from locally solicited sources. The party bureaucracy was becoming virtually indistinguishable from the government bureaucracy. On the other hand, elected officials of the regional and district committees were described by Bienen as loosely-knit, localised 'political oligarchies'.[7] They had considerable status but somewhat limited control over resources. Their status rested on being part of a powerful nationwide political organisation. Thus their localism was of a contradictory nature, neutralised by a national identity that was regularly reinforced by their attendance at biennial national party conferences.

Trade unions were a different matter. With the formation of the Tanganyika Federation of Labour in 1955, the trade union movement was posited on a nationalist ideology. However, there was a strong tendency for trade union branches to break away effectively from their headquarters, fail to remit dues and adopt their own policies. Mismanagement of funds and pilfery were common. Salaries of trade union officers were not guaranteed. Dues often had to be used to pay bills and salaries.

The trade union movement as a whole came to loggerheads with the government over the issue of Africanisation. The state was committed to Africanisation but at a gradual rate, trying to ensure peformance standards in the process. The Tanganyika Federation of Labour demanded much faster Africanisation. The contentious issue may well have been merit versus patronage. Africans' wage employment opportunities were not keeping pace with the growing numbers of job seekers. The pressures on neighbourhood patrons at their places of work to engage in nepotistic hiring practices were undoubtedly great in many sectors. In 1964, the Africanisation issue was abruptly resolved in favour of the state when some of the leadership of the Tanganyika Federation of Labour were implicated in the army mutiny and arrested. The Tanganyika Federation of Labour was banned and replaced by the party-affiliated National Union of Tanganyika Workers (NUTA). It was inevitable that it would be adopting a stance more in line with the party's nationalists in the future.

Local government, already established in some places during the final years of colonial rule, was adapted to the post-colonial state's government/party structure and extended nationwide. District councils' revenues were derived primarily from local rates as well as poll tax and produce cesses. Financial irregularities were common. Bienen described a councillor's job as follows:

> District and town councillors are not paid officials . . . being a councillor means that one is 'in on' projects under consideration in the district. The benefits can be substantial if one is a councillor and has some connection with building or supplying for local government . . . many government complaints about misappropriation of district council funds come about because some district and town councils think they are entitled to kickbacks. While downright embezzling has occurred, it is probably more common for district councillors to get remunerations for favors done or anticipated. The district council has the power to rebate school funds and allow nonpayment of tax in hardship cases. These are areas where the members of the finance or education committee are able to feather their own nests. Being a district or town councillor also confers status.[8]

Official expenditure was clearly more attuned to local pressures for the expansion of social service infrastructure than the production programmes of the state. In 1969, the central government withdrew the district's taxation powers and a Regional Development Fund was set up which annually distributed much smaller funds to the regions.

In 1972, the centralisation tendency reached its logical end through the ironically named decentralisation policy. The district and ward elected councils were abolished and replaced with regional, district and ward development committees that were staffed by central government appointees with technical expertise. All funds were centrally controlled, but forward and backward lines of communication and participatory decision-making were supposed to characterise the various committee levels.

What is evident in these three institutions is the contradiction between local populism and nationalism. Populism became synonymous with the dynamics of welfare-oriented, face-to-face encounters between patrons and local clients. The content of local populism was a natural outcome of the existing level of material development, reflecting the very basic uncertainties which people experienced as well as their perception of new opportunities for improvement of their standard of living. Neighbourhood social pressure enveloped clients' appeals to local patrons. When a patron did not respond, he risked rejection or non-compliance from his clientele.

In contrast, nationalism's need for wider social and political loyalties to support nation-building required less immediate and more impersonal responses to demands. The infrastructural investment plan promised material gratification at some future date rather than the imperative present. Bureaucrats of the central government and party had a more nationalist outlook, informed largely by the models of Western constitutional government and socialist party structure from abroad, rather than the immediate material conditions of the country. Their mission was seen as the technical execution of policies and plans and they enjoyed the security of well-paid employment. As first generation urban-dwellers, they did not escape the demands of neighbourhood clientage. Various commentators have noted a decline in accountability of the post-colonial government compared with the colonial government indicated by the increase in improper use of government vehicles, unaccounted loss of stores, peculation, etc.[9] However, when comparing central government and party performance with that of the less bureaucratised employees of the trade unions, local governments and cooperatives, there is far less evidence of clientage practices. During the period under review, government and party officials tended to approach their work with relatively more impersonal professionalism and consistently adopted policy measures that were aimed at curtailing neighbourhood clientage.[10] As far as the state was concerned, neighbourhood clientage was a threat to national welfare.

2. COOPERATIVES AND CLIENTAGE EXCHANGE

Amongst the new social organisations, the cooperative movement was the most powerful at independence by virtue of its strong populist base as well as its strategic importance to the national economy. The cooperative movement was vital to TANU's spread during the independence struggle, so the newly-installed government had a political debt to it. Furthermore, it played a profound role in rendering Native Authority clientage networks obsolete.

2.1 Cooperative development and the national economy

Not too long before independence, Nyerere publicly mused:

> supposing I were given the alternative of turning the whole of Tanganyika into a sisal estate or turning the whole of it into a KNCU. I know what I would do. Easy. I would multiply the KNCUs all over Tanganyika. If we multiply the KNCUs we become the envy of the outside world. We become the envy of the rest of Africa. . . . If we turn the whole of Tanganyika into sisal estates I do not know how many times we would multiply the labour force and give the big job to Rashidi Kawawa, a job he would never be able to handle at all . . . of those two, one has no foreign capital whatsoever, none. The other has foreign capital. . . . Multiply the KNCUş; see the people using the natural resources; organising them and getting the best out of them.[11]

In effect, TANU's rural economic policy for fifteen years was precisely this. African cooperative membership multiplied six times between 1948 and 1960, largely through grassroots initiatives that were legitimised by the Registrar of Cooperatives. The cooperative movement did not spread to the northeastern and coastal plantation zone nor to the labour reserves; cooperative development took place alongside rather than in place of the plantations. However, as the movement gained momentum it began surpassing the plantations in importance. After independence, the post-colonial state embarked on a nationwide cooperative programme. Societies were established in the more economically marginal areas, which frequently did not have a viable export crop. Thus many of the new cooperatives were based on food as a cash crop. These were far less successful than the coffee and cotton cooperatives of the northern and lake regions and were always viewed by the local peasants as the government's societies, not evidencing much popular participation.

2.2 Peasant attitudinal change and the rise of the cooperative patron

Peasants' commodity prices had been lifted out of a decade-long trough during World War II, but it was the inflationary effect of the Korean war and a world commodity price boom that gave Tanganyikan peasants' their first whiff of prosperity. Suddenly peasants could afford to buy consumer durables like bicycles, radios and corrugated iron for roofing their houses which provided convenience and comfort, and broadened awareness. There were now good reasons for engaging in income-generating activities, besides paying one's taxes and bridewealth payments. Peasant acquisitiveness and the cashcrop boom went together and had far-reaching social implications.

Up until the 1950s, there was very little differentiation in living standards and income amongst peasants with the exception of the chief and Native Authority personnel. As cashcropping became more prevalent, this began to change. Individuals' differences in skills in farming and marketing led to variation in income and some of the most successful could begin rivalling chiefs in wealth. These men were innovative, upwardly-mobile and usually relatively young. Migot-Adholla argues that they were in situation of 'status inconsistency', because their wealth was based on individual achievement, yet they lived in societies which, consistent with the survival ethic, upheld mutual support as a moral virtue.[12]

Frequently these men had extended their activities beyond farming to trade or lorry transport, but farming remained their main source of income. As members of local peasant communities, they were subject to the neighbourhood kinship loyalties and the moral dictates of sharing described above. They were destined to become a particular form of neighbourhood patron, the 'cooperative' patron.

The innovating farmer-cum-trader/transporter was the dynamising force behind the spread of the cooperatives during the 1950s as well as the natural candidate for cooperative leadership. Given the formidable competition that Asian traders posed for emergent African traders, African entry into produce marketing had to be a collective one and required political aggressiveness to succeed. Mass peasant support for cooperatives and their leaders was readily mobilised around the highly emotive race issue.

Marketing cooperatives provided a material foundation for the operation of clientage networks. At the village level, the elected committee members steered the affairs of the primary society. They generally were successful farmers with at least basic literacy and numeracy. They were assisted by a salaried secretary who was educated and had usually received some special training for the job. Committee members could also ration out other paid employment opportunities associated with the society's operations. The society's main activity was crop purchasing and, after independence, credit allocation.

The cooperative union was usually situated in a small town. The union had its elected committee, but the elections were proportional rather than direct and frequently allowed the entrenchment of powerful regional cliques.[13] Cooperative patrons at the union level were one step removed from their peasant clients. They were more urban in outlook and often less acceptable to the peasant producer, but nonetheless a vital link in the chain as far as peasant producer prices and credit allocation were concerned. The union was the site of inter-regional conflict over the division of cooperative resources.

2.3 Cooperative clientage exchange relationships

The cooperative patron represented a source of the means of improved production and consumption to the peasant, either indirectly through his facilitation of crop marketing or directly through the grant of special favours such as the preferential supply of fertiliser, tractor ploughing, etc. As an elected committee member, he enjoyed prestige as a local *mkubwa*.[14] Unless he was also of a ruling clan or held a ritual leadership position, the respect he commanded was of an entirely secular nature. His prestige derived from being an affluent member of the rural community who had economic and political power to influence the welfare of less advantaged peasants. In addition, he together with his fellow committee members could allocate themselves *posho*[15] and *zawadi*[16], that is, allowances and bonuses of various sorts. The rank and file membership usually knew about these perks but condoned them as befitting men of importance.[17] There was also the unsanctioned siphoning of cooperative funds and resources which tended to be blamed on the salaried secretaries, but increasingly it was believed that committee men were also involved.[18]

Official cooperative marketing margins had an enforced ceiling for most of the period under review, that of the Grain Storage Department's and later the National Agricultural Production Board's into-store price, but the floor was a matter of negotiation and approval. During the mid- and late 1960s, all unions had to forward their costs estimates to their Regional Commissioners which were then sent on to the Commissioner of Cooperatives. Once these costings were approved they were binding and cooperative unions and societies were expected not to exceed their stipulated margins and obliged to pay farmers the residual which became the established producer price for that area. Thus there was an inverse relationship between the size of the cooperative margin and the level of producer prices. The size of cooperative margins was the object of much criticism by economic commentators. Temu identifies the cooperatives as the 'villain' of inflated marketing costs.[19] René Dumont was particularly scathing:

> Since 1962, and because of the co-operatives, the prices paid to the producers have greatly fallen. At Lushoto, a ton of maize, bought at Shs. 400/- by the Marketing Board, only brings the producer Shs. 220/-. *We have never seen anywhere in the world, such high deductions* reaching half the value of the product . . . The reasons for such bad management seem to us so numerous that it seems difficult to classify them in order of importance. Certainly *lack of honesty* and of incompetence seem amongst the more serious[20] (Dumont's emphasis).

The combination of decreasing world commodity prices, the state's expanding use of peasant marketed production as a source of tax revenue, and peasants' growing awareness of marketing margins, particularly for food crops, had the potential of creating discontent during the 1960s. It is unclear whether inefficiency on the part of cooperative staff, and *posho* payments and peculation increased substantially during the 1960s or whether they were just more noticeable because there were far more cooperatives in existence.[21] The rapid expansion of the cooperatives, subject to less government supervision and with less well trained staff, made increased inefficiencies likely. Peculation may have been on the increase as the vested interests of the clientage networks deepened. Cooperative staff at society level were complaining about low wages. *Posho* payments were still widely accepted as legitimate sources of income for committee members. After independence, cooperatives became the channel for government-sponsored agricultural credit schemes and input supply, offering expanded scope for local patronage.[22]

A successful local patron was one that succeeded in steering more goods and services to his society over that of the others. Different cooperative societies competed against each other for shares of the credit available from their unions. The management of credit within the society tended to be haphazard. In some places almost every one sought loans often for the mere sake of having one. Farmers and their societies tended to be late placing their input supply orders. Accounting systems were very rudimentary and debts frequently went unrecorded. In such instances the union was in the habit of imposing an extra levy on all crops sold. Thus the virtuous were left subsidising the defaulters, compounded by the fact that larger farmers tended to have obtained larger loans and hence bigger outstanding debts.

2.4 Vying for peasant popularity

At independence, the state viewed the cooperative movement as its most essential organisational tool in developing Tanzanian agriculture; by 1966, the government was beginning to see the cooperatives as a threat to development. Corruption by local cooperative officials was known to be all-pervasive. A presidential committee, appointed to investigate the cooperatives, took the view that the inefficiencies and 'corrupt' practices of cooperative personnel and associated low producer prices were an active disincentive to peasant commodity production.[23] It recommended increased government supervision of cooperatives. The powerful VFCU in Sukumaland was dismantled at this time. These measures kept cooperatives in existence but attempted to restrict cooperative patrons' maneuverability. Tax versus *posho* was at issue. Government taxes and patrons' clientage practices put competing demands on peasant commodity production.

The reforms did not engender any marked improvement in cooperative performance. Financial mismanagement continued to be widespread. Approximately 40 per cent of all societies in the three years between 1967 and 1969 had annual net deficits and 20 per cent of the societies were insolvent.[24]

Similar to the state bureaucracy's reaction to the incidence of neighbourhood clientage in the party, trade unions and local government, the cooperatives were served with a 'bureaucratisation or perish' order. However, the cooperative movements' sheer size and history made it a force to reckon with. It took ten years for the state's bureaucratic encroachment to culminate in the complete abolition of cooperatives. Over those ten years, the state increasingly turned to the village as the focus of development rather than the cooperative society. In 1973, when villagisation became a nationwide programme, the cooperatives were effectively doomed, although cooperative unions were not officially dissolved until 1976. The cooperative movement, Tanzania's strongest bastion of neighbourhood clientage, was the last to fall to the nation-state's centralising and bureaucratising tendencies.

There were a number of hitches in the state's efforts to develop peasant agriculture without local cooperative patrons in the latter part of the 1960s and the early 1970s under the *ujamaa* policy. First, cooperative patrons tended to be the most technically innovative farmers in the rural areas, the so-called 'progressive farmers'. While research stations produced improved seed varieties and implements, it was the wealthier than average farmers who usually paved the way for rural household adoption of these improvements. They were the peasant farmers who could afford to experiment without jeopardising their families' subsistence.

Second, the level of material development in the countryside did not augur well for the successful benefaction of an impersonal state. People were used to having a patron locally accessible to receive their appeals. Often these appeals demanded very little time, effort or material disbursement on the part of the patron, but they were nonetheless vital to the well-being of the peasant and to his perception of his well-being. In essence, the patron ran a low-cost, multipurpose service centre that could include amongst other functions: an insurance agency, citizen's advice bureau, transport service, productive input supplier, etc. Being a very new form of clientage, neighbourhood clientage had untested limits. Nonetheless, as long as the cooperative patron was allowed his *posho* and input supply from union headquarters continued, he had sufficient means to secure 'cheap popularity' amongst the peasants and further his own agricultural and business endeavours.

The state, in contrast, had ambitious plans for transforming the rural areas and peasant production which required massive expenditure to improve the social service and productive infrastructure of rural areas. Hoping to gain widespread popular appeal amongst peasants, the *ujamaa* programme embodied this promise. *Ujamaa* villagers were to receive priority allocation of government services and supplies of productive inputs delivered by well-salaried, efficient bureaucrats or dutiful party cadres. This was 'pricey popularity', which did not offer the face-to-face accountability that peasants saw as so vital.

The peasants' preference for men of 'cheap popularity' is vividly illustrated by the electoral fate of Paul Bomani, one of the original founders of the cooperative movement in Sukumaland. He became a highly successful statesmen in the post-colonial state and one of the most outspoken national leaders on rural development policy, yet failed to win his local parliamentary seat during the first election after independence in 1965.[25]

Finally, state expenditure on rural infrastructure had to be weighed against the demands of urban areas, demands which state decision-makers were more acutely aware of, being urban-dwellers themselves.

14 Urban Growth and Food Adequacy

Between 1950 and 1973, urbanisation proceeded at the rate of 10.5 per cent per annum, raising the proportion of Tanzania mainland's population living in settlements of over 20 000 people from 1.4 per cent to 7.0 per cent. As growth proceeded, urban areas displaced plantations as the main source of food demand in the economy.

African migration was the main cause of urban growth. The European and Asian populations which constituted 27 per cent of the urban population in 1952 declined to approximately 13 per cent by 1967. In contrast to 1950 when only Dar es Salaam and Tanga numbered over 20 000, by 1967 there were a profusion of small towns. The primate city, Dar es Salaam, grew at the rate of 7.5 per cent between 1950 and 1967, whereas the aggregate growth of small towns speeded ahead at 15.4 per cent per annum. As crop-bulking points, small towns were direct beneficiaries of the cashcrop boom. However, when considering the small towns individually, only Arusha's growth rate superceded that of Dar es Salaam. The towns with the largest preponderance of men in the early 1950s experienced the fastest growth, as female migration served to even out the sex ratio progressively.

1 URBAN FOOD SECURITY

Food demand in urban areas expanded. There was a notable tendency towards the replacement of the traditional staples by the so-called preferred cereals. Maize meal was substituted for sorghum, millet and plantains, a pattern already well-established on the plantations. African consumption of the more expensive staple foods like rice and wheat was on the increase in urban areas.

Nonetheless, the 1969 household budget survey revealed the persistence of racially-distinct consumption patterns.[1] At middle levels of expenditure African consumption bore more in common with the lower levels of African expenditure than with the comparable middle levels of non-African expenditure. Africans with rising incomes had a tendency to hold to a starch-based diet with roughly equal expenditure on maize and rice and restricted consumption of dairy products in comparison with non-Africans.

Available evidence suggests that urban food supply was secure. Household budget surveys between 1950 and 1973 consistently indicated that only one half to two-thirds of low-income African expenditure was on food, significantly less than what prevailed in the decade to follow.[2] In the higher-income bracket, one-third to one-quarter of household income was spent on food. The formally employed could take food adequacy for granted. The cost of living allowances for civil servants continued to keep pace with the cost of living index during the first half of the 1950s. When the index started to decline there were official utterances that the time had at last come to phase out the civil service's cost of living allowances.[3] In 1956, in conjunction with a general reform of the civil service salary structure, the allowances were abolished without much ado. Urban food prices were exceptionally stable during the 1960s and their rise only began to supercede that of non-food commodity prices in 1971 (see Table 14.1).

2 SOURCES OF FOOD SUPPLY

The 1950s and 1960s saw increasing regional specialisation and greater peasant production of food for sale. For the years between 1950 and 1970 in which data is available, official purchases of maize exceeded sales in 9 out of 14 years (see Table 14.2). There are no statistics on parallel market sales, which varied over time. Even for the officially marketed production, it is impossible to know what proportions were contributed by peasants as opposed to settlers and African capitalised producers.

2.1 Specialised domestic production: settlers

Settler production of staple foods, which was launched with state support in the 1940s, reached its zenith in the 1950s. It was concentrated in the Northern Province and Eastern Province. The Land Utilization Board allocated settlers land in Kilosa and Morogoro districts for maize production and in Arusha and West Kilimanjaro for wheat production. It is ironic that land policy became more pro-settler during the final decade of colonial rule. Under Twining's governorship, land alienation in certain highly fertile, but relatively unpopulated areas was justified by the government in terms of its

TABLE 14.1 *Food and non-food cost of living indices, 1963–83 (1963 = 100)*

Year	*Food retail price index – wage-earners, DSM*	*Cost of living index – middle-grade civil servants*	*Non-food retail price index – wage-earners, DSM*	*Non-food cost of living index – middle-grade civil servants, DSM*
1963	100	100	100	100
1964	100	102	111	108
1965	108	113	114	111
1966	112	115	124	119
1967	112	119	132	125
1968	115	125	145	128
1969	113	125	163	130
1970	118	128	163	131
1971	123	134	164	135
1972	136	139	182	141
1973	144	154	211	153
1974	196	200	254	178
1975	270	294	454	218
1976	360	321	434	247
1977	426	354	497	281
1978	510	417	539	341
1979	529	484	605	417
1980	634	589	682	473
1981	797	787	942	613
1982	1001	1052	1093	704
1983	1191	1288	1498	895

SOURCES
Compiled from:
Bank of Tanzania, *Economic and Operations Report* (June 1975) p. 86.
Bank of Tanzania, *Economic and Operations Report* (June 1984) p. 90.

efforts to develop the country agriculturally.[4] Nearly 60 per cent of government revenue derived from non-African sources.[5]

The European settlers were organised into a number of different farming associations which tended to become highly politicised, bent on keeping the forces of nationalism from encroaching on their farms and way of life.[6] The district production committees liased with the government to facilitate the apportionment of guaranteed minimum returns to large-scale European grain producers. As nationalist consciousness grew, the blatant racial discrimination of these payments became a source of unease for the government, but they continued until 1955.

European settler farmers were greatly favoured over Africans with agricultural loans. African loan funds set up in the 1950s annually disbursed less than one-tenth of what European farmers received through the Land Bank. However, the settlers' favourable investment climate quickly evaporated after independence. The increase in agricultural labourers' wages, input supply difficulties and declining producer prices, all adversely affected farm profits. In 1972, President Nyerere was asked by the Chairman of the Kilimanjaro Farmers Association what lay ahead. Nyerere replied: 'If I tell you that there is any future for individual large scale farming in Tanzania, I will be cheating you. Tanzania is different from Kenya, because here we have the Arusha Declaration to implement.'[7] During the course of the next three years, most settler farms were nationalised. Thereafter very few European farmers remained in the country.

2.2 Specialised domestic production: African capitalised farmers

At the beginning of the 1950s a new type of African farmer emerged from the peasantry in a few 'frontier' localities, notably Ismani in Iringa, and Hanang and Northern Iraqw in Arusha. These were areas that had previously been underpopulated. In Arusha, tsetse clearance had opened up more land, whereas in Ismani lack of perennial sources of water had been the constraint. The rise of the capitalised farmer was stimulated by the improved producer prices of the 1940s and early 1950s, the example of the agricultural methods of the settler farmers and the higher producer prices offered by the Grain Storage Department for grain delivered in 3-ton lots which encouraged large-scale grain production by those with lorries.

The African capitalist farmers had a great deal of land at their disposal and proceeded to farm on a land-extensive basis, maximising productivity per unit of labour rather than land. Farms were sometimes over a hundred acres in size, a far cry from the two to three acre holdings of the average peasant farmer. Tractor mechanisation and hired labour enabled farmers to cover such expanses. In Arusha, where the climate was appropriate for wheat, its cultivation was well-suited to mechanisation. Although the first African commercial wheat farmers who appeared in Karatu in 1942 used ox-ploughs, by 1950, there were five African-owned tractors in the area.[8] In 1962, in Hanang district of Arusha region, local government allocated 20–60 acre plots to African farmers who could grow wheat on a mechanised basis.[9]

Tractorisation of maize was far more limited in scope such that

TABLE 14.2 *Official grain purchases and sales, 1949/50–1984/85 (tons)*

	MAIZE			*RICE*			*WHEAT*		
Year	*Purchases*	*Sales*	*Balance*	*Purchases*	*Sales*	*Balance*	*Purchases*	*Sales*	*Balance*
GSD									
1949/50	15831	111050	–95219						
1950/51	54840	43424	11416						
1951/52	61838	36809	25029						
1952/53	39995	74280	–34285						
1953/54	22386	61219	–38833						
1954/55	71611	47035	24576						
1955/56	116963	7061	109902						
1956/57	2977	1614	1363						
NAPB									
1963/64	108890								
1964/65	80430	83800	–3370	24516	22153	2363			
1965/66	69550	89500	–19950	12880	23600	–10720	29000	38900	–9900
1966/67	107820	74800	33020	24310	31700	–7390	28000	40000	–12000
1967/68	105125	93100	12025	19630	34400	–14770	33000	50600	–17600
1968/69	130181	104500	25681	29705	35200	–5495	23300	60100	–36800
1969/70	47000	123400	–76400	38870	41800	–2930	24600	56700	–32100
1970/71	186400	116600	69800	60800	52100	8700	43000	59700	–16700
1971/72	43000	160000	–117000	44600	75800	–31200	56800	88600	–31800
1972/73	106400	154000	–47600	47500	88000	–40500	46900	53900	–7000

NMC									
1973/74	73800	209700*	–135900	38700	82300	–43600	27900	66400	–38500
1974/75	23900	202700	–178800	14800	42900	–28100	14400	62800	–48400
1975/76	91100	137800	–46700	11900	34700	–22800	24500	60300	–35800
1976/77	127500	125800	1700	15100	52300	–37200	27100	68700	–41600
1977/78	213200	103300	109900	35100	74600	–39500	35300	88000	–52700
1978/79	220400	156000	64400	33000	70100	–37100	28900	96300	–67400
1979/80	161100	223000	–61900	29000	61300	–32300	27200	54800	–27600
1980/81	104600	295000	–190400	13000	77600	–64600	26900	42400	–15500
1981/82	89400	287000	–197600	15000	77800	–62800	24100	53100	–29000
1982/83	68700	208300	–139600	20900	71900	–51000	30900	54800	–23900
1983/84	71000	244300	–173300	22000	79100	–57100	28300	34300	–6000
1984/85	90000	220000	–130000	12200	58000	–45800	33200	67000	–33800

NOTE

* Note *sembe* maize flour included in maize sales total. When MDB has not specified a maize equivalent, I have calculated *sembe* at a 95 per cent extraction rate: 1 ton maize = 0.95 *sembe*.

SOURCES

Compiled from:

1. Tanganyika, Grain Storage Department, *Annual Report of the Grain Storage Department, July 1956–July 1957* (DSM: Government Printer, 1957) p. 14.
2. Kreisel *et al.*, *Agricultural Marketing*, p. 21.
3. Coopers and Lybrand Assoc. Ltd, *Grain Storage and Milling Project*, vol. II, DSM (1977) Tables A 1.17, A1.22, A1.27, A1.36, A1.37 and A1.38.
4. Tanzania, MDB, 'Price Policy Recommendations', vol. I: Maize, Rice and Wheat (DSM, 1981) apps 2.1 and 3.1.
5. Livingstone, I., 'Production, Price and Marketing Policy for Staple Foodstuffs in Tanzania', *ERB* Paper 71.16, 32.
6. Tanzania, MDB, 'Price Policy Recommendations', vol. I: Maize, Rice and Wheat (DSM, 1981: apps 2.1, 2.3, 3.1–3.2, 4.1; 1983: pp. 46–8; 1984: pp. 52–5; 1986: pp. 10, 17.

farmers did not branch into specialised maize production in Arusha. In Ismani, climate and soils precluded wheat. In 1949, when large-scale maize production began, hired labourers, particularly famine-stricken peasants from Gogoland, were employed. Within a few years, investment in tractors took place here as well.[10] By 1953, an estimated 15 square miles of former bush-land was under maize and maize sales jumped from 500 to 4000 tons between 1950 and 1952.[11]

African capitalised farmers distanced themselves socially from other producers. Using hired labour rather than more communal forms of labour removed them from the bonds of reciprocal exchange. The Ismani capitalised farmers were often non-resident, the core group being successful mechanics, lorry transporters and small shopowners in Iringa town. Feldman notes that they operated on the basis of *de facto* individual land tenure contrary to customary law.[12] They were not popular amongst the peasants who actually settled in the area and in 1971 when Nyerere made a call for the formation of ujamaa villages peasants saw this as a means of ousting capitalised farmers from their midst. In Arusha, the capitalised farmers were usually resident, but interestingly, they had found another way of distancing themselves from the rest of the local Iraqw population. Raikes mentions in a passing footnote that most of them were members of the Roman Catholic temperance society.[13] By not participating in the local drinking sessions which occupied a large part of the male peasant's social world, they not only saved time and money, they also avoided the numerous clientage exchange relationships that laced drinking sessions.

While the small nucleus of African capitalised farmers' agricultural methods and social stance bore more in common with settler farmers rather than neighbouring peasants in several respects, there were, however, important features that distinguished them from the settler farmer. First, and especially in the case of the Northern Iraqw, they were over-capitalised. The African loan schemes of the 1950s and 1960s favoured 'progressive farmers'. Farmers' loans on average did not exceed TShs. 2000 during the 1950s and only about 150 African farmers obtained them. But under the Agricultural Credit Agency established in 1962 African credit opportunities burgeoned. Over 4000 larger loans averaging TShs. 13 300 each were dispensed.[14] Credit continued to expand with the founding of the National Development Credit Agency which facilitated lending through the cooperative movement and later the establishment of the Tanzania Rural Development Bank in 1971. But credit agencies had few ways of enforcing repayment because African capitalised farmers were still subject to customary land laws, making land and property dispossession impossible.

The second major difference was that African capitalist producers tended to produce all their own food needs rather than purchase from the market. Third, African capitalised farmers were engaged in non-farm activities of an economic and political nature to a far greater extent than settler farmers. Many ran shops, restaurants, bars or taxi services, or were involved in local politics. Such dispersion of activity could be considered a risk-minimisation strategy, in view of the uncertainty of the state's agricultural policies.

The colonial state began to take note of the existence of African capitalised farmers during the early 1950s. While admiring their entrepreneurial initiative, on the other hand, the state deemed their methods of farming, particularly in Ismani, to be detrimental to soil conservation. But as the 1950s progressed, the colonial state became more supportive of large African farmers through half-hearted attempts to give them agricultural credit. After independence, as Nyerere's rural development strategy unfolded, African capitalised farmers became an anomaly that could not be tolerated for too much longer. In the late 1960s and early 1970s, they were, however, still thriving.

The call for *ujamaa* village development in Ismani was the first and most pointed confrontation between the state and the African capitalised farmers. The farmers took a belligerent line and the conflict culminated with the murder of Dr Klerruu, the zealous Regional Commissioner who was bent on uncompromising execution of the government's villagisation policy. In the aftermath of this event, the capitalised farmers appear to have shunned the headlines. With their diversified economic interests they had other options and could afford to keep a low profile when their land holdings became an issue during villagisation.

It should be emphasised that the African capitalised grain farmers were few in number.[15] They operated on a different economic logic from that of the neighbourhood patron. Like the neighbourhood patron, they were viewed by the Tanzanian state as a target for elimination and were far more vulnerable because they did not enjoy local popular support.

2.3 Specialised domestic production: state farms

State farms' cereal production was insignificant during the 1950s and 1960s. In 1951, the government established Lupiro farm on an experimental scale for paddy production in the Kilombero valley. After three good harvests it was decided to mechanise and enlarge the project and operate a commercial accounting system. Over the course of the next three years, the scheme did not prove to be economically viable. Game depradation and the failure to adapt mechanisation to the erratic flooding of the Kilombero river led to the abandonment of the farm at a loss of £15 000.[16]

State farms did not begin to play a significant role in staple food supply until the 1970s. In 1969, the National Agricultural and Food Corporation parastatal (NAFCO) was established within the Ministry of Agriculture. It was to serve as the holding company for a number of agriculturally-based enterprises, amongst them the Canadian Basotu Wheat Scheme in Arusha, which had been operated by the National Development Corporation. More than 50 large staple food farms and coffee estates in Kilimanjaro region, mostly owned by expatriates, were nationalised in 1973. The majority of these were handed over to cooperative unions. Nationalisation of the large settler wheat farms of Arusha was announced the following year. Chinese aid was also obtained for large-scale irrigated paddy production at Mbarali and Ruvu. The belief was that agglomeration of holdings into state farm operations would rationalise production. The early 1970s was a period of unproven optimism concerning the possibilities of state farm production of staple foods.

2.4 Non-specialised domestic production by peasants

The phenomenal growth of peasant commodity production was stimulated by the same social and economic forces that triggered the appearance of capitalised African farmers. The Korean war commodity price boom sparked off peasant commodity production levels that proved beyond a shadow of a doubt peasants' price responsiveness under conditions of fair weather and sufficient market and productive infrastructure. As prices dropped, peasant market participation was sustained by new-found purchased needs as well as the declining importance of migrant wage-labour as a source of income for tax payment.

Peasants outside the cotton and coffee zones were beginning to adopt new cash crops such as cashewnuts or tea, or they were attempting to produce food surpluses of the so-called 'preferred cereals' that had a ready-market in the burgeoning urban areas. The areas that were specialising in the preferred cereal production were of two types. Either they were areas particularly suited for the production of the crop by climate and soil type, such as paddy production in the Rufiji delta area, maize in Iringa, and wheat production in Hanang and Mbulu, or they were areas that were not suitable for the production of any of the major export crops and so by default took up marketed production of food, attempting to produce surpluses of their staple foods and succeeding in doing so in good harvest years, Dodoma and Singida being the prime examples of this. Obviously, the former areas generated a more regular supply than the latter.

Since peasant households were still producing their staple food needs as before[17] and the productivity of staple food production had not noticeably increased, there was a need to augment land, labour and capital resources of the household to produce an additional amount for the market. Most places still had available land. Where there was a decline in male out-migration, e.g. Iringa, additional labour resources were available. However, capital-intensification in the form of tractor-hiring schemes offered by Native Authorities, settlers and, later, African capitalised farmers and cooperatives was the most notable feature of areas with peasant commercial food crop production.

Tractor hiring always posed a number of logistical problems in terms of the scheduling of services, the transport of tractors from area to area, their mechanical maintenance and the collection of service fees. One by one, over the 1950s, the Native Authorities were forced to close down the schemes because of their lack of economic viability. The cooperatives' tractor schemes proved just as unwieldy. In Iringa and Arusha, settlers or capitalised African farmers offered tractor services whereas in the Rufiji there was no alternative service at hand once the Native Authority and cooperative schemes broke down. One of the major drawbacks faced by the peasant hiring a tractor was that his fields were ploughed only after the tractor owner's fields, often resulting in late planting and comparatively lower yields.

During the 1950s and 1960s, the agricultural policy of the state was aimed at helping to boost peasant households' commodity production over and above their normal subsistence food production. It was generally acknowledged by the government that such a policy would contribute to the tendency for fallow periods to be shortened. The 1955 East African Royal Commission, highlighting the need for the transformation of shifting cultivation to more intensive systems of agriculture, prompted the Department of Agriculture to coordinate the work of the country's agricultural research stations more effectively. Maize-breeding projects were directed at providing locally improved varieties. During the 1960s higher-yielding Ukiriguru and Ilonga maize composites were developed. Local experiments on fertiliser response were giving positive results as well. Both the colonial and post-colonial governments had similar research objectives *vis-à-vis* peasant agriculture and both pursued these objectives through local and East African-based research stations.

The main difficulty faced by both governments was in the realm of peasant agricultural extension. Not only was the peasantry very dispersed, its household labour constraints and lack of money to invest usually led it to be unwilling or unable to follow extension officers' suggestions. The Sukumaland Development Scheme, beginning in 1947 and lasting over the next ten years, was the colonial government's most ambitious agricultural extension effort. It and the Mbulu Development Scheme, the Uluguru Land-Use Scheme and other programmes in the Usambara and Pare mountains rested on the assumption that peasants had to be penalised for not adhering to government agricultural directives. Labour-intensive tie-ridging, terracing and manure application became mandatory. In 1955 peasants rioted against enforced conservation measures in the Uluguru mountains. The government, challenged by farmers and nationalists, abandoned its insistence on labour-intensive terracing and tie-ridging and embarked on a new 'focal point' approach whereby the extension officer's role as policeman gave way to that of teacher. In this approach, the peasant farmers most receptive to change were targeted for extension with the hope that they would set a convincing example for the others to emulate. At the same time, a few settlement schemes were initiated on former Groundnut Scheme land, the aim being to create yeoman farmers that would eventually farm extensive acreages.

At independence, agricultural 'teaching' was to take two forms: the 'improvement approach', similar to the 'focal point' approach in its reliance on farmers already inclined to the adoption of new farming techniques, and second, the 'transformation approach' which amounted to attempts at spoonfeeding peasants. This entailed the establishment of settlement schemes in a few special areas, placing peasants in a new physical environment which, it was considered, would spur their acceptance of new agricultural practices.

The improvement approach became increasingly at odds with the post-independent government's egalitarian goals whereas most of the settlement schemes were shortlived, and suffering severe organisational and supply problems. With a record of heavily supervised production, frequent over-capitalisation and mismanaged mechanisation, the government decided to abandon the settlement scheme programme in 1966.

1967 was a year for bold policy assertions. In his paper, 'Socialism and Rural Development', Nyerere rejected the 'improvement' approach and restructured the transformation approach into a far more ambitious rural development programme centering around an all-out call for the establishment of *ujamma* villages.[18] In the years that followed, spoonfeeding often became force feeding as 'operations' to villagise peasants in Rufiji (1969), Mtwara (1970), Iringa (1971), Dodoma (1971–2), Chunya and Kigoma (1973) took place. Most of these places were marginal commodity producing areas often subject to floods or droughts leading to food shortages and hence the operations were often carried out in the vein of disaster prevention. It was felt that agricultural extension would be easier in villages that had nucleated settlement. In 1972, the National Executive Committee of the party issued the policy statement *Siasa ni Kilimo* which adopted the stance that improving peasants' agricultural technology usage and productivity throughout the country was imperative.[19]

2.5 Imports

The years between 1950 and 1972 were characterised by an overall net import of grain averaging roughly 270 500 quintals of maize, rice and wheat per annum. Until independence, the annual average was 119 400 quintals as opposed to 421 500 between 1962 and 1972. These quantities were considerably in excess of the annual average deficit of 26 800 quintals prevailing from 1920 to 1950 (see Table 3.1).

Breaking the deficit down into separate grain categories: maize, the country's most important staple, registered an annual net import of only 18 400. This however disguises the extreme difference between an average annual net export of 107 600 quintals between 1950 and 1961 and a net average annual import of 144 500 during the post-colonial period. The low overall average but inter-year volatility of maize contrasts markedly with wheat, which had a high overall annual net import of 246 000 quintals with relatively little change in volume during the colonial and post-colonial period at 202 800 and 289 500 quintals respectively.

Between 1950 and 1973 there was a net annual rice import of 21 200 quintals with a net average export between 1950 and 1961 of 400 quintals annually and a net average import of 42 700 during the post-colonial period. If one considers rice and maize together, the overall net import was only about 40 000 quintals per annum. Thus, it was Tanganyikan consumers' newly found, but steady and mainly urban, demand for wheat which accounted for the bulk of net imports over the years rather than major deficits of domestically produced maize.

3 STAPLE FOOD MARKETING STRUCTURES

The 1950–73 period was one of relatively good food availability. The food security concerns of the state reflected this. No longer overtaxed with efforts to ensure supply to rural and urban areas under conditions of scarcity, the state became preoccupied with policies to stabilise producer and consumer prices for foodstuffs. Given the wide fluctuation of staple food production over time and space in Tanganyika, price stabilisation was no small task, but the colonial and post-colonial state felt it was warranted to ensure domestic stability in both an economic and political sense.

There are three distinct stages of food marketing structures between 1950 and 1973; that of the Grain Storage Department, 1950–57; private grain marketing, 1957–63; and the National Agricultural Board in conjunction with the regional marketing cooperatives, 1963–73.

The main aim of the Grain Storage Department (GSD) was to serve to even out the fluctuation of supply and price through a government-managed storage scheme handling maize/*mtama* and to a lesser extent paddy. At its peak, storage capacity was over 40 000 tons. The GSD refrained from engaging in widely dispersed marketing operations, buying grain from licensed traders and large-scale farmers in large amounts at railheads.

1949 and 1953 were drought years and the GSD ran at a loss but was generally recognised as providing invaluable service in meeting the challenge of regional shortages. In the intervening years until

1955, the GSD, although acknowledged to be operating efficiently, was frequently criticised for its pricing policy. 1955/6 was a bumper harvest and the tonnage of grain that was offloaded on the GSD was overwhelming (see Table 14.2). The surplus was exported at a loss of over £1 million. The government had to absorb the financial loss. Steps were immediately taken to wind up the operation of the GSD and finally ceased to exist in 1957.

In 1957, the Produce Control and Price Control Acts were repealed and the Milling Act of 1952 was amended so that only the licensing of wheat milling was retained. Traders were required to carry out their purchasing in accordance with Native Authority market regulations and pay market cesses, but otherwise they were free of restrictions. The only food security measure the central government continued was the maintenance of a small grain reserve for famine relief supervised by the Department of Commerce and Industry. Asian traders dominated the grain trade at all levels of the marketing chain. African participation was restricted to retailing in small amounts.

The late 1950s were fair weather years with very satisfactory food production overall whereas the early 1960s were not. 1961/62 was a drought year that severely affected central parts of the country, causing consumer prices to rise and engendering public resentment against traders just as the country gained political independence. These developments were to reverberate quickly in the post-colonial government's marketing policy.

In 1963 the National Agricultural Products Board (NAPB) was established for the single channel marketing of an array of products, namely: maize, rice, wheat, cashewnut and oilseeds. African public demand had been instrumental in bringing about this move. In addition to general resentment over the rise of food prices in the wake of the 1961/62 drought, the difficulties that cooperative societies were facing from the competition of Asian produce buyers in maize and rice trading made the establishment of the NAPB under African management popular. Furthermore, the post-colonial government saw this measure as an integral part of its food security function. 'Food crops are directly concerned with the feeding of the Nation and as such should come under the direct control of Government which has this fundamental responsibility.'[20] The NAPB was obliged to provide purchasing services throughout the country, buy all the produce that was offered to it, and keep a famine reserve stock for distribution to needy areas.

The goals of the NAPB were identical to the GSD; that of national food security and price stabilisation. Like the GSD, the bane of NAPB's operations was the financial losses incurred from trading in the world market while following a course of national price stabilisation. Within the financial confines of the NAPB, it seemed that the realisation of national food security was incompatible with price stabilisation. In the years when national food security was most successfully achieved, price stabilisation, which served to ensure food security at the level of the individual, was most threatened because heavy losses were incurred on domestic grain export. At these points, either the NAPB was allowed to include an export-loss fund in the following year's costings or the Treasury had to intervene with a subsidy or both.

The predicament facing the NAPB would have been enviable to past and present-day policy-makers wrestling with Tanganyika's food shortages. Despite relatively low producer prices, the NAPB was faced with over-abundant stocks. Abundance was reflected in the existence of the parallel market as a cheaper source of marketed food supply for waged workers; household budget data showing that food expenditure took up less than two-thirds of low-income household earnings; and limited use of the famine reserve. There were no serious food shortages in the country, even though peasants were growing increasing amounts of cash crops.

Unfortunately, security suddenly vanished in 1972. The 1971/2 harvest was extremely poor, necessitating an historically unprecedented amount of food imports (see Tables 3.1 and 14.2). This event took place alongside other adverse economic indicators. Between 1969 and 1971, the balance of trade had slid into a deficit position for the first time since independence (see Table 14.3). This was not due to a decline in export earnings; they registered a 4 per cent increase. Rather the import bill had ballooned by a full 79 per cent largely because machinery imports increased by 130 per cent under the Second Five Year Plan. In 1972, the trade imbalance widened with the increase in food imports.[21] Meanwhile, fundamental changes were taking place in the world market. Between 1969 and 1973 the price of oil doubled.

Within this inhospitable climate, the government and party were pursuing ambitious economic and social reform with the attitude that state organisation and planning could supercede external economic setbacks and eliminate the limitations of domestic peasant production and high costs of cooperative marketing. The state embarked on the drastic restructuring of state agencies through such policies as decentralisation in 1971 and marketing reform in 1973. Following the record-breaking food imports of 1972, the NAPB was dissolved and the National Milling Corporation was elevated to serve as the axis of the single-channel marketing system. It was clearly an effort to cut out duplication of functions by eliminating more than one node of the marketing chain. The NMC was to deal directly with cooperative societies in cases where the cooperative unions were especially ineffecive. The cooperatives became the mere executing agents of NMC parastatal marketing.

TABLE 14.3 *The value of net import/export, 1922–83 (TShs. 000000s)*

Year	*Imports*	*Exports*	*Balance*	*Year*	*Imports*	*Exports*	*Balance*	*Year*	*Imports*	*Exports*	*Balance*
1922	27.7	26.0	– 1.7	1951	562.4	786.9	224.5	1973	3139.5	2238.3	– 901.2
1923	35.9	33.0	– 2.9	1952				1974	5429.7	2537.4	–2892.3
1924	41.3	51.6	10.3	1953	568.5	690.9	122.4	1975	5288.1	2548.6	–2739.5
1925	57.3	57.2	– 0.1	1954	639.2	725.0	85.8	1976	4751.8	3815.0	– 936.8
1926	63.0	59.9	– 3.2	1955	870.6	723.8	–146.8	1977	6161.3	4393.8	–1767.5
1927	73.4	65.2	– 8.2	1956	717.7	896.1	178.4	1978	8797.7	3631.7	–5166.0
1928	74.7	76.3	1.6	1957	785.5	789.5	40.0	1979	8941.0	4313.2	–4627.8
1929	85.7	73.7	– 12.0	1958	671.4	834.1	162.7	1980	10210.5	4700.0	–9740.5
1930	79.7	51.8	– 27.9	1959	689.1	905.7	216.6	1981	9739.5	4705.8	–5033.7
1931	49.9	31.7	– 18.2	1960	756.3	1096.5	340.2	1982	10529.7	4143.9	–6385.8
1932	37.4	40.6	3.2	1961	793.7	973.0	179.3	1983	8876.5	4138.6	–4737.9
1933	38.9	46.9	8.0	1962	796.3	1024.8	228.5				
1934	46.9	47.0	0.1	1963	808.4	1271.1	462.7				
1935	59.8	61.5	1.7	1964	879.5	1402.2	522.7				
1936	67.1	80.5	13.4	1965	1000.9	1255.6	254.7				
1937	78.5	88.9	10.4	1966	1285.0	1582.1	297.1				

1938	69.0	38.4	– 30.6	1967	1300.5	1553.6	253.1
1939	60.8	38.3	– 22.5	1968	1531.7	1585.4	53.7
1940	60.0	79.4	19.4	1969	1418.8	1666.8	248.0
1941	73.1	89.6	16.4	1970	1939.2	1688.7	–250.5
1942	73.8	121.6	47.8	1971	2414.4	1735.4	–679.0
1943	92.5	108.1	15.6	1972	2597.6	2027.2	–570.4
1944	112.8	139.4	26.6				
1945	134.9	154.5	19.6				
1946	162.5	169.2	6.7				
1947	274.5	214.7	– 59.8				
1948	451.5	314.6	–136.9				
1949	551.5	384.7	–166.8				
1950	480.0	475.4	– 4.6				

SOURCES
1. Tanganyika Blue Books, 1922–48.
2. East African Annual Trade Reports, 1949–76.
3. Tanzania Annual Trade Reports, 1977–83.

Summary of Part V

A number of tendencies are evident in the period between 1950 and 1973. Most significantly, the African population in both rural and urban areas was not subjected to the same degree of food insecurity as had prevailed between 1919 and 1950. Although food importation increased in the country as a whole, this was related to the expansion of the urban population and their new-found demand for wheat rather than an increased incidence of rural food shortages, famine and urban scarcity. Both the colonial and post-colonial states endeavoured to ensure urban food security through cost of living allowances and later through food price stabilisation policies, such that the African urban population became reliant on a regular marketed supply of food. This alleviation of the burden of food insecurity provided a necessary condition for the blossoming of the social division of labour.

The extremely rigid tripartite racial division of labour began to disintegrate, superceded by an urban/rural divide and the beginnings of regionally-specialised peasant agriculture and intra-village class differentiation. The development strategy of the Tanganyikan state approximated the export crop strategy advocated by W.A. Lewis. A reasonable degree of success was being achieved until the beginning of the 1970s as indicated by the favourable balance of trade in contrast to the preceding and subsequent periods (see Table 14.3). The economy was capable of supporting a proliferation of African occupational specialisations. The food supply for the expanding numbers of urban-dwellers rested to a considerable extent on food import rather than increases in peasant food output, but such food imports were affordable within the context of the peasant cash crop boom.

Households, with less likelihood of having to cope with rural famine and with an increase in cashcropping, generally had more cash in hand and were beginning to experience the effects of enhanced educational opportunities for youth and rural outmigration. An age schism became apparent in the clientage relations of the Native Authority. The clientage networks of cooperatives sprouted alongside the power of the chief and his retainers in the main cash crop producing areas. The cooperatives were pivotal to the nationalist movement, affording TANU an organisational base in many rural areas. After independence the cooperative movement was generously rewarded by the state, which formally abolished the Native Authorities and invested in the expansion of the cooperative movement to all areas of Tanzania in conjunction with the removal of Asians from rural produce-buying. The physical departure of Tanganyika's Asian market agents left a vacuum that was filled by cooperatives and state trading corporations. Cooperatives which encouraged rural/small town mobility and the cash nexus were functional in breaking down tribal identity which stood in the way of the development of a national identity, and linked the nation-state to the peasant household via neighbourhood-based clientage networks. Increasingly over the 1960s, the state viewed cooperatives and their clientage relations as a sticky mess to clean up rather than as a vital adhesive between the urban-based bureaucracy and rural peasantry.

The state during this period had expanded the numbers on its payroll and its ambitions to spur peasant production. The state bureaucrat differed from the cooperative official because he was usually based in an urban area and had a salary that covered his immediate family's basic needs as well as modest improvements to his standard of living. Thus he was comparatively more insulated from clientage pressures. A sense of bureaucratic duty during the first decade after independence was maintained more or less intact in the party and government, a phenomenon which was related to Nyerere's elaboration of African socialism as an moral code which bridged the ethics of peasant household survival needs and the bureaucratic duty of state officials serving in the vanguard of nation-building activity. Capitalist profit and patrons' perks were antithetical to the tenets of African socialism as well as being seen as a drain in the state-managed fund for nation-building. It was this attitude in combination with the worsening of Tanzania's terms of trade in the world market which was to underly the state's frontal rural development programme from 1973 onwards.

Part VI
Urban Food Insecurity and the Undermining of Occupational Accountability, 1973–85

The preceding section documented the rapid development of labour specialisation, the ascendancy of the state *vis-à-vis* the market and the changing nature of clientage networks under conditions of relatively secure national food supply. In contrast, this section examines the erosion of labour specialisation and the enroachment of clientage on the state under food supply stress.

15 Merger of the State and Clientage

By 1973, the post-colonial state's systematic attempts to crush clientage practices had resulted in a wide sphere of government supervisory control over the cooperatives, local government and trade unions. This section analyses the aims of state control, then focuses on why clientage practices began to displace bureaucratic administration as the *modus operandi* of state agencies.

1 STATE DEVELOPMENT PROGRAMMES AND INTERVENING OBSTACLES

In 1973, the state embarked on a nationwide villagisation programme which sought to undermine peasants' shifting cultivation practices, bringing them into nucleated settlements in which they would practice 'modern' agriculture. A sense of urgency underlined the programme.

The relocation exercises took place in 'operations' organised on a regional basis under government and party supervision, often prodded by the militia and in some cases the Field Force Unit. Between 1973 and 1976, millions of peasants were moved into nucleated settlements, usually along accessible roads, to facilitate the state provisioning of productive and social service infrastructure.

Peasant agricultural transformation was all the more imperative in view of the state's industrialisation programme. Despite the disavowal of rapid industrialisation in the Arusha Declaration and the stated priority given to agriculture, the nationalisation of key industries in 1967 and the Second Five Year Plan (1969–74) pointed Tanzania on the path of industrialisation aimed at establishing a good mix of foundational industries. In the Basic Industries Strategy of the Third Five Year plan between 1975/76 and 1976/77, industrial expenditure leapt from 1.9 per cent to 7.4 per cent of the national budget.[1]

The similarities between the strategies of Preobrazhensky's Soviet Union and Tanzania during the 1970s are striking. State commitment to industrialisation and intervention in peasant agricultural production and marketing underlined by extreme optimism about the invincibility of the state characterised both. In Tanzania's case the realisation of these policies was thwarted by several obstacles.

Amidst the villagisation campaigns, the oil crisis hit with full force. 1974 oil prices were 350 per cent higher than the previous year causing Tanzania's fuel import bill to rise by TShs. 200 million.[2] The impact of higher oil prices was ubiquitous, raising international shipping as well as domestic transport costs for export crops and peasant incentive goods. The value of Tanzania's imports rose by 73 per cent while exports only increased by 13 per cent between 1973 and 1974 (see Table 14.3). Inadequate rainfall in 1973/4 and especially 1974/5 in combination with the dislocating effects of villagisation and transport constraints, led to food shortages in rural and urban areas. The all-time-high level of net food imports in 1975 reflects this (see Table 3.1).

Despite these blows, the country made a marked recovery in 1976 and 1977. Food imports fell back and the deficit in the balance of trade was considerably reduced, even though the liberalisation of imports policy under World Bank direction and the launching of the Basic Industries Strategy kept imports high (see Tables 3.1 and 14.3). But reprieve was brief. In October 1978, the country became embroiled in war with Amin's Uganda. Imports shot up to support the war effort and, to a lesser extent, exports declined as the country's transport system was adversely affected by the commandeering of public and private vehicles for use by the army. The war ended in May 1979, but economic recovery was nowhere in sight as the second oil crisis hit. Again the value of the oil import bill went up while volume declined. The transport system shrivelled, causing the effects of poor rainfall in 1979/80 to be magnified (see Table 3.2). Food shortages led to renewed high net imports of grain (see Table 3.1). The years that followed were characterised by a vicious downward spiral reflected in all economic indicators.

Besides the logistical difficulties of a collapsing transport system, the performance of the party and government bureaucracy was undermined by the disincentive effects of declining real wage and salary levels (see Table 12.1). Wages and salaries were raised in 1974 to counteract the effect of inflationary price rises following the first oil crisis, but on H.A. Turner's recommendation, the government froze the minimum wage for the next five years and restrained civil service salaries. The real purchasing power of wage earners quickly eroded. By 1983 the purchasing power of the minimum wage was at a par with the 1939 level. Urban families struggled to meet their basic needs on what amounted to a bachelor wage. As peoples' material expectations became increasingly frustrated and economic uncertainty loomed large, clientage practices on the part of the government and party bureaucracy became prevalent.

Clientage relations during this period had distinctive features. They were pervasive in all realms of the state and market, but just as cooperative clientage epitomised clientage during the 1950s and 1960s, it will be argued that parastatal clientage characterised the 1970s and 1980s.

2 PARASTATALISATION

2.1 Its establishment and organisational structure

Parastatals in Tanzania are defined as establishments in which the government has at least 5 per cent of the equity and the accounts are calculated on a profit-loss basis. Clark estimates that already in 1964 the government had parastatal assets worth TShs. 606 million. The Arusha Declaration of 1967 prompted the government to nationalise a number of key industries and commercial enterprises with assets worth TShs 362 million, 37 per cent in industry, 33 per cent in agriculture, 27 per cent in finance and 3 per cent in commerce.[3] The private sector's reluctance or inability to invest in large infrastructural and industrial projects made parastatals an attractive option for the government. Furthermore the government's attempts at planning the economy, it was thought, would be enhanced by the expansion of the parastatal sector.

The number of large national parastatal firms grew from 64 in 1967 to 190 in 1980.[4] In the Second Five Year Plan parastatal investment was projected to be over ten times greater than private sector investment.[5] The parastatals' contribution to total capital formation peaked at over 50 per cent in the first half of the 1970s.[6] Between 1966 and 1980, its contribution to GDP expanded from 3 per cent to 22 per cent. The parastatal sector was a motley assortment of enterprises which included: investment banks, import/export agencies, an insurance corporation, crop marketing boards, trading corporations, holding companies for productive enterprises, and companies directly involved in production and corporations for the servicing of public transport and communications.

Whatever their specific function, parastatals shared a similar organisational structure. Each parastatal had a parent ministry. A Board of Directors had overall responsibility for the corporations' operations and investment decisions. The day-to-day management and hiring was in the hands of the General Manager, assisted by sectional managers depending on the nature of parastatal operations.

This structure was nested in a wide array of regulatory agencies. The President had ultimate control of the establishment of new parastatals, the reorganisation of existing ones and the appointment and dismissal of top level personnel. Nyerere was known to inspect parastatals personally, particularly the ones involved in essential goods supply. The Standing Committee on Parastatal Organisation (SCOPO), established in 1967, was charged with designing and enforcing a code of conduct as well as setting standard salary levels and fringe benefits. A number of different bodies had supervisory functions over accounts including the Parliamentary Accounts Committee (est. 1978), the Treasury, the Bank of Tanzania, the Tanzania Audit Corporation and the Party Committee for Supervising Parastatal Activities. Major investment decisions were subject to the approval of the parent Ministry and the Economic Commission of the Cabinet. The Price Commission set fixed prices for parastatal products, the Central Bank controlled parastatals' access to foreign exchange and licensed imports, and parastatals were answerable to the party for their employees' working conditions. Despite all these controls, the general complaint outside the parastatals was that accountability was lacking and that the division of responsibility between ministries, boards, management, workers and party organs was not clear or that technical decisions were left to uninformed politicians.

The financial performance of parastatals, promising at first, deteriorated drastically over the 1970s. Published parastatal accounts were notoriously unreliable. Any aggregate statistics were at best indicative of trends. However, some parastatals were profitable, primarily those dealing in finance or commerce rather than industrial or agricultural production. Part of the parastatals' financial problems were traced to under-capitalisation at the time of their establishment.[7] In general, there was a tendency for over-capitalisation of fixed assets and under-capitalisation of working capital. Parastatal profits took a nose dive in 1974, while negative cash balances mounted. In the Third Five Year Plan disappointment was expressed at the failure of the parastatal sector to generate adequate investible surpluses. Over time parastatals drew more and more heavily on local borrowing to cover debts which led to rapid expansion of the money supply and inflation.

Not surprisingly, indicators were that factor productivity was extremely poor. Kim found that on average parastatal firms required two to three times more capital to generate a unit of output than private firms.[8] A UNIDO study identified widespread excess capacity.[9]

As the parastatal sector expanded, its 'socialist' versus 'capitalist' nature was heatedly debated.[10] The critics of capitalist penetration slated the introduction of management models derived from American business schools and the role of McKinsey and Co. in the reorganisation of the National Development Corporation and the State Trading Corporation.[11] Foreign management contracts were identified with the drain of profits outside the country, the biasing of choice of technology towards capital-intensification and financial irregularities.[12] Tanzanian management experts were at pains to point out the socialist nature of parastatal management in terms of planning goals and participatory decision-making.[13] But the debate pivoted on the capitalist or socialist *form* of the parastatal sector and ignored the *content* of parastatal operations, which did not conform to the norms of a state bureaucracy of socialist or capitalist description and were not suggestive of market rationality. They were primarily conducted on the basis of patron-client relations of managers and employees.

2.2 Parastatal managers, directors and employees

By the early 1980s there were over 400 parastatals, usually headquartered in Dar es Salaam and of a highly centralised nature involving the planning and coordination of economic activities throughout Tanzania. Parastatal management personnel were expected to be imbued with business professionalism as well as being committed to the national development goals of socialism and self-reliance.[14] Each parastatal had a presidentially-appointed General Manager. The basis for their selection was never made explicit, but political rather than professional credentials of the candidates often took precedence.[15]

Members of the board of directors of each parastatal were usually appointed by the concerned Minister whereas the board's chairman was a presidential-appointee. Board members were generally either high-ranking politicians or civil servants. While the extent of their influence varied from one parastatal to another, it is generally argued that they were ineffective because of their lack of business know-how, their appointment to too many boards,[16] the infrequency of their meetings and their indifference arising from the low monetary remuneration they received.[17] Ghai describes them as 'largely redundant', maintaining that managerial accountability was to the Minister not the board.[18]

While superior educational attainment generally separated management from both white- and blue-collar employees, the social background of all three groups was remarkably similar. They were all first generation urban dwellers who maintained contact with rural kin. According to von Freyhold's Dar es Salaam survey, the higher income management stratum had the strongest links in terms of rural visits and remitting money. More than half of both groups expected to hold land rights in their rural home areas indefinitely, although most intended to stay in Dar es Salaam for the majority of their lives.[19]

Parastatal employees received higher wages than government employees of the same occupational rank. But whereas their earnings were considered way above the average in the 1960s, SCOPO-enforced rigid salary scales kept them from escalating during the 1970s. Bonus schemes to boost salary productivity had to be approved by the Permanent Labour Tribunal and managements were reluctant to initiate them. Parastatal managers' salaries were supplemented by numerous perks which varied over time, including entertainment allowances, travel and nights out allowances, company cars, trips abroad, houses, and overseas training. Parastatal employees' perks were far less generous, namely lunch vouchers or subsidised canteen lunches, and company buses to transport them to and from work.

3 PARASTATAL CLIENTAGE PRACTICES AND NETWORKS

Whether socialist or capitalist objectives are imputed to the parastatal sector, expectations regarding the formal behaviour and work performance of managers' and employees' are essentially the same, i.e. the professional execution of their jobs in an efficient, hierarchically coordinated manner to achieve planned targets of production and to generate investible surpluses for the national economy. There were numerous external agencies that could regulate and impose checks on parastatal performance. However, so many of the checks could not be enforced in the absence of up-to-date audited accounts which the vast majority of parastatals continuously failed to produce on time.[20] Indeed, few parastatals kept careful account of their financial transactions and stocks, making annual audited accounts an impossibility.[21] The parastatals with the most out-of-date accounts tended to be the ones with the biggest overdrafts and were rumoured to be the most corrupt. Nonetheless, banks continued to be willing to loan to parastatals disregarding their creditworthiness and failure to produce audited accounts, particularly in the case of the crop authorities, which were seen as strategic to national welfare.

Parastatals were riddled with clientage practices which grew more profuse and ingenious as the national economic crisis deepened. The general manager, his retinue of supporting managers and the accounting staff had the best access to parastatal resources. They could engage in a long list of malpractices including: misuse of public vehicles, dubious imprests, falsification of records on purchases particularly with private customers, favouritism in allocating goods, lack of proper procedures in the application of funds from Treasury, misappropriation with fraud, poor control and management of movable fixed assets, fraudulent accounting, negligence, theft and embezzlement,[22] inadequate project feasibility studies resulting in the acceptance of uneconomic projects which involved kickbacks, and the accumulation of large outstanding debts.[23] Moshi's extensive research on parastatal operations led him to conclude that: 'the PEs [public enterprises] turned out to become instruments for privatisation of benefits and for socialisation of costs (losses). This explains why PE managers are usually healthier than the organisations they are managing.'[24]

Stock control was very lax, allowing pilfering.[25] Those employees who had poor access to either finances or stocks could always neglect to do their jobs.[26] Arriving late for work, reading newspapers, chatting and absence during the day to do errands unconnected with work were the norm. Under a perpetual 'go-slow', workers could extract small bribes for merely agreeing to 'speed-up' execution of their normal work tasks.[27] Statutory security of employment made job dismissal an infrequent occurrence. One cannot conclude, however, that more lowly-placed workers were completely isolated from the big rake-offs. For example, the messenger and a guard that were implicated in the 1984 Bank of Tanzania fire were, it was rumoured, acting on behalf of people higher up who had reason to seek the destruction of the Bank's financial records.[28]

Quantitative measurement of clientage practices is impossible. The Bank of Tanzania fire is perhaps indicative of what lengths could be taken to cover up activities. But an impression of their extent can be gleaned from newspaper accounts of frauds and the National Audit Board reports on incomplete submission of parastatal accounts. The enormous bank overdrafts that most of the parastatals had are suggestive of malpractice.

Unlike Native Authority and neighbourhood clientage, parastatal clientage was pursued with a certain amount of discreetness, even secrecy, because it was knowingly a transgression of professional conduct and often the law.[29] The dynamic underlying parastatal clientage relations differed from that which had prevailed under Native Authority and cooperative clientage. The material insecurity was still the motive for initiating clientage practices, but rather than mutual support between patrons and clients with clients bestowing prestige on patrons in return for favours, managers and employees plundered parastatal resources at will. They had to be willing to participate to some degree in a conspiracy of silence, turning a blind eye to each others' exploits.[30]

The conspiracy of silence was lubricated by nepotistic practices. Besides overmanning in parastatals, it was constantly rumoured that managers placed relations or friends in posts within their enterprises.[31]

Clientage relations within the parastatal cohered on the basis of combined material insecurity and fear. Face-to-face accountability rested more on mutual fear of exposure than close identification between management and worker. But the accountability of parastatal employees *vis-à-vis* the rest of the population was very limited, particularly with respect to the peasantry. As consumers of parastatal goods and services peasants suffered from the serious inefficiencies of the erratic delivery service and high prices. As producers, they received low prices for their crops. As service takers, they received scant attention and as taxpayers they were over-burdened by the bank overdrafts that ultimately came down on their shoulders.

What most distinguishes parastatal clientage from that of the Native Authorities and cooperatives is that its networks largely failed to engulf the rural areas, despite the fact that the parastatals had been designated as the main provisioners of the modern, improved means of production and consumption that peasants sought. Based in urban areas and shielded from the public behind a facade of corporate business procedures, the face-to-face accountability that the peasantry had exercised over the cooperative patrons had less chance to be exerted. Clientage no longer adjusted the processes of market and state surplus extraction. Over-extraction through a decline in peasant producer prices and a rise in consumer prices and a marked deterioration in the rural standard of living was evident.

Parliamentary committee reviews of parastatal performance were to little avail. Over the latter part of the 1970s the press began to take an active role in trying to uncover corrupt practices in the government and parastatals, eagerly reporting the investigations of the government's Anti-Corruption Squad.[32] President Nyerere, under the instigation of the party, was increasingly exercising his right to dismiss managers. An anti-corruption campaign was launched following a 1981 NEC extraordinary party meeting to discuss essential goods shortages.[33] For Nyerere it was a matter of weeding out certain corrupt individuals in an otherwise sound governmental and parastatal system: 'We must introduce a little bit of hell in our fight against corruption in Tanzania'. . . . We have not found out that one parastatal organisation is the source of corruption for another'.[34]

There were limits to this, however. Some government and party officials widely suspected of gross misconduct were not netted, and it was rumoured that they were too powerful for such treatment.[35] The campaign's firing squad was in danger of getting a return volley with unpredictable consequences for state stability. The government's emphasis switched from an anti-corruption theme to economic efficiency, appointing a special commission in January 1983 to look into the activities and performance of parastatal corporations with a view to reducing operating costs. However, just before the completion of his last term of office, Nyerere, in his characteristic see-saw style of policy-making, appealed for management autonomy.[36]

Parastatal clientage practices probably resulted in a net value transfer from rural areas to the urban areas, since most parastatal employees were urban dwellers. Ellis' work suggests that this was true of the marketing boards which had the largest bank overdrafts in the parastatal sector.[37] Considering that most of this money probably went into the private pockets of parastatal employees, how did they spend it?

After 1975 urban incomes were declining at a faster rate than rural incomes (compare Tables 12.3 and 15.1). Since so much of peasant consumption was self-provisioned, urban residents were evidently

TABLE 15.1 *Peasant income index, 1952–81 (1963 = 100)*

Year	*Estimated real income of commercial cotton producer*[*]	*Estimated real income of commercial maize producer*[+]
1952	99	
1953	101	
1954	116	
1955	117	
1956	119	93
1957	105	84
1958	103	86
1959	101	80
1960	103	69
1961	109	96
1962	104	99
1963	100	100
1964	98	87
1965	93	94
1966	88	81
1967	87	84
1968	87	83
1969	86	75
1970	87	78
1971	86	61
1972	81	71
1973	79	69
1974	69	69
1975	66	68
1976	69	77
1977	65	71
1978	65	69
1979	64	67
1980	65	67
1981	61	61

NOTES

* Assumes 40 per cent of income derives from subsistence production and is not subject to price changes, whereas the rest of the farmer's income is solely derived from sale of cotton produce. Cotton prices are deflated by the Non-Food Retail Price Index for Dar es Salaam (1963 = 100).

+ Assumes 40 per cent of income derives from subsistence production and is not subject to price changes, whereas the rest derives from sale of maize. Maize prices are deflated by the Non-Food Retail Price Index for Dar es Salaam (1963 = 100).

SOURCES
Cotton Prices:
1952–68: Helleiner, G.K., 'Agricultural Marketing in Tanzania: Policies and Problems', *ERB* Paper 68.14, UDSM (1968) p. 25.
1969–74: Odegaard, K., 'A Study of Agricultural Producer Prices', Office of the Prime Minister and Second Vice-President (1974) Annex Table No. I.10.
1975–84: Tanzania, MDB, 'Price Policy Recommendations for the July 1982 Agricultural Price Review: Summary', DSM (July 1982) app. 7.
Maize Prices:
1956–69: Kriesel, H.C. *et. al.*, *Agricultural Marketing in Tanzania: Background Research and Policy Proposals* (East Lansing: Michigan State University, 1970) p. 38.
1970–74: Odegaard, K., 'A Study of Agricultural Producer Prices', Office of the Prime Minister (1974) Annex Table I.4.
1975–86: Tanzania, MDB, 'Price Policy Recommendations for the 1984 Agricultural Price Review: Summary (1984) app. IV.

experiencing a much more drastic decline in their accustomed standard of living than peasants. It is likely that a great deal of the value transfer was used to try to stave this fall in urban material welfare. Secondly, the money could have been used for ostentatious consumption but strict import controls throughout this period imposed limitations. There was investment in house building, but cars, boats, expensive liquors, holidays abroad, etc. were very difficult to obtain. Furthermore, since most of Tanzania's elite were first-generation urban dwellers, they tended not to have aspirations for the trappings of a 'bourgeois' lifestyle as defined by European consumers. Non-essential consumption was more on the traditional lines of drinking large quantities of beer, as well as a growing incidence of cigarette smoking. Bottled beer and cigarettes were subject to enormous sales tax and constituted one of the largest sources of government revenues. Outside of the infamous chicken farms of government and parastatal *wakubwa*,[38] it is very difficult to gauge how much was productively invested. The stringent controls on property ownership imposed by the Leadership Code, which applied to all middle and high income personnel, put a damper on investment possibilities.

The imposition of peasant face-to-face accountability on parastatal patrons was not completely undermined. Peasant demands could be lodged through household channels. Rural-based peasant branches of the extended family could and did make demands on their urban kin, often for consumer goods that were unobtainable in the rural areas or for lodging rights in the urban areas for schooling children or for ill members seeking urban hospital services.

In summary, parastatal clientage like the other forms of clientage represented inter-personal exchange relations under conditions of extreme material insecurity. Unlike earlier forms, its inter-personal dealings were conducted by people who identified as urban wage-earners and salaried professionals purportedly adhering to the norms of corporate business impartiality and legality. Under these circumstances, clientage practices became more secretive. Furthermore, the urban location of the patrons put them out of the range of face-to-face accountability with the peasants. Thus, urban occupational accountability was undermined in almost all respects, which had grave implications for the viability of labour specialisation in the national economy.

16 Parastatal Staple Food Management

Increasing domestic production and marketed supply of food were necessary pre-conditions for successful industrialisation and attendant urbanisation. As state policy aims, their importance was reinforced by the drought, domestic food shortages and massive food imports of the mid-1970s. With a sense of urgency and confidence in its own organisational capability, the state embarked on a number of measures in line with Preobrazhensky's theories.

1 STATE-REGULATED PEASANT PRODUCTION

In 1973, President Nyerere publically announced: 'To live in villages is an order.'[1] For decades, peasants' dispersed settlement and shifting cultivation had been seen as the greatest obstacle to the country's agricultural development. Unlike the preceding *ujamaa* village policy, the villagisation programme carried out between 1973 and 1976 was directed at nucleating settlement rather than collectivising production. The rationale was that once peasants were aggregated, they could more easily be provided with improved inputs and social services, and their fields, whether or not they were collectively cultivated, could be contiguous, facilitating mechanisation and fertiliser and insecticide application.

There were two powerful forces exerting pressure on Tanzanian peasant agriculture during the period under review. The first was purely domestic, namely the state's efforts to modernise agriculture through its villagisation programme and the imposition of numerous state regulatory measures. The second was the economic crisis triggered by drastic price changes in the world market and its economic and political reverberations in Tanzania. Even in the absence of the latter, it is not very probable that the state's plan for peasant agriculture could succeed as intended. The hope of many urban-based bureaucrats was to create factory-like production on the part of peasant households in a three-staged process.[2] First, the state would provide the peasants with improved productive inputs, initially at a subsidised rate to promote their adoption, but eventually remove the subsidy. Second, the household would use these inputs to produce improved yields. Third, the output would be sold to state marketing agencies at an incentive price, but one well below world market prices. Thus, the state would serve as the production and marketing manager of peasant household units, advancing the capital to combine with peasants' land and labour inputs, then marketing the output. There were, however, innumerable things that could and did go wrong.

The state's input delivery system had numerous shortcomings. Because of Tanzania's large geographical area and input expense, village coverage was always restricted. Untimely delivery and poor storage of inputs reduced the effectiveness of the inputs' effect. Many of the inputs were clearly wrong and sometimes even harmful, for the specific environmental conditions of Tanzania's different agro-economic zones.

Peasants experienced a number of problems in utilising the inputs, the most notable being the lack of household labour for additional tasks connected with input application. Villagisation had compounded the labour shortage situation. Peasants had to spend more time walking to and from fields which were more liable to crop destruction by vermin. The semi-urban atmosphere of the now larger nucleated villages created a youth sub-culture amongst the male youth who flaunted urban tastes and disdained rural life and agricultural toil. Much of the increased workload associated with agricultural intensification fell on the women.[3] Furthermore, the implementation of the Universal Primary Education caused a large reduction in the availability of child labour.

A major pitfall in the 'state factory' schema was the peasants' ability not to deliver the output to state agencies. The peasantry could eat their surplus if it was in the form of food, or sell it outside official state marketing channels. It was for these reasons that, like Preobrazhensky, the Tanzanian state saw peasant agriculture as extremely cumbersome and preferred the more direct control of large-scale state farming.[4]

What actually happened to peasant agriculture after villagisation? Villagisation made the continuation of shifting agriculture impossible. By nucleating population, villagisation artificially raised critical population densities[5] to the point at which agricultural intensification and technological change in the Boserupian sense became imperative. Kjaerby argues that villagisation engendered a 'land-use crisis' which pre-empted most of the traditional preventive and regenerative responses to loss of soil fertility.[6] The concentration of population in villages put more pressure on the soils, pasture land and firewood availability. Various animal grazing patterns in combination with dispersed, shifting settlement were no longer possible. People could no longer move when soil fertility was depleted or when insect and rodent infestation and the build-up of plant, livestock and human diseases became serious.[7] Furthermore, it saved peasants' time to intensify production on the fields closest to the settlement.

Throughout Tanzania, peasants turned away from export crop production. Coffee, cotton and cashew, the main export crops, declined. It would be a mistake to attribute this directly to the effects of villagisation since real export values as well as domestic prices were declining.[8] Instead peasant agriculture concentrated on food production, spurred by higher relative prices as well as a re-emphasis on household food self-sufficiency.

Despite the impact of villagisation and government agricultural programmes, the adoption of improved inputs by peasants in the nation as a whole was still very limited. Fertiliser distribution increased from 0.9 kg to 6.6 kg per rural resident between 1962 and 1980, boosted by the state's substantial fertiliser subsidy.[9] Similarly between 1974 and 1980 distribution of improved seed expanded. However, a significant portion of this would have gone to the large-scale farming sector rather than peasant producers. By the early 1980s peasant usage was registering a noticeable decline. In 1982, for example, out of 8029 tons of improved seeds produced by TANSEED, only 32 per cent was purchased by the farmers.[10] As input subsidies were lifted, only the commercial food crop farmers could buy fertilisers and insecticides. The cultivation of hybrid maize was pursued mainly for cash rather than home consumption.[11] Peasants' were reluctant to improve the land with long-term fixed investments, thinking that their plots might be subject to reallocation in follow-up villagisation measures.[12]

Overall, did peasant agricultural productivity improve? In the absence of detailed yield data measuring the before and after situation, it is impossible to say. However, it seems likely that in the case of Southern Highlands productivity per land and labour unit probably increased owing to a combination of capital injection and the 'vent for surplus' effect created by improved transport conditions. Hybrid maize became the area's specialised cash crop. Improvements in productivity per unit of capital, however, are highly questionable, especially in view of the huge deficits in the parastatals servicing input supply and peasant marketing. In the Northern areas, Kjaerby conjectures that productivity per unit of labour declined[13] while it probably increased per unit of land and capital with the spread of ox-ploughing. At the aggregated level of total peasant output, it seems likely that the decline in export crop production was not fully compensated for in terms of increased food production, at least in value terms; the best evidence for this being the overall decline in standards of living of the Tanzanian population. Incentives for peasants to produce over and above subsistence levels were lacking due to the scarcity of purchasable consumer goods.

2 STATE FARMS

Despite the rapid expansion of the state farm sector and its importance to domestic marketed food supply, it is extremely under-researched. In Tanzania, the term 'state-farm' embraces a number of state institutions including those that attempt to produce food for their own internal needs, most notably the prisons, the army and many schools of higher learning, as well as the commercial state farms operated by the Ministry of Agriculture and various parastatals. Of the latter, the NAFCO group and it subsidiaries was by far the largest, being a holding company of over 20 different farms.

1973 marked the beginning of a clearly distinguishable state farm sector with the nationalisation of European and Asian farms in Kilimanjaro and Arusha. These farms were divided amongst the cooperatives, district development corporations and NAFCO. The rationalisation for expansion at this point was the incongruity of prosperous, large private farms with the tenets of the Arusha Declaration. Thereafter, state farm growth, although phenomenal, received little publicity. Following the food shortages of 1973–75, NAFCO was given the green light to expand as fast as foreign aid could take it in the spheres of wheat, rice and maize production. The aim was to bolster and regularise domestic marketed supply, much in the same way as the 1943 food shortages had led the colonial state to vest hope in large-scale capitalised farming over lower-yielding, erratic peasant production. In 1981, NAFCO reported wheat, paddy and maize hectarages of 18 013, 3373 and 1233 respectively with total tonnage output of 21 868, 23 792 and 3502. Between 1973/4 and 1981/82 the NAFCO cultivated area expanded from 5510 ha. to 30 346 ha (a 24 per cent annual growth rate) with cereal output increasing from 7715 tons to 68 203 tons (a 31 per cent annual growth rate).[14] As in the 1940s, capitalised wheat production received the most investment.

Besides their large-scale mechanised nature which distinguished them so starkly from the surrounding peasant farms, the NAFCO state farms were operated on bureaucratic principles of management, which some critics say was antithetical to viable agriculture. The farm management often had little knowledge of horticulture and sometimes refused to work outside of office hours. Many decisions had to be cleared with the NAFCO bureaucracy in Dar es Salaam before they could be implemented on site, resulting in the untimely execution of agricultural tasks.

Clientage practices as described in the preceding chapter were widely prevalent. Although NAFCO's financial account-keeping was of an above average standard for parastatals, this left room for a great deal of irregularities in cash disbursements and embezzlement.[15] Stock keeping was lax. Privileged supply of farm products to private individuals as well as local government and party officials was common.[16] Some managers allotted portions of state farm land to people of influence.[17] The biggest scandal, though not publicised, was the disappearance of approximately 10 000 tons of wheat between the Basotu farm and the NMC Arusha mill, undetected for some time because tonnage was only recorded at the place of delivery.[18] The transporters were suspected of the theft with possible collaboration from the state farm management.

Overmanning of administrative staff was very common. Personal loans to staff employees from company funds were frequent, as was borrowing and lending between NAFCO farms. The tendency was for these loans to be left outstanding for long-time periods, eventually being written off as bad debts.[19] Staff members benefited from the ruling that all of them should be allocated individual plots for the cultivation of their household food needs.[20] They could hire the state farm's tractors and other machinery on Sundays, which proved highly lucrative, since any surplus grain was sold on the parallel market.[21] Land conflicts between the villages and state farm employees, most of whom were non-local, were frequent.[22] In an extreme case the state farm employees were charged with burning peasants' homes to make them move.[23]

Operationally, state farm managers, not unlike peasant farmers, had to contend with the shortcomings of the wider economy. Transport constraints, the restricted availability of foreign exchange and productive inputs were all the more pressing given the capitalised nature of state farm production. Since all of NAFCO produce had to be sold through the official government marketing channels, government pricing and inter-parastatal debt defaulting were direct determinants of NAFCO's financial status.

In evaluating the performance of the state farms, it is important to recognise that two aims were accomplished, namely higher grain yields and a growing proportion of officially marketed grain came from the state farm sector. Wheat yields rose impressively from 700 kgs to 1750 kgs per hectare, under the Canadian research programme.[24] Maize yields at Mbozi increased from approximately one ton/ha in 1974 to four tons in 1982.[25] Rice at Mbarali was recorded as high as 7.5 tons/ha, three times higher than that of peasants nearby.[26] State farm production accounted for 96 per cent, 91 per cent and 7 per cent of officially marketed wheat, rice and maize, respectively, in 1982/83.

NAFCO and government officials were eager to point out that foreign exchange was saved by averting food imports.[27] But this was doubtful since so many of Tanzania's food imports were obtained on concessional terms during the period under review and state farm production was far more heavily dependent on imported inputs, notably fuel, than peasant production. Increasingly the economy's foreign exchange constraints impinged on the state farm's input supply. The cost of NAFCO's wheat and rice production in 1981/82 was estimated as 62 per cent and 63 per cent of import parity value.[28] Only 17 per cent of the sector's requests for foreign exchange were granted between 1978/9 and 1980/81.[29] This led to under-utilisation of capacity and financial losses.

Between 1975 and 1982 the NAFCO group's accumulated losses ranged between TSh. 0.7 million and TSh. 18.2 million, whereas the subsidiary companies had an accumulated loss of TSh. 62.8 million in 1983.[30] By 1982, state policy was primarily concerned with improving the state farm sector's efficiency rather than expanding its operations.

The majority of NAFCO's staff not only worked in the rural areas but also lived there, unlike most parastatal enterprises. But only a small minority of the white-collar and skilled staff were from the area, whereas most manual labourers were local people, generally hired on a casual basis. The administrative and technical staff were reported to be alienated from and disdainful of the local peasantry. Their mechanised methods of production were completely out of reach of the peasant.[31] Wages on the state farm were low creating problems of recruitment of labour.[32] However, workers did have a right to buy grain direct from the farm. Bantje argues that: 'the main impact of the state farm on the villages is the food security it provides by selling maize in times of food shortage. There are indications that the management uses this "food power" to persuade the villages to come and work, by refusing to sell maize to those that do not.'[33] Peasants' contributed labour service was being exchanged for food availability in times of need almost in the fashion of the Native Authorities. Thus, the state farm did function to some degree in the alleviation of peasant food insecurity. Peasants could also steal grain from the enormous fields of the state farms.[34]

3 FOOD MARKETING

In 1973, the government abolished the National Agricultural Products Board, handing over its staff, fixed capital and crop procurement activities to the National Milling Corporation (NMC). Government policy objectives in the realm of staple food marketing had not changed. The main preoccupation was still to achieve food security by ensuring stable consumer prices and incentive producer pricing. Eliminating the cooperatives' wide marketing margins rather than the NAPB per se was the aim of reorganisation. The NMC could by-pass inefficient cooperative unions and purchase directly from the cooperative societies, thus consolidating the principle of single channel marketing.

After the completion of the villagisation operations and the passage of the 1975 Village Act, the state abolished local cooperative societies in May 1976. The NMC was to procure staple food directly from village governments which were more numerous than primary cooperative societies. From village to central mill, the NMC had control. At the wholesale level, the Regional Trading Companies were generally in charge up-country and the parastatal, National Distributors Ltd. served Dar es Salaam. Only retailing of staple foods was not under direct state control.

NMC faced formidable circumstances during its early years as a marketing parastatal. First, the NMC inherited the NAPB's liabilities, including a large bank overdraft of TShs. 64 million.[35] Second, in 1974/5, the country experienced a severe shortfall of domestic food production and a drastic decline in marketed output (see Table 14.2). Rural famine relief had to be supplied by the NMC to a number of places. At the same time, urban food demand was expanding as a result of rapid urbanisation and posed a greater political threat than rural demand in the event of supply failure. NMC's sales became more and more focussed on Dar es Salaam and secondarily the other major towns with residual supply to the rural areas. 1974 and 1975 were characterised by unprecedented levels of grain importation (see Table 3.1).

The government's consumer pricing policy rested on the unswerving principle that controlled staple food prices had to be low enough to allow the basic nutritional needs of the minimum wage earner's nuclear household to be met. This principle became an adjunct of the wage policy. Between 1975 and 1980 the government refrained from raising the minimum wage despite its declining purchasing power (see Table 12.3). The controlled price of *sembe*, the main urban staple food, was held constant. After the oil shock of 1979, as inflation skyrocketed, the government had to relent and raise the minimum wage slightly, a measure which was reinforced by the lowering of the *sembe* price by 29 per cent. Until 1984, the minimum wage and *sembe* prices continued to be balanced such that the purchasing power of a day's minimum wage, measured in terms of kgs of *sembe*, never slipped below 7 kg.[36]

The *sembe* subsidy made NMC marketing margins impossibly slim.[37] The maize marketing margins between producer and ultimate *sembe* consumer price between 1964/5 and 1972/73 was 309 per cent, 110 per cent between 1973 and 1980 and only 37 per cent between 1980 and 1984. The NMC's bank overdraft consequently mounted steadily from the level inherited from the NAPB. Retailers' margins as well as those of the NMC were squeezed. Complaints were made that retailers refused to stock *sembe* in their shops or required customers to buy slow-moving items with any *sembe* purchase.[38] The *sembe* subsidy was lifted in 1984 under pressure from the IMF, causing a 320 per cent increase in the consumer price. Its removal was accompanied with a 35 per cent compensatory increase in the minimum wage (see Table 12.3), so that *sembe*'s price doubled in relation to workers' purchasing power.

The majority of NMC sales took place in Dar es Salaam and the secondary cities of the country. The urban growth rate was over 10 per cent per annum. Table 16.1, measuring NMC sales as a percentage of total urban requirements, shows a fairly steady decline at an annual rate of 9 per cent. Frequent urban food shortages were the inevitable consequence. Maize shortages were concentrated in the years of bad harvests and increased importation, 1973 to 1975 and

TABLE 16.1 *NMC sales of preferred cereals per urban resident, 1964/65–1983/84 (kg/capita)*

Year	*Maize*	*Rice*	*Wheat*	*Maize as % of Total*	*NMC sales as % of total urban requirements*[x]
1964/65	215.8	57.1			190
1965/66	204.3	53.9	88.8	59	242
1966/67	151.3	64.1	80.9	51	206
1967/68	166.9	61.7	90.7	52	226
1968/69	169.7	57.2	97.6	52	325
1969/70	181.5	61.5	83.4	56	227
1970/71	155.4	69.4	79.6	51	212
1971/72	193.2	91.5	107.0	49	273
1972/73	168.4	96.2	58.9	52	225
1973/74	207.7	81.5	65.8	56	247
1974/75	181.9	38.5	56.4	66	193
1975/76	112.0	28.2	49.0	59	132
1976/77	92.6	38.5	50.6	51	127
1977/78	68.9	49.8	58.7	39	177
1978/79	94.3	42.4	58.2	48	136
1979/80	122.0	33.5	30.0	66	129
1980/81	146.2	38.5	21.0	71	143
1981/82	128.9	34.9	23.8	69	131
1982/83	84.7	29.2	22.3	62	95
1983/84	90.0	29.1	12.6	68	92
Average 1964/65–1972/73	178.5	68.1	76.3	53	236
1973/74–1983/84	120.8	40.4	40.8	60	146

NOTE

[x] Total urban requirements are calculated with the assumptions that: 1) 40.4 per cent of the population are under 15 years of age (1978 census); 2) under-15s consume 90 kg of cereals per year; 3) adults consume 180 kg per year; and 4) the 1979–84 urban annual growth is the same as that recorded between 1967 and 1978.

SOURCES

1. As listed in Table 14.2.
2. Tanganyika, *African Census Report 1957* (DSM: Government Printer, 1963).
3. Tanzania, *1967 Population Census*, vols I and II (DSM: Bureau of Statistics, 1970).
4. Tanzania, *1978 Population Census*, vol. II (DSM: Bureau of Statistics, 1981).

then 1979 onwards, whereas shortages of rice and wheat were continuous features of the period gradually worsening over time (see Tables 3.1 and 14.2).[39] As supplies diminished, NMC sales became increasingly concentrated in Dar es Salaam. In 1974/75 Dar es Salaam accounted for 33 per cent of NMC's total maize sales; by 1983/84 the figure had risen to 57 per cent, disproportionately high relative to the 46.5 per cent of the nation's urban population living in Dar es Salaam.

Consumers grew accustomed to queueing at *dukas* for staple food purchases. In order to save their employees time, many ministries, parastatals and private firms made efforts to procure supplies in bulk from the NMC to sell to their employees on an ad hoc basis. In 1983, the government finally instituted a party-supervised rationing system. Ward party secretaries were responsible for collecting the daily allocations for their areas from the National Distributors Ltd for distribution to retail shops. Households registered with their neighbourhood retail shop and received a rationing card that entitled them to 1/2 kg of staple grain per capita per day. At first the system seemed to be an improvement. However, retailers' discretionary sales were not eliminated and eventually the rationing system procedures were themselves blamed for persisting shortages.[40]

By 1978, the NMC employed 4200 people, 1600 in Dar es Salaam. Apart from the highest echelons of management, its staff were poorly educated and trained, most having gained their positions through long service in the NAPB or cooperatives rather than formal schooling. It is impossible to know whether NMC staff performance was below the generally low standards of parastatals, but it is clear that the NMC's accounting system was particularly deficient and the lack of middle-level cadres supervising an overmanned and untrained labour force was very pronounced. Clientage practices proliferated in an atmosphere of declining salaries, gross inefficiency, poor management and lack of accountability. The staff were dealing in extremely valued food commodities and large sums of cash which led to frequent financial and commodity distribution irregularities.[41] The newspapers' reported cases of NMC staff involved in peculation, fraud and parallel marketing, were undoubtedly only the tip of the iceberg.[42] For example, the hiring of private cars for the transport of NMC executives and employees became a common practice as in most parastatals, but it was particularly abused at NMC's headquarters in Dar es Salaam.[43]

In 1984, government investigations into the problems of staple food distribution revealed corrupt collusion on the part of the senior management and rank and file workers of the National Distributors Ltd, the parastatal serving as wholesale trader for cereal products in Dar es Salaam. The appointment of a new General Manager resulted in 'workers . . . initiating a strike and writing letters threatening to physically eliminate the NDL new General Manager, Ndugu Abdul Buddy, who had instituted tough measures to curb laxity and apathy in the company'. The Chief Accountant, the Depot Manager and Chief Cashier were dismissed in connection with the disappearance of over TShs. 30 million.[44]

The combined effects of government's welfare-oriented policies and NMC's various operational failings culminated in an escalating bank overdraft. By 1981, NMC's overdraft was an astronomical TShs. 2.3 billion, topping the league of parastatal overdrafts. Over the years, a number of agencies and investigating committees scrutinised NMC's operations and finances.[45] In 1981, the government came to the conclusion that NMC was over-extended and in need of reorganisation. At this time it was proposed that the marketing cooperatives be reinstated to handle regional produce-buying. The Cooperative Bill was passed in parliament in 1982.

The return to cooperative buying was to be implemented gradually. Cooperative buying first resumed in some regions in 1984. Numerous problems over the division of financial and fixed capital assets bogged down implementation of the cooperative legislation. After relinquishing its role as primary produce-buyer, NMC was to continue as the country's bulk buyer from the cooperative unions, as principal miller, as manager of strategic grain reserves, as monitor of the national food situation and as provisioner of famine relief.

Meanwhile various measures were taken to reduce or contain the NMC's deficit and bank overdraft. From its enormous 1980 level, the *sembe* consumer subsidy was reduced through a cross-subsidy on sugar and compensating payments from the treasury.[46] Finally in 1984 the subsidy was removed having cost the government an estimated TShs. 1.2 billion.[47]

4 NATIONAL FOOD SECURITY: DOMESTIC FOOD SELF-SUFFICIENCY v IMPORTS

Through a number of seemingly conflicting policies, the government endeavoured to guarantee the Tanzanian population's food security.

Measures to achieve food security took two forms: long-term programmes and short-term expedients. Regarding the latter, when the Marketing Development Bureau investigated the NMC's financial disarray, it found: 'The overall justification explanation and rationale given on every topic was that NMC had such a critical role to play in the national economy that its main aim was to make sure every one had food, and every other consideration was incidental.'[48]

4.1 Sectoral planning

The aim of national food self-sufficiency was clearly enunciated in the Third Five Year Plan. However, food imports were massive in 1981 at the close of the Third Five Year Plan (see Table 3.1). Critics maintained that the Third Five Year Plan's investment concentration on the Basic Industries Strategy had diverted Tanzania from its expressed aim of developing peasant agriculture following villagisation. From independence until 1976, expenditure on industry was on average 2.2 per cent and on agriculture 10.7 per cent of the total government budget. From 1976 to 1981, under the Third Five Year Plan, industry's share spurted to an average 8.5 per cent and agriculture's declined to 9.7 per cent.[49]

National food self-sufficiency was the primary objective of the National Food Strategy, a Danish-funded, FAO-consulted plan which was commissioned by the government in 1982, and a central tenet of the 1982 Agricultural Policy.[50] The danger was that the food self-sufficiency strategy would detract from peasant export crop production. The import requirements for the country's major export crops was estimated at 27 per cent of the crops' export parity value in 1981/2, whereas import requirements for food crops were 51 per cent of food crops import parity value.[51] The figure for maize was 45 per cent; transport costs accounting for almost half. This suggests that a household food self-sufficiency strategy which minimised transport costs was the wisest policy. Under prevailing conditions, Tanzania clearly had a comparative advantage in the production of export crops. But national food self-sufficiency had been a treasured aim for so long that few planners accommodated this fact. In any case, long-term investment-demanding food strategies had a tendency of getting swept aside by the urgency of current food insecurity. Crisis-management policies took precedence over food sector planning.

4.2 National famine prevention measures

Amidst the food crisis of 1974–75, the MDB proposed a programme which entailed the storage of 100 000 tons of grain independent of NMC commercial stocks but under NMC supervisory control for use in times of severe food shortfalls. The assumption was that Tanzania would become broadly self-sufficient in maize and paddy over the following years and stocks would be replenished by local surpluses. But the actual implementation of the project in 1978 was based on pledges of food aid, and reliance on food aid continued. The lack of storage facilities separate from the NMC commercial stocks, and Tanzania's failure to secure surplus stocks of the preferred cereals meant that the strategic grain reserve existed in name rather than fact.[52]

The Early Warning and Crop Monitoring Programme (EWCMP), a small unit of FAO-funded experts attached to the Ministry of Agriculture instituted in 1978, was more successful. It developed a reporting system for rainfall and crop growth based on weekly and monthly reports from regional agricultural officers and meteorological department personnel. Its ability to forecast food-deficit districts facilitated the timely delivery of government famine relief. It advised the NMC on the anticipated size of crop harvests and the need for food imports.

4.3 Food imports

Relatively large net imports of grain prevailed in every year except 1973 and 1979 (see Table 3.1). The average annual net import was roughly 2 million quintals, half of which consisted of maize with wheat and rice each accounting for a quarter. This contrasts with the period between 1950 and 1973 when imports were mainly wheat. Per capita import reached historically unprecedented levels in 1975 of almost 30 kg per person (see Figure 5.1).

The priority accorded food security by the government was most poignantly expressed by Nyerere, when he declared that he was willing to import South African maize if necessary, despite Tanzania's militant opposition to apartheid.[53] The costs of food import during the 1974–75 crisis weighed very heavy on the economy. World market prices for grain were high and shipping costs were escalating. Tanzania, hitherto recepient to only small amounts of international food aid, succeeded in getting some assistance, but at that time most

TABLE 16.2 *Food aid 1974/75–1983/84 (metric tons 000s)*

	Food aid					
Year	*Maize*	*Rice*	*Wheat*	*Total*	*Commercial and food aid imports*	*Aid as % of total Imports*
1974/75	1.0		46.5	47.5		
1975/76	27.0		45.7	72.7	187.5	38.8
1976/77	7.0		33.6	40.6	80.5	50.4
1977/78	34.3	21.6	40.5	96.4	122.9	78.4
1978/79		20.2	45.5	65.7	102.5	64.1
1979/80		50.1	32.5	82.6	119.7	69.0
1980/81	86.5	51.0	48.7	186.2	388.5	47.9
1981/82	217.1	66.5	70.9	354.5	369.0	96.1
1982/83	106.4	29.4	2.0	137.8	164.2	83.9
1983/84	69.2	26.7	46.3	142.2	297.7	47.8

SOURCES
1974/75 NMC figures quoted in Tanzania Food and Nutrition Centre, 'Data Report on the Food and Nutrition Situation in Tanzania 1972/73–1976/77', DSM (1978) Table 21.21.
1975/76–1983/84 Tanzania, MDB, 'Price Policy Recommendations for the 1984 Agricultural Price Review', vol. I (1984) pp. 22–3.

food aid was being channeled to the Sahel. The NMC incurred a TShs. 500 million loss on importing grain at world market prices and selling it at low controlled consumer prices.[54] During the 1980s, the costs of food importation were prohibitive. The volume of food aid increased and in the process food aid dependence became a structural feature of the economy (see Table 16.2). The MDB explained the phenomenon thus: 'Tanzania's need for imports is influenced more by the balance of NMC purchases and historical sales levels to NMC's usual customers than by the overall food situation in the country.'[55] In other words, with subsidised consumer prices, effective demand for NMC's products remained high, whereas the operation of the parallel grain market was deflecting local supplies from the NMC.

A food aid scandal in 1981 indicated that clientage practices were pursued not only in very high echelons of the state but also in the extremely sensitive realm of national food security.[56] Rainfall that year was below-normal (see Table 3.2). The expatriate-staffed EWCMP started predicting a bad harvest in its regular reporting to the Minister and Principal Secretary of the Ministry of Agriculture and estimated a minimum food import requirement of 170 000 tons. This information was not communicated to the channels which would have started the machinery in motion for timely requests of food aid from donors. The expatriate in charge of the EWCMP revealed the urgency of the situation to a foreign journalist.[57] The State House and the President were informed through the journalist's enquiries. An emergency cabinet meeting was called in which the Ministry of Agriculture was ordered to solicit food aid. Donors responded with alacrity, thereby averting famine. A series of charges and counter-charges ensued. The Ministry of Agriculture dismissed the EWCMP expert from his job for conveying confidential information to an outside party. Soon afterwards, the Minister of Agriculture was removed in a cabinet reshuffle and some months later the Principal Secretary was replaced.[58]

It is unclear what the motive was for withholding information on the critical state of national supplies. The Principal Secretary had told the journalist in October that they anticipated stocks would run out in December–January and were looking into the possibility of purchasing food on the open market, an odd reply in view of Tanzania's desperate shortage of foreign exchange. Newspaper articles speculated that the Principal Secretary or the Minister or both wanted to negotiate a food aid deal from which they would profit; others believed that the aim was to discredit the government politically.[59]

4.4 Policies to ensure household food security

At least 80 per cent of NMC sales took place in urban areas and the *sembe* consumer subsidy was targeted at urban minimum wage earners. The government-controlled staple food market was the largest and most expensive urban food security measure but it did not exhaust state efforts. During the 1974–75 food crisis, the party launched the *Kilimo cha Kufa na Kupona*[60] campaign to get urban dwellers directly involved in cultivation. Government offices, factories and other places of work in Dar es Salaam were issued with land outside the city for cultivation by their employees. Problems of transport, time taken from normal working hours for cultivation and the inexperience and lack of coordination evidenced in the production effort limited the campaign's usefulness.[61] The campaign was not reinvoked during the 1980 food crisis, but the Prime Minister called on urban councils to allocate farming areas to town dwellers.[62] In 1985, the government announced that all DSM's unplanted valley areas would be taken over by the City Council and allocated to the unemployed for cultivation.[63] These were ad hoc measures, undoubtedly open to malpractice since land in and around Dar es Salaam was being cultivated on all sorts of individual and village usufruct terms as well as being subject to illegal and legal purchase agreements.

The government's attempts at containing urban growth were *en passant* directed at depressing urban food demand. The general policy was that urban residence should be restricted to waged workers and their families in line with the anti-vagrancy laws of colonial days. There was a strong current of thinking that anyone without a formal job was a parasite, unjustifiably using the city's amenities and consuming its food supply. From time to time in the 1970s adult urban residents were required to carry identity cards from their places of work and were subjected to house checks by militia. In 1983 this policy was more systematised with the passage of the Human Resources Deployment Act and the launching of the *nguvu kazi* campaign, which involved the militia in the stop and search of all males suspected of not having legitimate employment. If the man being questioned could not produce a valid identification card and proof of employment, he was to be sent to a rural area or one of the northern sisal plantations experiencing a shortage of labour. It was widely believed that many, if not most, of the rusticated people quickly made their way back to the city. More successful were the attempts to get the unemployed and unlicensed hawkers to settle and farm in the outlying areas of the town.[64]

17 Clientage and Crisis, 1979–85

Throughout the period under review, state and market activities, defined in a strict sense (Chapter 6), were disintegrating. Parastatal and government agents were increasingly involved in clientage practices. The state controlled market was progressively less able to service the population's basic needs. As indices of real wages (see Table 12.3), real producer prices, and food and non-food costs of living (see Table 14.1) show, by the late 1970s the standard of living affordable through official labour and commodity markets had deteriorated drastically. The real minimum wage in 1983 was at the same level as 1939, but now it was supposed to cover the needs of an urban nuclear family in contrast to the bachelor wages of pre-World War II (see Table 12.3). Urban residents and peasants lacked purchasing power and availability of essential goods – food being the most essential. Food insecurity was acute and, most significantly, experienced by virtually all sections of the population. Urban residents as well as rural dwellers faced uncertainty of supply and found a major portion of their income and working time devoted to food procurement. Findings of a 1980 Dar es Salaam household budget survey revealed that 85 per cent of expenditure in low income households was for food.[1]

The overall situation was instigated by international factors, notably skyrocketing oil prices and Tanzania's declining terms of trade, and exacerbated by domestic policies. The disruptions caused by villagisation, a premature and rapid industrialisation strategy, the disorganisation of the state marketing system as well as government efforts to eliminate private retail trading were all exacerbating factors. Operation Maduka, the national campaign to encourage villages to run cooperative shops in place of private *dukas*, began in 1976. Despite consumer complaints of inexperienced management and clientage practices, government-fostered cooperative shops continued to be formed in the following years, adding to the deteriorating supply of consumer goods.[2] As the availability of goods and services provisioned through the state and the state-controlled market declined, people had to devise ways and means outside of formal channels to procure their essential consumer requirements.

1 RURAL HOUSEHOLDS' SURVIVAL STRATEGIES

Peasants had to confront three main problems: first, what goods were essential and could not be foregone; second, how could the essential goods be obtained? Could they be produced directly or did they have to be bartered for or purchased? Third, how could one's cash income be raised for the purchase of such goods?

Two main responses developed in the rural areas, namely, a household-based strategy which involved autarkic production, food self-sufficiency and exchange of goods and services between rural and urban segments of extended households and second, an extra-household, clientage-based strategy of parallel marketing.

Autarky entailed a diminution in peasants' definitions of basic needs as well as a proliferation of their productive activities. NMC supplies to the rural areas, never plentiful, dwindled to virtually nothing by the early 1980s.[3] This reinforced the household's 'food-first' strategy. The 1976 Household Budget Survey reveals that 87 per cent of cereal consumption was of subsistence origin.[4] Some large consumer durables like radios, bicycles and spare parts for machinery and vehicles were not obtainable by any means. Peasants had to try to devise substitutes for soap and cooking oil, pressing their own oil seeds, or alternatively worked out informal networks of supply through urban-based members of the extended household. Certain items such as batteries or prescribed medicines could not be directly produced by the peasant and so requests were lodged with family relations or close friends who might have more ready access to obtain them. Such favours were repaid in kind more often than cash and payment tended to be deferred. There is no way to estimate the volume of intra-household exchange of essential goods, but casual observation would suggest that it was considerable and filled some very vital gaps in household consumer supply.

Increasingly, peasants' trading activities circumvented the official market.[5] Peasants exchanged grain and other agricultural produce for consumer goods by barter or cash sales. Barter offered the immediate receipt of desired scarce commodities. There is no way of measuring its extent. The incidence of parallel marketing was the subject of several speculative estimates based on fragmentary price data and interviews with peasant farmers in a few areas. In 1984, the Marketing Development Bureau's guesstimates of the proportions of marketed production going through parallel markets was 75 per cent of maize, 80 per cent of rice and 25 per cent of wheat.[6] In Kigoma, Loft and Oldevelt estimate that 80 per cent of farmers' marketed crops were sold in the parallel market, but only 13 per cent was marketed. Thus 10 per cent of total production made its way to the parallel market.[7] In Iringa (1983), Rasmussen estimates that 40 per cent of the maize was sold, almost all of it to private traders.[8]

There is virtually no documentation of how parallel marketing was carried out, but it is possible to piece together a plausible picture. Inter-regional parallel marketing of a substantial volume of grain required fixed capital for purchasing, transporting and milling as well as good relations with regional government officials. Road blocks to prevent the movement of parallel market goods were strategically placed throughout the country. There was variation in policy from region to region on what constituted illegal goods, but the specification for grain was usually a load greater than five bags.[9] It would have been expensive and hazardous to attempt bribery at each road block. Personal contact with district and regional government officials with their go-ahead for the free movement of grain would have greatly facilitated the trade. Urban-based Asian merchants who could offer large material incentives or the few African businessmen or more numerous African government/parastatal personnel who established friendships of mutual benefit with regional officialdom would have been well-placed to arrange to circumvent the roadblocks. Without the intercession of more powerful urban-based state officials or private individuals, local transporters/millers had to strike up understandings with regional, district and village officials. With the launching of the Anti-Economic Sabotage campaign in 1983, their risks increased.

The parallel market did not represent a 'market' in the classical sense of the term. The numerous inter-personal relations that encrusted the parallel market negated the operation of impersonal forces of demand and supply. The irregularity of the market's operation in time and space made it virtually impossible for peasant produce sellers or urban consumers to rely on it fully for their livelihood.

2 URBAN HOUSEHOLDS' SURVIVAL STRATEGIES

Residents of urban areas, like their rural relations, had to devise strategies to lessen the adverse effects of the lack of essential consumer goods and services distributed through state marketing channels. The peasant option of adopting a household autarky strategy was far less feasible. Increasing one's cash income to afford the purchase of price-inflated essential goods was of paramount importance. There was a rapid increase in the incidence of clientage practices in salaried employment, frequently involving the siphoning of money and commodities, during this period. There were gradations of involvement from large-scale fraud down to the pervasive non-performance of one's allocated work tasks, a habit that increased as people became involved in '*miradi*'[10] and devoted less and less time and energy to their official paid employment.

Almost all urban consumers preferred NMC because it was the cheapest source of supply, particularly for *sembe*. The 1976/77 Household Budget Survey reveals that in the poorest households *sembe* accounted for 17.2 per cent of the total value of their consumption declining in the successively higher income groups until it amounted to only 0.8 per cent in the highest income group. The mean was 5.2 per cent. Even after the subsidy was removed NMC *sembe* sales did not drop. Demand continued to exceed supply. Supplies of *sembe* as well as rice and wheat dwindled. No amount of patient queuing could bring about quantities sufficient for most households' requirements particularly in up-country towns.

People tried to gain privileged access to the limited NMC supply. The NMC at Dar es Salaam headquarters and most up-country go-downs were willing to supply in bulk to government/parastatal agencies or private individuals with a *kibali*[11] authorised by regional government officials and parastatal managers.[12] These customers avoided wholesale and retail marketing and transport costs. The growing complaint was that they were the higher-incomed with influential contacts and motor transport. Low-income consumers could only try to chat up the retailer to gain an advantage in the distribution.

The 1976/77 Household Budget Survey records that 49 per cent of household food consumption was direct farm supply unmediated by market exchange. The lowest income groups derived the greatest proportion of their total food consumption this way. The share decreases with successive income levels but a slight upturn is recorded with the top two income groups. As NMC shortages got worse, the proportion of non-market household supply of food increased, with possible differences in the rate of increase by income group according to access to transport, land and agricultural inputs.

In urban cultivation, land rather than labour was the scarce factor of production. Women's relative absence from the formal urban labour force made them a ready source of labour. Wives often farmed the household plot. Alternatively other family relations or hired labour were employed. Land proximate to one's residence was not usually readily at hand in Dar es Salaam and the larger secondary towns. Municipal authorities made some land available for plot allocation or lease sale, otherwise people resorted to more informal arrangements which included squatting on land or buying land illegally from individuals who claimed rights to it. Alternatively, in villages on the perimeter of the city urban residents sometimes used party or government contacts to gain access or even quasi-legal rights to the land, even though they lived outside the village boundaries.[13] As the town's agricultural frontiers were pushed further away from the city centre, transport became critical to whether or not a household could manage an 'urban' farm.[14] In Dar es Salaam, some government officials went as far as Bagamoyo district villages to get plots, sometimes hiring labour or working out a sharecropping arrangements with villagers who were provided with inputs in return for some of their output.[15] Frequently, government rather than private transport was used by the 'urban absentee farmer'. For those with extremely limited acreage, cassava was the favoured crop because of its high yield.

Urban households also sent family members to the household's rural home area for the periods of planting, cultivating and harvesting. Usually the family member would be a woman, that is, the wife or other unemployed women in the household. In a 1980 Dar es Salaam nutrition survey, 33 per cent of the high income earners and 44 per cent of those with low incomes had a farm either somewhere around Dar es Salaam or in their home areas.[16] Finally, a whole range of exchange relationships between rural and urban kin took place. Rural-based kin were often willing to supply a substantial portion of the grain requirements of the urban family in exchange for cash, goods or services.[17] Frequently, the grain was transported by members of the family travelling between the up-country home and Dar es Salaam for business or social reasons. During the food shortages of the 1980s, although road block checks were numerous, the government remained tolerant of the transport of one to five bags of food.

The parallel market was most people's last resort because of its higher prices. For many consumers, it was the only market option. Except for Dar es Salaam, parallel-marketed maize was available year-round in most towns, but the supply of rice was more erratic. Northern towns, particularly around Lake Victoria, paid two to three times the price for maize than southern towns.

In some cases, parallel market sales took place in the shops of licensed merchants who were either to get a higher margin or to compensate for higher prices they had had to pay to corrupt state wholesale agents.[18] Parallel marketed supplies were often available in central town markets. The higher prices were an open secret or tacitly condoned by officials whose first concern was to keep the town supplied.[19] Some towns, Dar es Salaam in particular, tried to enforce rigid bans on sale of uncontrolled grain. Some traders, licensed or unlicensed, managed to circumvent the ban by selling in markets in the town perimeters.[20] They were subject to periodic official swoops. The Prime Minister, Sokoine, took a strong anti-trader stance maintaining that traders' profiteering went unchecked because too many people without proper retail premises had been given trading licenses.[21]

The importance of household and clientage-based sources of staple foodstuffs explains why the removal of the *sembe* subsidy in 1984 and the consequent 320 per cent rise in the official price was not followed by food riots or any other visible form of political protest. People complained, but the majority of urban consumers no longer solely depended on NMC supplies and the new official price was still 40 per cent below the mean annual price for parallel marketed maize grain.

The urban households' food self-sufficiency strategy probably contributed to Tanzania's continuing political security but there were costs. Labour specialisation was sacrificed both in terms of the attention and actual time that it took away from one's paid employment.[22] Furthermore, urban dwellers were usually very amateur farmers: '[Nyerere] said he was impressed that many people in DSM, including intellectuals, had taken to agriculture but expressed concern over lack of farming expertise evident in almost all the farms he visited. "There is no expertise at all. They (farmers) plant crops anyhow."'[23]

3 THE STATE'S RESPONSE TO THE CRISIS

3.1 The economic situation

There were three dimensions to Tanzania's economic crisis: first, the marked deterioration of the balance of payments resulting in an acute shortage of foreign exchange; second, the decline of economic sectoral performance, notably that of agriculture and industry; and third, the near collapse of public finance.

The serious deterioration in the trade balance that began in 1979 sprang from the worsening of Tanzania's international terms of trade and declining export volumes. The value and volume of imports, on the other hand, increased as a result of import requirements for the Ugandan war, the second oil price shock and the government's liberalisation of import controls in 1977–78 upon the advice of the International Monetary Fund (IMF). The trade deficit widened to an unprecedented level, despite attempts to cut imports to the barest minimum (see Table 14.3). As the crisis deepened, Tanzania had to increasingly resort to short-term loans and suppliers' credit.

The volume of fuel imported declined to crippling proportions, while road, rail and vehicle maintenance deteriorated. By 1981 only 9 per cent of foreign exchange requests for the transport sector was being granted.[24] Industry was recepient to 27 per cent of investment during the Third Five Year Plan.[25] The Basic Industries Strategy required large imports of intermediate and capital goods. However, industry's foreign exchange allocations were slashed by more than half between 1977 and 1981. Capacity utilisation in some factories was as low as 20 per cent by 1980.[26]

Poor sectoral performance took a heavy toll on public finance. In 1978/79, the government's budget slid into a deep deficit over two times greater than that of the previous year.[27] Expenditure on defence rose astronomically as a result of the Ugandan war. Although defence spending shrunk the following year, the effects of the oil crisis, Tanzania's heavy commitments to government development programmes, the financing of flagging parastatals and the provision of producer and consumer subsidies kept government expenditure high.

Government revenues meanwhile stagnated. Tanzania had been heavily dependent on export taxes and as agricultural exports declined, alternative sources of revenue were not forthcoming. Excise taxes fell in step with the decline of industrial output. The tendency for farmers to increase their subsistence output and production for untaxable parallel markets caused the state's tax base to shrink. Sales taxes, particularly on luxury items like cigarettes and beer, were raised to very high levels. Most significantly, beginning with the Ugandan war and continuing over time, the government had to rely on bank overdraft facilities. Consequently, the money supply expanded on average by 26 per cent between 1978 and 1983, followed by an even higher rate of inflation in the economy.[28] At current prices gross foreign aid disbursements increased from $362 million to $696 million between 1978 and 1982, but most of this was project aid that Tanzania could not use for balance of payments support.

In 1979, the Tanzanian government was forced to seek IMF assistance. In July 1980 a major programme was negotiated for a three-year stand-by facility, but this agreement collapsed in November of the same year because Tanzania exceeded the domestic budgetary ceiling imposed by the IMF. For the next five years there was a continuous deadlock between the IMF and Tanzania regarding IMF conditionality. Throughout this period the IMF withheld financial assistance.

3.2 The undermining of state agents' occupational accountability and the national ideology impasse

As the economic crisis deepened, government and parastatal personnel experienced the perpetual decline of the purchasing power of their salaries. This had a detrimental impact on their work performance. The spread of clientage practices undermined occupational accountability and bureaucratic professionalism.

During this period, Nyerere and the CCM party continued to exhort the socialist path. In 1981, the party issued guidelines aimed at instilling moral fibre in staff performance and generally reasserting socialist public accountability. The socialist ideology, as it had been defined by Nyerere, rested on the tenets of cooperation and brotherhood, not unlike the unsanctioned but all-pervasive ideology of clientage. However, Nyerere's socialism was first and foremost a nationalist ideology, in which the notions of cooperation were to extend beyond face-to-face encounters to the entire citizenry. Clientage, therefore, was an opposing outlook and social force, which the advocates of a socialist public morality simply condemned as corrupt. Clientage practitioners were labelled wrongdoers that had to be apprehended and punished. It is not surprising that this period witnessed public campaigns against clientage.

But while party stalwarts pursued their struggle for socialist purity, clientage practices became all the more apparent in every avenue of state and market activity and all the more demoralising for those removed from any influence over the channelling of goods and services.

Nyerere raised the theme of socialist morality to the level of international debate when he attacked the IMF's antagonism to

Tanzania's socialist development strategy.[31] Just as state 'service' was contrasted with market 'greed' at the domestic level, 'socialist' Tanzania was contrasted with the 'capitalist' IMF at the international level. This depiction had the unintended effect of winning some Tanzanians, particularly frustrated management-oriented professionals or aspirant merchants, to the side of 'capitalism'.[32]

Clearly, the debate had been reduced to an over-simplistic dichotomy between the state and market, with the loaded terms 'socialism' and 'capitalism' volleyed back and forth. Ironically, during this period, the operational content of both the state and market in Tanzania were straying so far from the classical definitions of these two institutions (see Chapter 6) that it was analytically difficult to identify either of them anymore. The debate was extremely myopic. The economic crisis had reduced the vast majority of the population whatever their occupational role in the society to giving priority to the basic needs of the household, notably food. Clientage networks incorporated elements of state and market operations but were primarily informed by the logic of basic need fulfillment, rather than capitalist profit or socialist cooperation. Nonetheless, the vociferous opponents in the state/market debate continued to thrash out the usual arguments for or against the state. Clientage was not being analysed nor realistically addressed through policies. Campaigns to root out clientage practices were futile because the practices were not restricted to isolated individuals; they had become the *modus operandi* of the economy in which everyone participated in different capacities to a greater or lesser extent.

3.3 State policy retreat

The Ugandan war had lasted only seven months and had been won with a fairly minimal loss of life, but its financial cost to Tanzania was estimated at between TSh 3.6 and 4.0 billion.[33] In addition there were various destabilising after-effects: the agricultural marketing situation was no longer being effectively managed within the confines of parastatal marketing arrangements owing in part to the disruption in crop transport that had taken place during the war; more than ten thousand soldiers had been promised jobs by the state as a reward for their military services;[34] troop disarmament was not thorough and guns and ammunition in the hands of ex-soldiers and other civilians caused the incidence of robbery and lawlessness to rise very markedly.

Government policies were increasingly couched in terms of tactical and emergency measures to free a besieged economy. The patriotic rallying slogans of the Ugandan war were transferred to the economic front. In 1981, the state initiated the National Economic Survival Programme (NESP),[35] which involved a TSh. 6 billion export target that all government and parastatal institutions were expected, but failed, to implement. In 1982 the emphasis switched to cutbacks and prioritising expenditure to optimise output with the launching of the three-year Structural Adjustment Programme (SAP).[36] The SAP demarcated the areas of the economy that had first claims on scarce foreign exchange. One of the main aims of the programme was to provide agricultural inputs and incentive goods to farmers. In industry, priority was to be given to those industries supplying basic amenity and incentive goods. Over 200 development projects were suspended for lack of funds and non-economic industries were slated to be closed down.[37]

While the economic planners tried to optimise the utilisation of the country's extremely meagre capital resources, the party campaigned against individuals who were thought to be undermining Tanzania's economy. They targeted first the 'economic saboteurs', those who were dealing in illegal marketing and corrupt practices; and second, the urban unemployed and under-employed defined as all those who did not have a formal job or were engaged in unlicensed market activity. In 1983, under the Economic Sabotage Act, a 12-member tribunal for the hearing and conviction of 'economic crimes' was set up. By the end of 1983, 1745 cases had been filed before the National Anti-Economic Sabotage Tribunal.[38] In 1984, the Human Resources Deployment Act was passed in conjunction with the *nguvu kazi* campaign that involved the rounding up of all noticeably unemployed in the towns and small unlicensed market vendors, who were then sent to the rural areas for resettlement. Thousands were arrested.[39]

As these measures to halt economic decline proceeded, the government was also engaged in reversing a number of policies that had hitherto been considered landmarks of Tanzania's development strategy. Thus in 1982, marketing cooperatives were reinstated and the 1971 Decentralisation policy and the 1975 Village Act were superceded by the Local Government Act which reinstituted local councils. New national and party constitutions were promulgated which reduced the President's leverage, giving the elected Parliament more power. Meanwhile, steps were being taken to accord more recognition of private property and the private sector. The 1982

Agricultural policy specified that villagers should be given 33-year leases to their land. In 1981, the Minister of Agriculture had stated that large-scale private farming was welcomed by the government. By the mid-1980s private investments in farming were being actively encouraged and positively reported by the press and the ban on rented private property was lifted.[40] Furthermore, the government liberalised external trade, allowing Tanzanians to import goods without having to state how they obtained the foreign exchange.

In his 1981 New Year address Nyerere had blasted the IMF demands as an affront to national sovereignity, but increasingly, over time, government policy was incorporating measures recommended by the IMF.[41] Nyerere's position was not a complete rejection of IMF policies, but rather an insistence on deciding their intensity and timing. In Nyerere's words: 'I cannot sign [an agreement with the IMF] and then have riots on the streets. . . . You [the IMF] may be the economic experts but I am the political expert – allow me at least to say how much the people can take'.[42]

Tanzania did have small devaluations four times between 1981 and 1985.[43] Social services were cut back drastically, partly out of default and partly out of conscious policy. Subsidies on *sembe* and fertiliser were removed in 1984. Parastatal budgets were severely limited. Despite all these measures, which were precisely what the IMF wanted, Tanzania and the IMF remained at loggerheads throughout Nyerere's presidency because the IMF maintained that these measures and currency devaluation had to be more drastic. Thus Tanzania continued to be denied the IMF special drawing rights that were so desparately needed to bridge the balance of payments problem.[44]

Summary of Part VI

In 1973, the urban population constituted roughly 7 per cent of the national total, a percentage which was to double over the next eleven years. It was in this context that the state embarked on its ambitious industrialisation and agricultural transformation programme, bearing strong resemblance to measures advocated by Preobrazhensky. Villagisation, single-channel state marketing and the Basic Industries Strategy were implemented by the government's growing ranks of civil servants and parastatal employees. Despite the high profile given to peasant agricultural development in Tanzania's official policy declarations, industrial investment superceded agricultural investment and state farm initiatives gained importance in Tanzania's agricultural strategy.

Some, notably the IMF, when offering explanations for Tanzania's economic crisis would cite the state's dominance over the market as the most deleterious factor. Many Tanzanian critics, including the government itself on occasion, blamed inefficient or corrupt state agents. No matter how much weighting is placed on domestic policies and their implementation, they cannot be divorced from exogenous factors, namely the 1973/74 and 1979 oil booms, the droughts of 1973–75 and 1979/80, and the Ugandan war. The fact that Tanzania's import/export balance plunged so radically following each oil crisis strongly suggests that the instigating forces in Tanzanian economic decline were of an external nature, while domestic factors tended to reinforce the downward slide.

The 1973–75 drought was met with successful state measures to guarantee food security in rural and urban areas. Heavy food importation made up for the deficit in domestic production and large wage and salary increases adequately covered increased food costs for urban dwellers. From 1979 onwards the situation was different. Tanzania had to become increasingly reliant on food aid because of its severe shortage of foreign exchange. Although the *sembe* subsidy was an attempt to guarantee urban residents' food security, it failed in one important respect: the NMC could not meet urban demand and several towns were simply not supplied with anywhere near per capita requirements. Even in Dar es Salaam, which had supply priority, severe shortages were frequent. Salaried and waged workers were adversely affected by the lack of purchasable basic staple foods and the inflationary prices of the parallel food market.

It is not difficult to argue that food insecurity, the most basic uncertainty that the population faced during this period, had a profound effect on the social division of labour. The division of labour was contracting in a number of respects. The occupational accountability associated with professionalism and the complex division of labour of the urban society, quickly eroded under material stress. The lack of bureaucratic accountability on the part of government and parastatal agents was particularly apparent. Parastatal clientage came to the fore. In comparison with the other variants of clientage described in preceding chapters, parastatal clientage's networks and face-to-face accountability did not extend as effectively down to peasants in the rural areas. Even within the parastatals, face-to-face accountability was based more on fear than mutual reciprocity and the exchange of prestige and security between patron and client. Parastatal clientage was far more fragile as a network and far less effective as a distributive channel for productive goods and services than cooperative clientage. Unwittingly, the government's call for adherence to a socialist morality merely served to call attention to the spread of clientage practices rather than putting a check on them.

Parastatals were not succeeding either as public service agencies nor profitable concerns. In addition, they were increasingly unable to provide their employees with salaries that covered their basic consumer needs. The large deficits that the parastatals were incurring jeopardised the national economy. The performance of civil servants in government ministries was following a similar course. The fact that Tanzanian government policy had vested so much in state control of the economy at every level and every sector meant that poor performance of state agents had an all-pervasive effect. Industry and agricultural output slumped and the produce marketing network under parastatal control became more and more erratic.

As the state marketing infrastructure crumbled, everyone, peasants and urban dwellers alike, had to become increasingly reliant on localised household and clientage survival strategies. This had direct implications for the functional division of labour. Besides the formal employment lay-offs that started taking place in the early 1980s, informally the occupational division of labour was eroding as people took time off from their formal jobs to engage in non-sanctioned income earning activities and farming.

Thus this period in Tanzania's history witnessed a failure to launch industrialisation and a peasant agricultural transformation programme, as well as deterioration in the existing functional division of labour to such an extent that the occupational division of labour between rural and urban areas was undermined. The lack of sufficient agricultural surplus to feed Tanzania's existing urban settlements and an associated complex of occupational specialisation was never more apparent.

Part VII
Food Insecurity and the Social Division of Labour

18 Summary and Conclusions

Aspects and dimensions of food insecurity in Tanzania during the British colonial and post-colonial period under Nyerere's leadership have been explored in the preceding chapters. In Part II, the physical causes of food insecurity were outlined. Tanzanian peasant producers have faced a highly vagarious physical environment and their household pattern of production has necessarily given primacy to food self-sufficiency. High fertility rates have led to rapid population growth. There is evidence that, in a Boserupian fashion, the peasant household has responded to increasing rural population density with changes in agricultural technology and the intensification of the working day, the latter it appears has been especially borne by women. Food production capability has gradually risen roughly in correspondence with the increase in the rural population, contrary to Malthusian thought. But agricultural adaptations have not succeeded in eliminating the fluctuation of supply due to weather variability, as indicated by the wide spatial and temporal incidence of food inadequacy in peasant households over the past 66 years. It is evident from this that although the level of food production capability in Tanzanian peasant production has supported rapid growth of the rural population it provides an extremely tenuous basis for the territorial supply of food to the non-peasant population.

Part III juxtaposed Tanzania's three main extra-household social institutions: the state, the market and clientage networks. Between 1919 and 1950, the state was dominated by Europeans, the market by Asians and clientage networks by African rural dwellers. The incidence of food stress was restricted primarily to Africans. Europeans and Asians rarely were directly exposed to food insecurity. African household food insecurity was mediated by Native Authority clientage networks that operated on the basis of the moral obligations of highly localised societies, involving continuous face-to-face encounters between patrons and clients.

Part IV reviewed the food supply arrangements for the expanding African wage labour force between 1919 and 1950. A combination of ad hoc state measures, market activity and a not inconsiderable amount of self-provisioning by the labourer himself under the *kipande* system took place during the interwar period. During the 1940s, African marketed food demand rose sharply as the wage labour force grew and urbanisation accelerated. Domestic food supply fell far short of demand. Food importation increased. The state imposed controls on food marketing, offered cost of living allowances to ensure African state employees' basic nutritional needs and tried to spur increased domestic supply by supporting European capitalised food production at the expense of peasant producers. In this way, food insecurity was minimised in the urban areas, whereas African agriculture stagnated.

Part V traced the elimination of the racial division of labour and the dismantling of the European state and the Asian market under relatively good weather conditions and favourable international terms of trade between 1950 and 1973. The performance and accountability of the newly-installed, urban-based African state bureaucracy was supported by relatively high incomes in comparison with the rest of the African population, a strong national identity and the ethos of African socialism. The market, on the other hand, started to disintegrate during this period. Asian traders were edged out and replaced by the cooperatives and state trading corporations. The cooperatives operated on the basis of clientage networks extending from regional towns downwards to village level. A 'neighbourhood' sense of identity replaced tribal identity. The network was conducted on the basis of face-to-face accountability. Patrons were no longer vested with magico-religious powers, but the new goods and services they offered peasant producers gave them a magnetic attraction. The modernising state was impatient with both the inefficient ways that cooperatives operated as well as the way agricultural surpluses were eluding state control.

Part VI, covering the period between 1973 and 1985, described the state's abolition of the cooperatives and the parastatalisation of the economy. The government's ambitious plans at the outset were set at no less than peasant agricultural transformation and industrialisation. But the intervention of drastically declining international terms of trade, the Ugandan war and adverse weather undermined the state's development programme as well as the state marketing and productive and social service delivery systems. State and parastatal agents, who had been charged with executing the programme, became increasingly demotivated as the purchasing power of their salaries declined to a point at which basic requirements like food were threatened. Clientage practices on the part of state and parastatal agents proliferated as food insecurity mounted. Parastatal clientage lacked effective conduits down to the peasants. Peasants were increasingly marginalised from the goods and services that the parastatals distributed officially or unofficially. A growing proportion of the exchange that took place between urban and rural areas was channelled through extended households. As the supply of state-provisioned goods and services dwindled, both rural peasants and urban dwellers had to resort to survival strategies characterised by increasing household self-sufficiency in food production. Households and clientage networks encroached more and more on the terrain of the state and market.

Having summarised each Part, it remains to tease out the theoretical implications of the Tanzanian case in relation to the general problem of increasing a nation-state's food supply at the turning point between agrarian and industrial social organisation. It has been argued that over the decades since 1919, Tanzania's development evidenced elements of the Ricardian and W.A. Lewis 'comparative advantage' approach, whereby reliance was placed on food importation and peasant export cashcropping. More latterly during the 1970s, the Preobrazhensky state marketing and state-led industrialisation strategy held sway. But during the 1980s, the positive results of these approaches were dimmed by the serious inadequacy of Tanzania's domestic food supply, giving credence to Malthusian gloom, at least in the short run. Had it not been for a large increase in per capita food imports, some parts of the population, notably those in urban areas would have experienced life-threatening shortages of food.

The inadequacy of domestic food supply resulted from rapid increases in demand arising from population growth, de-agrarianisation and the development of occupational specialisation and urbanisation on the one hand, and insufficient development of agricultural productivity on the other. Tanzania's declining terms of trade exacerbated the effect of these tendencies, as well as calling into question the viability of Tanzania's urban areas and the occupational specialisation that they represented.

The assumption made by Ricardo, Preobrazhensky, Lewis and most social scientists of the present day, namely that the operation of the state and the market determine national production and distribution, cannot be applied uncritically in the Tanzanian case, particularly under conditions of food stress. When household food insecurity is as rampant as it was in the 1980s and most importantly, when food insecurity pervades urban as well as rural households, state and market operations contract as clientage network practices become more prevalent.

It has been argued that the peasant household is Tanzania's basic unit of production and in the rural areas the division of labour has been premised on household and clientage social organisation. Under British colonial rule, a rigid racial division of labour was superimposed in conjunction with the entrenchment of a European-controlled state and an Asian-controlled market. The struggle for independence and post-colonial state policies represented a frontal attack on the colonially-constructed extra-household racial division of labour. The state and the market were Africanised. The state adopted a bureaucratic mode of operation similar to the one followed by the British, whereas the market deviated from the competitive, profit-maximising model set by the Asians and absorbed the aims of rural neighbourhood clientage networks. Meanwhile, little was being done to change the internal rural household division of labour based on sex and age. The state, adverse to localised clientage practices and keen on deepening nationalist consciousness, promoted a secular public morality in the form of 'African socialism'. Under Nyerere's leadership African socialism became an ethos equally meaningful to peasants and educated urban-dwelling civil servants. On the foundation of this configuration of social institutions and public accountability, the state embarked on agricultural transformation and industrialisation during the mid-1970s.

Food insecurity arising from adverse weather and the declining purchasing power of urban wages in the wake of Tanzania's drastic deterioration in international terms of trade put an end to the state's ambitious plans. Urban occupational accountability was undermined and neither of Durkheim's notions of 'organic solidarity' or of 'mechanical solidarity' was applicable. Durkheim had used the term 'organic solidarity' to denote the social interaction of people under the influence of market complementarity and a complex division of labour, whereas 'mechanical solidarity' had referred to a more simplified division of labour under the direction of a coercive state. In the Tanzanian case, once food insecurity became an all-pervasive feature of the economy, the impersonal state and the market ceased to dominate extra-household exchange.

Perhaps the term 'basic solidarity' is most appropriate to the situation that prevailed. The division of labour was eroding to its elemental basis that of age and sex in the household. Clientage networks were serving as the main distributive channels. Interpersonal association arising from one's immediate neighbourhood, place of work, place of birth or family ties functioned as the basis for ad hoc exchange and distribution, underpinned by face-to-face social accountability. Professional ethics declined as membership in an occupation-based moral community took second place to membership in the consumption-based social unit of the household. In addition to its role as a consumption unit, the urban household was increasingly taking on subsistence farming and other productive activities. Under these circumstances 'family morals' took precedence over professional job performance. As Durkheim so sagely observed, professional ethics are contingent on the stability of the professional social groups. When their material security is threatened they cease to be accountable and self-regulating.

The effective operation of the state and the market require a certain level of economic surplus capable of supporting occupational labour specialisation. In the absence of a sufficient surplus, 'basic solidarity' arises. The satisfaction of essential household need and inter-household prestige rather than carrying out the tasks of an impersonal state bureaucracy or market profit-maximisation become state and market agents' preoccupation. Thus, consistent with Durkheimian theory, food insecurity, as it has been experienced by the Tanzanian population particularly in the late 1970s and 1980s, has affected the social division of labour with respect to: one, the involution of occupational specialisation; two, the erosion of occupational accountability; and three, the realignment of the main social institutions, the state and the market, being increasingly undermined by the smaller scale inter-personal relations of the household and clientage networks.

The question remains how can Tanzania move from basic solidarity to what might best be termed 'balanced solidarity', i.e. a complex division of labour arising from a balanced, interactive state and market. The fundamental precondition for this to happen is more favourable international terms of trade, whereby Tanzania's exports become remunerative *vis-à-vis* essential imports, notably fuel. After this vital precondition is met, a resolution to the problem of balancing national food supply and demand as the proportion of the population engaged in agriculture shrinks must be sought in domestic policy. This will require the refinement of agricultural packages to localised climatic and soil conditions. It will require the provisioning of an efficient productive, transport, credit and social service infrastructure to the peasants by professionally-minded agents. On the demand side, it will require slowing down the population growth rate which *inter alia* entails an improvement in rural women's social and economic status. It will necessitate an urbanisation policy that keeps urban growth at a manageable rate. These requirements are easy to list, but exceedingly difficult to translate into measures that can be combined in a balanced fashion and realistically implemented with the resources and personnel on hand.

Ricardo, Lewis and Preobrazhensky never put time limits on how long the resolution of the problem of erratic and inadequate national food production takes in the transition from agrarian to industrial social organisation. It is clear that each society has not only its own speed but its own way of solving the problem. The Tanzanian case illustrates that there are serious obstacles to the goal's attainment. Positive change is most likely to arise out of policies that avoid dichotomising the role of the market and state and which do not ignore their functional interaction with household and clientage networks. The state and the market require stable institutional foundations through which the social division of labour can expand. State and market operations cannot be assumed, they must be created and solidified. In the meantime, the omnipresent logic and practices of clientage networks are inevitable and necessary for human survival.

Notes

1 The Population/Food Production Capability Balance at the Outset of Industrialisation

1. Malthus, T.R., *An Essay on the Principle of Population and Summary View of the Principle of Population* (Middlesex: Penguin, 1970 (1798 & 1830)).
2. Ricardo, D. (ed.) (intro. by J.H. Hollander and T.E. Gregory) *Notes on Malthus and Principles of Political Economy* (Baltimore: Johns Hopkins Press, 1928) p. xxxix.
3. Ricardo, D. (ed. J. Bonar) *Letters of David Ricardo to Thomas Robert Malthus, 1810–1823* (Oxford: Clarendon, 1887) p. 34.
4. Deane, P. and Cole, W.A., *British Economic Growth 1688–1959: Trends and Structure* (Cambridge: Cambridge University Press, 1962) pp. 7, 16.
5. Preobrazhensky, E. (trans. B. Pearse; intro. by A. Nove) *The New Economics* (Oxford: Clarendon, 1965).
6. Kerblay, B., 'Peasant Family Economy in the USSR Today', in E.J. Hobsbawm, W. Kula, A. Mitra, Raj, K.N. and Sachs I. (eds) *Peasants in History: Essays in Honour of Daniel Thorner* (Calcutta: Oxford University Press, 1980) p. 73.
7. Lewis, W.A. *Growth and Fluctuations 1870–1913* (London: Allen & Unwin, 1978).
8. Lewis, *Growth and Fluctuations*, p. 223; Lewis, W.A. (ed.) *Tropical Development 1880–1913* (London: Allen & Unwin, 1970); Lewis, W.A. *The Theory of Economic Growth* (London: Allen & Unwin, 1955).
9. 'Attempts at putting economic history into a set of dynamic equations are doomed to failure. . . . The world economy is a back drop against which the individual peripheral countries stage their very different performances. To make a model in which their rates of growth are determined primarily by events in the international economy – growth of world trade, international lending, migration, terms of trade – would be to omit the sociology of development' (Lewis, *Growth and Fluctuations*, pp. 167, 176).

2 The Relationship Between Population, the Social Division of Labors and Food Supply

1. Durkheim, E., *The Division of Labor in Society* (New York: The Free Press, 1964 (1933)).
2. Durkheim, *Division of Labor*, p. 262.
3. Durkheim, *Division of Labor*, p. 38.
4. Durkheim, *Division of Labor*, p. 227.
5. Durkheim, E., *Professional Ethics and Civic Morals* (London: Routledge & Kegan Paul, 1957).
6. Durkheim, *Professional Ethics*, p. 14.

7. Durkheim, *Professional Ethics*, p. 31.
8. Durkheim, *Professional Ethics*, pp. 8, 13.
9. Durkheim, *Division of Labor*, p. 271.
10. Boserup, E., *The Conditions of Agricultural Growth* (London: Allen & Unwin, 1965).
11. Sahlins, M. *Stone Age Economics* (London: Tavistock, 1974).
12. Boserup, E. *Women's Role in Economic Development* (New York: St Martin's, 1970).
13. Boserup, E. *Population and Technology* (Oxford: Basil Blackwell, 1981).
14. Boserup, *Population*, pp. 188–210.
15. Durkheim, *Division of Labor*, p. 271.

3 Physical Determinants of Food Insecurity and Settlement

1. The 1976/7 Household Budget Survey indicated that 81 per cent of a sample of rural households' food by weight is of subsistence origin (Tanzania, Central Statistical Bureau, '1976/77 Household Budget Survey' (HBS), Unpublished Computer Print-out Tables, 1983).
2. 39 per cent of total food consumption by value and 75 per cent by weight (1976/77 HBS, Tables 3A.1 and 10A.1).
3. Tanzania, 1976/77 HBS, Table 3A.1, unpublished results.
4. Masefield, G.B., *Famine: Its Prevention and Relief* (London: Oxford University Press, 1963) pp. 16–17; Iliffe, J., *A Modern History of Tanganyika* (Cambridge: Cambridge University Press, 1979) pp. 6–20 and Gillman, C., 'Population Problems of Tanganyika Territory', *EAAJ*, 11 (October 1945) p. 86.
5. Nieuwolt, S., 'Seasonal Droughts in East Africa', *EAAFJ* 43(3) (1978) pp. 208–22.
6. Mosha, A., 'Kuhifadhi na Kudunduliza Mazao Yaliyo Muhimu', *Tanzania Food and Nutrition Journal* 1 (1976) p. 8.
7. Golob, P. and Hodges, R., 'Study of an Outbreak of *Prostephanus truncatus* (Horn) in Tanzania', Tropical Products Institute, Overseas Development Administration (1982) pp. 1–23.
8. Walker, P.T., 'A Survey of the Use of Maize Stalk Borer Control Methods in East Africa', *EAAJ* 25 (January 1960) pp. 165–8.
9. Mgeni found a correlation between pesticide exposure levels and frequency of medical complaints (Mgeni, A.Y., *A Prospective Study of Pesticide Effects (Particularly Anticholinesterases) on Health of Exposed Workers in Tanzania*, University of Zagreb Masters Thesis, (1978)).
10. Keen, B., 'Presidential Address by Sir Bernard Keen, Director, E.A.A.F.R.O. at the Conference of the Medical, Agricultural and Veterinary Aspects of Food Production in East Africa,' *EAAJ* 20 (July 1954) p. 8.
11. e.g. Mufindi, Njombe, Loliondo, etc.
12. Allan, W., *The African Husbandman* (Edinburgh: Oliver & Boyd, 1965) pp. 162–206.
13. Anderson, D., 'Depression, Dust Bowl, Demography and Drought: The

Colonial State and Soil Conservation in East Africa during the 1930s', *African Affairs* (83)332 (July 1984) pp. 321–43.

14. Keen, 'Presidential Address', p. 7.
15. This low figure may reflect under-reporting or alternatively a tendency for peasant farmers to switch to pure stands, as they adopt improved seeds (Tanzania, *1971 Agricultural Census*, Table 5, pp. 161–85).
16. Tanzania, *1971 Agricultural Census*, Table 3, p. 49.
17. Kjaerby, F. 'The Development of Agro-Pastoralism among the Barbaig in Hanang District', *BRALUP* Research Paper No. 56, UDSM (1979) p. 64.
18. Schneider-Barthold, W. *et al.*, 'Farmers' Reaction to the Economic Situation in Tanzania with Respect to Production and Marketing: A Case Study of Five Villages in the Kilimanjaro Region's', German Development Institute mimeo, Berlin (1983) p. 66; Kajumulo-Tibaijuka, A., 'An Economic Analysis of Smallholder Banana-Coffee Farms in the Kagera Region, Tanzania', Report 240, University of Agricultural Sciences, Uppsala, Sweden (1984) p. 55; Iliffe, *Modern History*, p. 459.
19. Mascarenhas, O., 'Women's Control of Resources and Its Implications for the Food and Nutrition Status of their Family', Tanzania Food and Nutrition Centre/UNICEF Workshop on 'Hunger and Society', Soliwayo, Tanzania, p. 14; Community Development Trust Fund, 'Appropriate Technology for Grain Storage', DSM (1977) pp. 40–1; Kjaerby, 'Agro-Pastoralism', p. 123.
20. Gillman, 'A Population Map of Tanganyika', *Geographical Review*, XXVI(3) (1936) pp. 370–2.
21. Moore, J.E., 'Rural Population Carrying Capacities of the Districts of Tanzania', *BRALUP* Research Paper No. 18 (1971).
22. Boserup, E., *The Conditions of Agricultural Growth* (New York: Aldine, 1965).

4 Characteristics of the Peasant Household Farming Unit

1. Iliffe, *Modern History*, p. 283.
2. Tanzania, *Agricultural Census of Tanzania 1971/71*, vol. I, *Peasant Farming* (DSM, Bureau of Statistics, 1979) Table 15, p. 246.
3. Collier, P., Radwan, S., Wangwe, S. and Wagner, A., *Labour and Poverty in Rural Tanzania* (Oxford: Clarendon, 1986) pp. 41, 45.
4. Tanzania, *1978 Population Census*, vol. VIII (DSM, Bureau of Statistics, 1983) p. 476.
5. Boserup, E., *Women's Role in Economic Development* (New York: St. Martin's, 1970).
6. Kjaerby, F., *Problems and Contradictions in the Development of Ox-Cultivation in Tanzania*, Centre for Development Research, Copenhagen, No. 66 (1983) p. 63.
7. Tanzania, *1971 Agricultural Census*, Table 14.
8. Ruvuma: Lewin, R., 'Matetereka', *Mbioni* 5(3) (1969); Lushoto: Mbilinyi, M., 'The Changing Position of Women in Peasant Commodity Production: The Case of the Shambaa Kingdom', Symposium on

Women and Work in Africa, University of Illinois at Urbana-Champaign (1979); Mwanza: Ngalula, T.K.F., *Women as Productive Force in the Tanzanian Rural Society: A Case Study of Buhongwe Village in Mwanza District*, UDSM M.A. thesis, (1977); Oomen-Myin, M.A., *Involvement of Rural Women in Village Development in Tanzania: A Case Study in Morogoro District*, Department of Agricultural Extension, UDSM, Morogoro (1981); Bukoba: Storgaard, B., 'Women in Ujamaa Villages', *Rural Africana*, 29, (1976); Kilimanjaro and Bukoba: Swantz, M-L., 'Strain and Strength among Peasant Women in Tanzania, *BRALUP* Research Paper No. 49, UDSM (1977).

9. Rald, J. and Rald, K., *Rural Organization in Bukoba District, Tanzania* (Uppsala: Scandinavian Institute of African Studies, 1975) pp. 70–8.
10. Egero, B. and Henin, R.A., 'Fertility', *1967 Population Census*, vol. VI (1973) p. 192; Henin, R.A. and Egero, B., 'The 1967 Population Census of Tanzania: A Demographic Analysis', *BRALUP* Research Paper No. 19 (1972) p. 19; Tanzania, *1978 Population Census*, VI, pp. 318, 348–9. Note that the 1978 total fertility rate was regarded as possibly too low owing to an understatement of current births.
11. Kocher, J.E., 'Rural Development and Fertility Change in Tropical Africa: Evidence from Tanzania', *BRALUP* Research Paper No. 53 (1979) pp. 44–56.
12. Tanzania, *1978 Population Census*, vol. VI, pp. 291, 339.
13. The censuses before 1948 are suspected of being inaccurate.
14. Goldthorpe, J.E., 'The African Population of East Africa: A Summary of its Past and Present Trends', in *East Africa Royal Commission 1953–55 Report*, App. VII (London: HMSO, 1955).
15. Under the mandate of the League of Nations, the British colonial government was obligated to protect African rights to land, which constrained land alienation to European settlers.
16. James, R.W., *Land Tenure and Policy in Tanzania* (Nairobi: East African Literature Bureau, 1971) p. 22; Tanner, R.E.S., 'Land Tenure in Northern Sukumaland, Tanganyika: An Analysis of Present-day Trends in Two Parishes', *EAAJ* 21 (October 1955) p. 123; Iliffe, *Modern History*, p. 459.
17. Tanzania, Ministry of Agriculture, *The Agricultural Policy of Tanzania* (DSM: Government Printer, 1983) p. 110.
18. Tanzania, *1971 Agricultural Census*, Table 2.
19. Collier *et al.*, *Labour and Poverty*, p. 53. These figures would infer considerable under-reporting of land holdings in the 1971 Agricultural Census. Regional surveys differ widely on the size of average household land holdings, but in highland areas survey findings have been similar to those of the Agricultural Census, e.g. Bukoba, 1.0 ha. and Kilimanjaro, 1.2 (Kajumulo-Tibaijuka, 'Economic Analysis', p. 243, and Schneider-Barthold, 'Farmers' Reactions', p. 35).
20. Collier *et al.*, *Labour and Poverty*, p. 51.
21. Collier *et al.*, *Labour and Poverty*, p. 45.
22. Rudengren, J. and Swantz, M.-L., 'Village Skills Survey: Report of the Pre-Pilot and Pilot Surveys', *BRALUP* Research Paper No. 42 (1976) p. 29.

23. Bryceson, D.F. and Kirimbai, M., 'Subsistence or Beyond? Money-Earning Activities of Rural Women in Tanzania' *BRALUP/UWT* (1980) p. 156; McCall, M., 'Heavier Burdens and Lower Status: Some Implications of Villagisation for Women in Tanzania', Technische Hogeschool, Twente, The Netherlands, (1984) p. 14; Mascarenhas, 'Women's Control of Resources', p. 23.
24. Reining, P., 'Social Factors and Food Production in an East African Peasant Society: The Haya' in P. McLoughlin (ed.) *African Food Production Systems* (Baltimore: Johns Hopkins Press, 1970) pp. 78–83; Kajumulo-Tibaijuka, 'Economic Analysis', p. 77.
25. Havnevik, K.J., 'Economy and Organization in Rufiji District: The Case of Crafts and Extractive Activities', *DERAP* No. 112, Bergen, Norway (1980) p. 29.
26. Schneider-Barthold *et al.*, 'Farmers' Reactions', p. 65.

5 The Incidence of Household Food Inadequacy

1. Latham, M.C., 'A Clinical Nutrition Survey of Certain Areas of the Dodoma and Kondoa District', *East African Medical Journal* 41(2) (1964) p. 76; Latham, M.C., 'A Clinical Nutritional Survey of Certain Areas of the Rufiji District of Tanganyika', *East African Medical Journal* 40(3) (1963) p. 93.
2. Jerrard, R.C., *The Tribes in Tanganyika, Their Districts, Usual Dietary and Pursuits* (DSM, Government Printer, 1936); Culwick, A.T. and G.M., 'A Study of Factors governing the Food Supply in Ulanga, Tanganyika Territory', *East African Medical Journal* 16 (1939) pp. 43–61.
3. Mohamed, S.A. and McKeag, J., 'The History of Human Nutrition Activities in Tanzania', Human Nutrition Unit, Ministry of Health, DSM (1970).
4. In a 1956 study of Maposeni village in Songea, 76 per cent of the school boys had signs of protein deficiency (Robson, J.R.K., 'Malnutrition in Tanganyika', *TNR* 58/59 (1962) p. 263); Results from surveys in the 1960s showed the percentage of under-5s with protein calorie deficiency as: Kisarawe (1965), 31 per cent; Dodoma (1965), 22 per cent; Tabora (1967), 8 per cent; Bukoba (1967), 12 per cent; and Kilimanjaro (1968), 24 per cent (Maletnlema, T.N., Mhombolage, R. and Ngowi, G.E., 'Family Food Consumption Surveys in Rural Tanzania', *TNR* 73 (1974) p. 52); Kreysler, J.V., 'Nutrition' *The Young Child Study in Tanzania*, UNICEF, DSM (1973); Latham, M. and F.J. Stare, 'Nutritional Studies of Tanzania (Tanganyika)', *World Rev. Nutritional Dietetics* 7 (1967) pp. 31–71; Seshmani, L., 'Food Consumption and Nutritional Adequacy in Iringa – A Case Study of Four Villages', *ERB* Paper 81.5 (1981).
5. Carswell, F. *et al.*, 'Nutritional Status, Globulin Titers, and Parasitic Infections of Two Populations of Tanzanian School Children', *American Journal of Clinical Nutrition* 34(7) (1981) pp. 1292–9.
6. Countrywide: Maletnlema *et al.*, 'Family Food Consumption', p. 47: Kilimanjaro: Swantz, M.-L., Henricson, U.-S. and M. Zalla, 'Socio-Economic Causes of Malnutrition in Moshi District', *BRALUP* Research Paper No. 38, UDSM (1975) p. 32; Rufiji: Bantje, H., 'Food

Flows and Dietary Patterns in Ikwiriri Village', *BRALUP* Research Paper No. 74 (1982) p. 12.

7. Kilimanjaro: Swantz *et al.*, 'Socio-Economic Causes', p. 25; von Freyhold, M., Sawaki, K. and Zalla, M., 'Rural Area-Moshi District', *The Young Child Study in Tanzania*, Dar es Salaam, UNICEF (1973) pp. 175, 183, 199.
8. Kilimanjaro: Swantz *et al.*, 'Socio-Economic Causes', p. 28.
9. Kilimanjaro: von Freyhold, 'Rural Area-Moshi District', p. 178.
10. Songea: Robson, 'Malnutrition', p. 263.
11. Countrywide: Culwick, G.M., 'Nutrition in East Africa', *Africa* 14(7) (July 1944) p. 402; Kilimanjaro: von Freyhold *et al.*, 'Rural Area-Moshi District', p. 182; Rufiji: Bantje, 'Food Flows', p. 17.
12. Tanzania and UNICEF, 'Analysis of the Situation of Children and Women and the Priorities for Child Survival and Development', UNICEF, DSM (1985) pp. 151–2.
13. Tanzania and UNICEF, 'Analysis of the Situation of Children', p. 394.
14. Packed lunches away from home or the purchase of cooked food or packaged snacks to take away and eat on the agricultural work site are foreign to the rural areas of Tanzania. Generally, women cook once a day in the evening and the leftovers are eaten the following morning. There are no materials like plastic or paper bags or wrapping paper that could be used for packing a lunch.
15. Kilimanjaro: Swantz *et al.*, 'Socio-Economic Causes', pp. 36, 43; general: TT, 'Commission for Human Nutrition: Preliminary Survey of Nutrition among the Natives of Tanganyika Territory', Government Report of Committee, DSM (1937); Kilimanjaro: von Freyhold *et al.*, 'Rural Area-Moshi District', p. 173.
16. TT, 'Commission for Human Nutrition, p. 4.
17. Bantje, H., 'Seasonal Variations in Birthweight Distribution in Ikwiriri Village', *BRALUP* Research Report No. 43 (1980) p. 21.
18. Brooke, C., 'Types of Food Shortages in Tanzania', *Geographical Review* LVII(3) (1967).
19. Mascarenhas, A.C., 'Aspects of Food Shortages in Tanganyika, 1925–1945', *Journal of the Geographical Association of Tanzania* 3 (1968) pp. 50–1; Mascarenhas, A.C., 'Agriculture, Food and Population Change in Tanzania', in J.E. Kocher (ed.) 'Social and Economic Development and Population Change in Tanzania', *BRALUP* Research Paper No. 36 (1975) pp. 51–4; Brooke, 'Types of Food Shortages', p. 350.
20. Sumra, S., 'Changes in Agricultural Practises among the Peasants of Handeni District during the British Colonial Period', Social Science Conference of E. A. Universities, UDSM (December 1976) p. 8.
21. Swynnerton, R.J.M., 'Some Problems of the Chagga on Kilimanjaro', *EAAJ* 14 (January 1949) pp. 123, 126.
22. Brooke, 'Types of Food Shortages', p. 341.
23. Fleuret, P. and A., 'Nutritional Implications of Staple Food Crop Successions in Usambara, Tanzania', *Human Ecology* 8(4) (1980) pp. 311–27; Iliffe, *Modern History*, p. 350.
24. Brooke, 'Types of Food Shortages', p. 347.
25. Savile, A.H., 'A Study of Recent Alterations in the Flood Regimes of

Three Tanganyika Rivers', *EAAJ* 11 (1945); Bantje, H., 'The Rufiji Agricultural System: Impact of Rainfall, Floods and Settlement', *BRALUP* Research Paper No. 62 (1979) pp. 28–9.
26. Bantje, 'Rufiji Agricultural System', pp. 2, 35.
27. Bantje, H., 'Flood and Famines, A Study of Food Shortages in Rufiji District', *BRALUP* Research Paper No. 63 (1980) p. 12.
28. Brooke, 'Types of Food Shortages', p. 350.
29. Kavishe, F.P., 'A Safari Report on the Food Crises in Central Mwanza and Shinyanga Regions', TFNC Report No. 883, Project 15, DSM (1984) p. 1–14; Paula Park, Oxfam, personal communication, November 1984.
30. Kjaerby, 'Agro-Pastoralism', p. 31.
31. Brooke, C., 'The Heritage of Famine in Central Tanzania', *TNR* 67 (1967) pp. 15–22; Mbogoni, L.E.Y., *Labour Migration and Famine in Dodoma District*, UDSM, B.A. History Dissertation, (1977); Ndorobo, B., 'Famine Problems in Dodoma District', *Journal of the Geographical Association of Tanzania* 8 (1973); Patton, M., 'Dodoma Region 1929–1959: A History of Famine', *BRALUP* Research Report No. 44 (1971); Rigby, P., *Cattle and Kinship among the Gogo* (Ithaca: Cornell University Press, 1969).
32. Thiele, G., 'State Intervention and Commodity Production in Ugogo: A Historical Perspective', *Africa* 54(3) (1984) p. 96.
33. Thiele, 'State Intervention', p. 101; Sachak, N., 'Creating Employment Opportunities for Rural Women: Case Study of Dodoma Rural District', *BRALUP* Workshop on Women's Studies and Development, Paper No. 6 (1979) p. 5.
34. Latham, M.C., 'A Clinical Nutrition Survey, p. 76; Mwaluko, E.P., 'Famine Relief in the Central Province of Tanganyika, 1961', *Tropical Agriculture* 39 (1962) pp. 163–8.
35. Bryceson, D.F., 'Colonial Famine Responses', *Food Policy* (May 1981) p. 97.
36. Brooke, 'Types of Food Shortages', p. 345.
37. Sumra, 'Changes in Agricultural Practices', p. 14.
38. Arhem, K., K. Homewood and A. Rogers, 'A Pastoral Food System: The Ngorongoro Maasai in Tanzania', *BRALUP* Research Paper No. 79 (1981) cited in Petit, A., 'Report of a Nutrition-Status and MCH-Coverage Baseline Survey in Nainokanoka Ward, Ngorongoro District, Arusha Region, Tanzania', Oxfam (1984) p. 3.
39. Kjaerby, 'Agro-Pastoralism', pp. 55–8.

Part II: Summary

1. Tanganyika, Department of Agriculture Annual Reports; East African Statistical Department, 'Tanganyika: Report on the Analysis of the Sample Census of African Agriculture 1950 (Revised)', (Nairobi, East African Statistical Department, 1953) p. 34; Acland, J.D., *East African Crops* (London, Longman, 1975).

6 Defining Extra-Household Social Institutions

1. Feierman documents how the household became the essential social unit during colonialism, replacing the corporate action of the lineage and the still earlier clans (Feierman, S., *Concepts of Sovereignty among the Shambaa and their Relation to Political Action*, Oxford, D. Phil. Thesis (1972) p. 48).
2. Weber, M., *Economy and Society* (Berkeley: University of California Press, 1968) pp. 956–8.
3. The dates for these stages of clientage are not precise but rather rough approximations because the decline of one organisational form always over-lapped with the gradual rise of the next.

7 The British Colonial State

1. During the interwar years, there were on average only 150–170 administrative officers in the country, including those on leave (Heussler, R.W., *British Tanganyika, An Essay and Documents on District Administration* (Durham, N. C.: Duke University Press, 1971) p. 23).
2. Cameron, D., 'Sessional Paper No. 2: Instructions to Administrative Officers in regard to Native Labour and the Production of Economic Crops', DSM, Government Printer, 1926.
3. Furse, Sir R., *Aucuparias: Recollections of a Recruiting Officer* (London: Oxford University Press, 1962) pp. 239–41.
4. General meetings held outside for all to come, usually in the form of a short address made by the visiting dignitary followed by a question/answer period.
5. Translated 'farms'.
6. Tanganyika, Department of Agriculture Annual Report, 1937, p. 17.
7. Young, R. and Fosbrooke, H., *Land and Politics among the Luguru* (London: Routledge & Kegan Paul, 1960) p. 125.
8. Wakefield, A.J., 'Address to Colonial Office Summer School, Cambridge, August 1948', RH Mss. Afr.s.348–53, 2.
9. Savory, B., in Heussler, R.W., 'British Colonial Service in Tanganyika', 1965, RH Mss. Br.Emp.s.480/4, p. 8.
10. White, E.G., 'Brief Domestic Reminiscences of Life in Tanganyika, 1929–34', RH Mss. Afr.s.172, (n.d.) p. 2.
11. Hall, Lady Lorna, 'A Bushwife's Progress: The Life of a Colonial Officer's Wife in Tanganyika, 1932–53', RH Mss. Afr.s.1834 (1982) pp. 12–21.
12. Leslie, J.A.K., Transcript of 'Interview upon his Service as D.O.; Commissioner, Social Development; and Permanent Secretary in Tanganyika, 1946–54', RH Mss. Afr.s.1516, pp. 42–3; Hall, RH Mss. Afr.s.1834, pp. 40, 55.
13. Governor's Secretariat Minute, 27 January 1931, notes that the event would be reported to the Permanent Mandate Commission of the League of Nations (TNA SMP 13252).
14. Translated 'hunger'.
15. Letters from Lumley, Assistant District Officer to Chief Secretary,

6 August 1930 and 2 February 1931, and Letter from Lukiko Nyamiaga, Bugufi to Maguire, District Officer, 26 November 1928, TNA SMP 13252.

16. Director of Agriculture's Secretariat Minute, 11/10/41, TNA SMP 13252.
17. Rowe, E.G., 'Interview concerning Colonial Service in Tanganyika, 1928–1958', RH Mss. Afr.s.1698, p. 64.

8 The Asian Market

1. TT, *Non-Native Census, 1921, Report* (DSM: Government Printer, 1921).
2. TT, *Report on the Census of the Non-Native Population taken on the Night of 25 February, 1948* (DSM, Government Printer, 1953).
3. Delf, G., *Asians in East Africa* (London: Institute of Race Relations, 1963) p. 30.
4. Ghai, D.P. and Y.P. (eds) *Portrait of a Minority, Asians in East Africa*, (Nairobi: Oxford University Press, 1970); Mangat, J.S., *A History of the Asians in East Africa c. 1886–1945* (Oxford: Oxford University Press, 1969); Honey, M.S., *An Economic History of Asians in Tanzania and Zanzibar c. 1840–1940*, Ph.D. thesis, UDSM (1982).
5. Economist Intelligence Unit, *A Survey of Wholesale and Retail Trade in Tanganyika* (London, 1962).
6. Translated 'shops'.
7. Translated 'shopkeeper'.
8. Chief Secretary, to All Senior Commissioners and District Administrative Officers, Circular Letter No. 3998/35, 29 July 1926, TNA SMP 3998; Director of Agriculture to Chief Secretary, 1 December 1930, TNA SMP 10138.
9. Economist Intelligence Unit, *Survey*, pp. 127, 172.
10. With reference to the *dukawallahs*, Gillman wrote in his diary: 'The idiotic policy of letting East Africa with its comparatively speaking innocent and certainly far from decadent, native population be invaded and inflicted by the scum of India' (23/1/1921, RH Mss. Afr.s.1175). In the *dukawallah*'s defence, V.M. Nazerali, an unofficial LegCo. Member responding to the Governor's call to *dukawallahs* to enhance their salesmanship, had this to say:

    Your Excellency has referred to the duka wallahs. Sir, it is the first time that this miserable species of human being has got some recognition from the Governor of the Territory. Generally amongst the Government circles – and some other circles as well – these duka wallahs have been considered as parasites and that attitude still persists . . . seen under impartial and reasonable light, these duka wallahs have sacrificed their own and their families' health, their children's education and their standard of living in trying to open up the country by penetrating in peaceful manner and opening our trade for which they receive very little, if any credit and very little if any recognition up to this time that Your Excellency has mentioned them' (LegCo. Proceedings, 25th Session, 15/11/50, 21).

11. Except for sugar which was used for brewing. During the 1950s, however, the Sukuma became the exception to this general rule when specialisation in cotton production became a viable proposition (Economist Intelligence Unit, *Survey*, p. 155).
12. 'Trade in Districts Policy', TNA SMP 3998; 'System of Marketing of Produce', TNA SMP 10138.
13. TT, Sessional Paper No. 2 of 1943, 'Famine Finance', PRO/CO852/428/17630.
14. e.g. Dudbridge, B., 'Report on the 1949/50 Famine in the Maswa District', RH Mss. Afr.s.880.

9 Native Authority Clientage

1. I use 'tribe' to refer to societies where economic organisation and access to land are based on kinship (Mair, L., *An Introduction to Social Anthropology* (Oxford: Clarendon, 1983) p. 14).
2. Chagga: Liebenow, J.G., 'Tribalism, Traditionalism, and Modernism in Chagga Local Government, *Journal of African Administration* 10(2) (1958) p. 74; Sukuma: Cory, H., *The Indigenous Political System of the Sukuma*, (Nairobi, East African Literature Bureau, 1954) p. 11; Kimbu: Shorter, A.E.M., *Chiefship in Western Tanzania: A Political History of the Kimbu* (Oxford: Clarendon, 1972) p. 106.
3. Wright, A.C.A., 'The Transition from Native Administration to Local Government', Paper prepared for the Government of Tanganyika (1952) 3 (Cory Collection No. 402, UDSM).
4. Fosbrooke, H.A., 'Tanganyika, the Application of Indirect Rule to Chiefless Societies', Rhodes-Livingstone Conference Proceedings, RH (1959) pp. 22–3; Ranger, T., 'European Attitudes and African Realities: The Rise and Fall of the Matola Chiefs of Southeast Tanzania', *Journal of African History* 20 (1979) p. 82.
5. To Cameron, indirect rule was a matter of using 'their own indigenous institutions in order to promote higher standards of civilization'. Whereas one former district officer and resident magistrate summarised the policy as: '(A) Bringing the African people to respect their gerontocracy and (B) making the gerontocracy worthy of that respect. (A) depended very considerably on (B), but (B) was often difficult to implement' (Cameron, Sir D., 'Native Administration in Nigeria and Tanganyika', *Journal of the Royal African Society* XXXVI (1937) p. 9.)
6. Hartnoll, A.V., 'Prayer for Rain in Ugogo', *TNR* 13 (June 1942) p. 59; Sukuma, Hehe, Nyamwezi, Luguru: McCallum, D., 'Rain-making in Tanganyika', *TNR* 52 (March 1959) p. 53.
7. Whatever administrative arrangement had transpired under German rule the rituals endured (Luguru: Young, R. and Fosbrooke, H., *Land and Politics among the Luquru* (London: Routledge & Kegan Paul, 1960) p. 84; Sukuma: Ntundu, Y., 'The Position of Rainmaker among the Wanyiramba', *TNR* 7 (June 1939) p. 86).
8. Gogo: Adam, V., 'Rain Making Rites in Ihanzu', Paper presented at the East African Institute of Social Research Conference, DSM (January 1963) p. 15; Feierman, S., *Concepts of Sovereignty among the Shambaa*

and their Relation to Political Action, Oxford, D.Phil thesis (1972) p. 398.

9. TT, *Native Authority Memorandum, No. 3* (1930) p. 15–(i).
10. Aplin, H.D., *Report on Native Administration in Tanganyika Territory* (Zomba: Nyasaland Protectorate, 1931) [RH] p. G18.
11. Mitchell, Sir P., *African Afterthoughts* (London: Hutchinson, 1954) p. 126.
12. Unomah, A.C., 'Indirect Rule and the Nyamwezi Traditional System in the Tabora Province of Tanganyika', *Tarikh* 3(3) (1970) p. 59.
13. TT, Bukoba District Annual Report, 1920/1.
14. TT, *Native Authority Memorandum, No. III*, 15–(i) (1930).
15. Cory, H., *The Indigenous Political System of the Sukuma* (Nairobi: East African Literature Bureau, 1954) p. 27.
16. Sturdy, D.S., Transcript of 'Interview concerning Agricultural Services in Tanganyika, 1926–45', RH Mss. Afr.s.1331 (1969) pp. 14–15; Tomlinson, G.A., Miscellaneous Papers: 'Memorandum on Indirect Rule' RH Mss. Afr.s.370 (1937) p. 2–3; Perham, M., 'The System of Native Administration in Tanganyika', *Africa* 4 (1931) p. 310.
17. Culwick, A.T., 'What the Wabena Think of Indirect Rule', *Journal of the Royal African Society* 36 (1937) pp. 186–92.
18. Savory, B., 'Answers to Questionnaire received from R. Heussler, Esq.' in Heussler, R.W., RH Mss. Br.Emp.s.480/4, p. 23.
19. Cameron, 'Native Administration', p. 9.
20. e.g. Bagshawe diary (Kondoa District) 22/4/19, 21/1/20, RH Mss. Afr.s.281; PC, Eastern Province to Chief Secretary, 11 August 1939, TNA SMP 27245; TT, *Second Convention of Representative Chiefs of Tanganyika* (DSM: Government Printer, 1958) p. 3.
21. Savory, B., in Heussler, RH Mss. Afr.s.480/4, p. 24.
22. Longland interview reported in Heussler, R.W., *British Tanganyika. An Essay and Documents on District Administration* (Durham, N. C.: Duke University Press, 1971) p. 57.
23. Tomlinson, RH Mss. Afr.s.370, p. 5.
24. Adam, 'Rain Making Rites', p. 18.
25. TT, *Native Authority Memorandum No. VIII* (DSM, Government Printer, 1929) pp. 20–3; Young and Fosbrooke, *Land and Politics*, p. 86; Liebenow, J.G., 'Some Problems in Introducing Local Government Reform in Tanganyika', *Journal of African Administration* 8(3) (1956) p. 135.
26. TT, *Native Administration Memorandum No. 1* (DSM: Government Printer, 1930) pp. 21–2.
27. Heussler, *British Tanganyika*, p. 55; TT, *Second Convention of Representative Chiefs*, p. 3.
28. Salaried headmen, upon the discretion of the chief, could receive modest monthly, quarterly or half-yearly salaries based on 3 per cent of the taxes paid by their village, whereas further down those with less than 100 taxpayers did not receive remuneration (TT, *Native Authority Memorandum No. 3* (1930) 15–(iv).
29. Savory, B., in Heussler RH, Mss. Br.Emp.s.480/4, p. 19.
30. Winnington-Ingram, C., Miscellaneous Papers: 'N. Mara district annual report', RH Mss. Afr.s.1749 (1950) p. 10.

31. Gulliver, P., *Labour Migration in a Rural Economy: A Study of the Ngoni and Ndendeuli of Southern Tanganyika* (Nairobi: East African Literature Bureau, 1955) p. 29.
32. Leslie, J.A.K., Transcript of 'Interview upon his service as D.O.; Commissioner, Social Development; and Permanent Secretary in Tanganyika, 1946–54', RH Mss. Afr.s.1516, p. 27.
33. Rowe, E.G., Transcript of 'Interview concerning colonial service in Tanganyika, 1928–58', RH Mss. Afr.s.1698 (1969) pp. 36–44.
34. Young and Fosbrooke, *Land and Politics*, p. 86.
35. Cory, *Indigenous Political System*, p. 19; Feierman, *Sovereignty among the Shambaa*, p. 348.
36. Wright, 'Transition from Native Administration', p. 2.
37. Tukuyu District Annual Report, 1919–20.
38. In some cases it was pointedly stipulated that livestock owners were expected to sell their cattle before being eligible for famine relief and tax defaulters were required to labour rather than receive famine relief food on credit (Letter from DO, Bagamoyo to PC, 23/1/34, TNA SMP 19454).
39. Unomah notes the consternation of Tabora peasants who were required to pay for famine relief food for the first time in 1925 (Unomah, 'Indirect Rule', p. 61).
40. Letter from DO, Musoma to PC, Lake Province, TNA SMP 13252; Elliot, Sir H.F., 'Food Situation in the Western and Southern Areas of Mwanza District', Safari Report addressed to the DO, Mwanza, 3/3/38, RH Mss. Afr.s.1430.
41. Letters from: Chief Secretary to PC, Mwanza, 10/9/34; PC, Lake Province to Chief Secretary, 30/10/34; Hall, Acting DO, Maswa to PC, Lake Province, 20/10/34; Acting Chief Secretary to PC, Lake Province, 13/11/34, TNA SMP 13252.
42. Cory, *Indigenous Political System*, p. 26.
43. TT, Circular No. 33 of 1930, (11)i, 2.
44. One district officer complained that cassava patches were planted right across the path he was likely to use on entering a village, but not elsewhere (Bagamoyo District Annual Report 1949, TNA Acc. 7).

10 Food Supply for an African Wage-Labour Force

1. TT (Cameron) *Instructions to Administrative Officers in regard to Native Labour and the Production of Economic Crops*, Legislative Council Sessional Paper No. 2 (DSM: Government Printer, 1926); Letter from Cameron, Governor of Tanganyika to Secretary of State for the Colonies, 14/7/25, PRO/CO691/78/152.
2. Orde-Browne, Major G. St. J., *Labour in the Tanganyika Territory* (London: HMSO, 1926) p. 72.
3. Labour Department Annual Report 1928, p. 9.
4. In 1927, total migrants numbered 72 000 and local casual workers were 60 000 (equivalent to 10 000 full-time labourers) (1927 Labour Department Annual Report). In the 1945 labour census, 51 per cent of the non-government labour, excluding women and children, were migrants. If women and children are included and counted as local (unfortunately

there is no specification of this), then the percentage of migrant labour declines to 45 per cent (Labour Census on 15 February 1945 reported in the Labour Department Annual Report, 1945); by the late 1950s the balance had definitely tipped in favour of local labour at 60 per cent to migrant labour's 40 per cent proportion (Hitchcock, E., 'Labour and Employment in an African Plantation', *Inter-African Labour Institute Bulletin* 6 (1958) p. 20).

5. Translated 'card'.
6. Enclosure F. Longland, 'Report on Labour Matters in Sisal Areas: No. I: Tanganyika', 29/3/36, TNA SMP 23544; TT, *Report of the Committee Appointed to Consider and Advise on Questions relating to the Supply and Welfare of Native Labour in the Tanganyika Territory* (DSM: Government Printer, 1938), 10; TT (By P.E. Mitchell) *Labour: Notes on Labour in Tanganyika* (DSM: Government Printer, 1933) p. 9.
7. Molohan, M.J.B., *Detribalization: A Study of the Areas of Tanganyika where Detribalized Persons are Living* (DSM: Government Printer, 1957) p. 14.
8. Maize production had been boosted by the distribution of Potchefstroom Pearl and White Congo seeds by the Agriculture Department in that year (TT, Agricultural Department Annual Report 1928/29, pp. 4, 8).
9. On the other hand, a high seasonality of labour supply was reported for mine workers, particular at Lupa where workers were in the habit of returning to their home areas for the planting and harvesting season.
10. Tanner, R.E.S., 'Subsistence Agriculture on the Tanganyika Coast', *EAAJ* 24 (1958) p. 72.
11. Bagshawe, F.J.E., 'Private Diaries', RH Mss. Afr.s.288 and 289, 23/6/29 and 9/8/30.
12. Kilimanjaro Planters Association: Memorandum on the Maize Growing Industry, August 1934, TNA SMP 19533.
13. D.W. Malcolm criticised Kenyan European subsidies which he identified as aping the South African model without the 'mountain of gold' to pay for it, with the result that European farming flourished on the 'backs of the Native Authorities' (Malcolm, D.W., Diary entry while assistant to Lord Hailey, 19/12/35, RH Mss. Afr.s.1445).
14. Director of Agriculture to Chief Secretary, 21/5/35, TNA SMP 19533.
15. Director of Agriculture to Chief Secretary, 15/4/36, TNA SMP 19533.
16. Indian Planters' Association, Kilosa District to Chief Secretary, 5/2/36, TNA SMP 19533.
17. In 1939, Tanganyika Railways carried 32 900 ton-miles per route mile in comparison with the Gold Coast Railways' 119 200; Kenya and Uganda Railways' 150 000; South Africa's 500 000; India's 598 000 and the UK's 868 000 ton-miles per route mile (TT, *Tanganyika Transport: A Review by J.R. Farguharson, Chief Engineer, Tanganyika Railways and Ports Services* (DSM, Government Printer, 1945) p. 6).
18. Hofmeier, R., *Transport and Economic Development in Tanzania* (Munich, Weltforum Verlag, 1973) p. 323.
19. Major Bown, LegCo., 5th Session, 23/10/31, p. 203.
20. Tanganyika, Labour Department Annual Report 1929–31.
21. Bagshawe, RH Mss. Afr.s.282–8.

22. TT, *Labour: The Recruitment, Employment and Care of Labour* (DSM, Government Printer, 1933) p. 13–14.
23. P.C. Mitchell to Governor, 1/11/30, TNA SMP 11306; Dundas, A. *Beneath African Glaciers* (London: H.F. & G. Wetherby, 1924) pp. 96–8.
24. TT, *Labour: The Recruitment*, p. 14.
25. Brinkworth, H. 'Tanganyika Safari Diary, 1946', RH Mss. Afr.s.788, p. 5.
26. Bagshawe diary, 21/9/29, RH Mss. Afr.s.288.
27. TT, Labour Department Annual Report 1927, p. 62.
28. Individual camps total annual occupancy ranged between 40 and 19 000 (TT, Labour Department Annual Report 1940, pp. 14–15).
29. Dickson, J., 'Lupa Diary, 1925', RH Mss. Afr.s.738.
30. Iliffe, *Modern History*, p. 294.
31. Pearson, N., 'Trade Unionist on Safari, 1949', RH Mss. Afr.s.394, pp. 68–70, 107.
32. TT, *Labour: The Recruitment*, p. 20; TT, Government Notice No. 144 of 1936.
33. Jerrard, Labour Inspection Report, Bombwera Estate (Tanga District), 17/6/38, TNA SMP 25908/1/66.
34. Charron, K., *The Welfare of the African Labourer in Tanganyika* (DSM: Government Printer, 1944).
35. TT, Labour Department Annual Report 1928, p. 47; TT, *Report of the Committee*, p. 28.
36. TT, *Report of the Committee*, pp. 28, 32–3; International Labour Office, *Studies and Reports. Series b Social and Economic Conditions*, No. 23, Workers' Nutrition and Social Policy (Geneva 1936).
37. Draft Report of Nutrition Committee (1940) TNA SMP 25987.
38. Mohamed, S.A. and McKeag, J., 'The History of Human Nutrition Activities in Tanzania', Human Nutrition Unit, Ministry of Health, DSM (1970).
39. i.e. the maize meal fed to rural labourers.
40. i.e. finely machine ground maize flour.
41. 'Report of Enquiry into Wages and Cost of Living of Low Grade African Government Employees in Dar es Salaam', Appendix C (1942) TNA SMP 30598.
42. Labour Commissioner Orde-Browne to Chief Secretary, 14/3/28, TNA Acc. 61/295.
43. In 1938, hawkers of dried fish and certain fresh foods were, however, exempted from the Itinerant Traders Bill after the investigations of the government-appointed Nutrition Commission. There was considerable opposition to this measure from some unofficial LegCo. members who claimed that most hawkers' produce was stolen from farmers' fields (Major Sir William Lead, LegCo., 12th Session, 29/3/28, 119–22).
44. Depelchin, J., 'The "Beggar Problem" in Dar es Salaam in the 1930's', History Department Seminar Paper, UDSM, (1978) p. 5.

11 The Systematisation of the Territorial Food Supply: 1939–50

1. There were 87 000 Tanganyikan Africans enlisted in the military forces, proportionally one of the highest in Africa (President's Address, LegCo., 20th Session, 2/12/46, 258).
2. President's Address, LegCo, 18th Session, 6/12/43, p. 5.
3. Bryceson, D.F., 'A Century of Food Supply in Dar es Salaam', in J. Guyer (ed.) *Feeding African Cities*, (International African Institute, Guildford, 1987) p. 177.
4. President's Address, LegCo., 19th Session, 7/12/44, p. 4.
5. President's Address, LegCo., 19th Session, 7/12/44, p. 3.
6. Orde-Browne, Major G. St. J., *Labour Conditions in East Africa* (London, HMSO, 1946) p. 10.
7. President's Address, LegCo., 19th Session, 7/12/44, p. 4.
8. Financial Secretary, LegCo., 19th Session, 14/12/44, p. 41.
9. TT, Cypher Telegram from East African Governors' Conference to Secretary of State, Colonies, 19/3/43, PRO/CO852/428/17600/II.
10. TT, Labour Department Annual Report 1943, p. 8.
11. This was later to be raised to 33 per cent, then 50 per cent (TT, Labour Department Annual Report 1945, p. 10).
12. Essup Dar es Salaam to Chief Secretary, 22/7/44, TNA SMP 29549.
13. Molohan, M.J.B. (Labour Officer, DSM) 'Unemployment and Wage Rates in Dar es Salaam', 27/9/41, TNA Acc. 61/443/1.
14. Europeans were earning over four times more than Asians and 16 times more than Africans (Circular Letter No. 45 of 1947 to all Heads of Department, 12/4/47, 'Revision of Cost of Living Allowances', in Stenhouse, RH Mss. Afr.s.417).
15. The 1950 price rise was accompanied by an increase of the minimium rate of pay for daily paid Government labourers from 1.60s to 1.75s (TT, Labour Department Annual Report 1949, p. 19; Press Release, 1/2/50, TNA SMP 39114).
16. TT, Labour Department Annual Report 1950, p. 32.
17. Iliffe, J., 'The Creation of Group Consciousness among the Dockworkers of Dar es Salaam 1929–1950', in R. Sandbrook and R. Cohen (eds) *The Development of an African Working Class* (Bristol: Longman, 1975) p. 68.
18. Annual Report of the East African Sisal Industry, 1946, TNA SMP 19417/3.
19. Orde-Browne, *Labour Conditions*, p. 22.
20. Miller, R.W.R., 'Rations for African Labour', *EAAJ* 12, (October 1946) p. 108.
21. Memorandum for Standing Finance Committee, 'Measures to Stimulate Production of Food', 6/3/46, TNA SMP 30626.
22. Memorandum No. 92 for Executive Council, 'Grain Prices and Price Guarantees', 8/49, TNA SMP 38804.
23. Director of Agriculture, LegCo., 20th Session, 12/12/46, p. 303.
24. Twining, President's Address, LegCo., 25th Session, 15/11/50, p. 9.
25. E.C. Philips, LegCo., 25th Session, 23/11/50, p. 65.

26. Acting Director of Grain Storage, 31/1/51, TNA SMP 35181.
27. Twining, President's Address, LegCo., 24th Session, 23/1/49, p. 4.

12 Reordering of the State and the Market

1. As a percentage of total labour, estate agricultural labour was 51 per cent in 1961 and 23 per cent in 1973.
2. Chief Secretary, LegCo., 35th Session, 18/5/60, p. 96.
3. Translated 'familyhood'.
4. Nyerere, J.K., 'Ujamaa – the Basis of African Socialism' (1962) in *Freedom and Unity* (Oxford: Oxford University Press, 1966) p. 162.
5. Nyerere, J.K., *Socialism and Rural Development* (DSM, Government Printer, 1967) p. 26.
6. (TANU, *T.A.N.U. Guidelines 1971*, reprinted in Coulson, A. (ed.) *African Socialism in Practice* (Nottingham: Spokesman, 1977) p. 37 (para. 15).
7. Tanzania, 'Annual Manpower Report to the President 1969', DSM, Government Printer (1969) p. 27.
8. An Area Commissioner was the district party secretary and the government's chief administrator in the district.
9. Nyerere had persistently maintained that Africanization of the civil service could not proceed more quickly than the development of education (Nyerere, Eastern Province, LegCo., 35th Session, 17/5/60, p. 90).
10. In 1952/3 there were an estimated 27 000 African traders, usually holding stocks worth not more than a few hundred pounds, frequently not over £50 (Wright, F.C., *African Consumers in Nyasaland and Tanganyika*, (London: HMSO, 1955) pp. 50–2).
11. J.K. Nyerere, LegCo., 34th Session, 27/5/59, p. 128.
12. von Clemm, M., *People of the White Mountain: The Interdependence of Political and Economic Activity amongst the Chagga in Tanganyika with special reference to Recent Changes*, Oxford D.Phil Thesis, (1962) pp. 350–5.
13. Tanzania, *1967 Population Census*, VI, p. 171.

13 Cooperatives and Neighbourhood Clientage Exchange

1. Gulliver, P., *Neighbours and Networks: The Idiom of Kinship in Social Action among the Ndendeuli of Tanzania* (Berkeley: University of California Press, 1971) p. 217.
2. Translated 'unfarmed bushland inhabited by wild animals'.
3. Leslie, J.A.K., *A Survey of Dar es Salaam*, (London: Oxford University Press, 1963) p. 107.
4. Leslie, *Survey*, p. 108.
5. Bienen, H., *Tanzania: Party Transformation and Economic Development* (Princeton: Princeton University Press, 1970) pp. 4–14, 63, 80; Iliffe, *Modern History*, p. 568.
6. Maguire, G.A., *Toward 'Uhuru' in Tanzania* (Cambridge: Cambridge University Press, 1969) p. 287.

7. Bienen, *Tanzania*, pp. 110–11.
8. Bienen, *Tanzania*, p. 108.
9. Chambers, D.V., 'Food and Cashcrops', RH Mss. Br. Emp.s.476, 14–15; Holmes-Siedle, Bishop J., Transcript of 'Conversation between Bishop Holmes-Siedle, Bishop of Kigoma in Tanzania, the White Fathers – and John Tawney', RH Mss. Afr.s.1595, p. 39.
10. Finucane, J.R., *Rural Development and Bureaucracy in Tanzania* (Uppsala: Scandinavian Institute of African Studies, 1974) p. 10.
11. Nyerere, J.K., LegCo., 34th Session, 27/5/59, 130. Note: at the time Rashidi Kawawa was a nationalist labour leader.
12. Migot-Adholla, S.E., 'Traditional Society and Co-operatives', in Widstrand, C.G. (ed.) *Co-operatives and Rural Development in East Africa*, (New York: Africana Publishing Corp., 1970) pp. 26–33.
13. Migot-Adholla, S.E., 'The Politics of a Growers' Cooperative Organisation', in Cliffe, L., Lawrence, P., Luttrell, W., Migot-Adholla, S., Saul, J.S., (eds) *Rural Cooperation in Tanzania* (DSM: Tanzania Publishing House, 1975) p. 243.
14. Translated 'big-man'.
15. Translated 'food ration'.
16. Translated 'gifts'.
17. There was a thin line between bonuses and peculation: '. . . the peculator on a scale large enough to make it worth while is too often the object of admiration of the very persons he has defrauded' (Tanganyika, *Annual Report on Co-operative Development 1958*, DSM (1959) p. 1); Migot-Adholla, S.E., 'Power Differentiation and Resource Allocation: The Cooperative Tractor Project in Maswa', in Hyden, G. (ed.) *Cooperatives in Tanzania* (DSM: Tanzania Publishing House, 1976) p. 51.
18. Tanganyika, *Report of the Presidential Special Committee of Enquiry in to Co-operative Movement and Marketing Boards* (DSM: Government Printer (1966) p. 9; Rutaguza, G.H.M., 'The Cooperative Leadership', in Hyden (ed.), *Cooperatives*, p. 33.
19. Temu, P., *Marketing Board Pricing and Storage Policy with Particular Reference to Maize in Tanzania*, Stanford Ph.D. thesis, (1975) pp. 81, 95.
20. Dumont, R., *Tanzanian Agriculture after the Arusha Declaration* (DSM, Ministry of Economic Affairs and Development Planning, 1969) p. 50.
21. Most observations made in the Department of Co-operative Development's Annual reports suggest that defalcation was far from rampant during the 1950s. In *1950* (p. 4): 'The high standard of honesty amongst the employees of co-operative societies occasions periodic surprise. It exists because every peculation becomes known without delay and unlike the peculation of public money, in which the public appear to feel no direct interest, causes resentment in the community in which the peculator lives.' In *1957* (p. 20): 'Fraud and peculations have increased but the standards of honesty are still surprisingly high when it is considered that some £7 425 273 was paid out in cash to members; in more advanced countries, where the major have bank accounts, most payments are made by cheque, thus reducing the enormous temptations which exist when large sums are paid out in cash. Furthermore, the majority are

illiterate, thus putting even greater temptation before the officials of the societies.' In *1958* (p. 1):' It is regretted that the incidence of dishonesty still causes concern. There were no major defalcations during the year but the general level of integrity leaves room for considerable improvement. . . . It is not enough to claim that the co-operative standards compare not unfavourably with those in other walks of life. They could, and should be a great deal higher.' In contrast in 1966, corruption, petty thievery and nepotism were cited as very widespread (Tanganyika, *Report of the Presidential Special Committee*, pp. 9–16).

22. Migot-Adholla, 'Power Differentiation', pp. 44–55.
23. Tanganyika, *Presidential Special Committee*, pp. 9–12.
24. Westergaard, P., 'Analysis of the Accounts of the Co-operative Societies in Tanzania for the Years 1967–69', *ERB* 73.2 (1973) p. 33.
25. Hyden, G., *Beyond Ujamaa in Tanzania* (London: Heinemann, 1980) p. 89; Bienen notes that in the 1965 parliamentary elections many incumbents lost on the basis of ceasing to be a 'local' (Bienen, *Tanzania*, p. 395).

14 Urban Growth and Food Adequacy

1. Tanzania, *1969 Household Budget Survey: Income and Consumption*, vol. I (1972).
2. Bryceson, 'Century of Food Supply', pp. 174–5.
3. President's Address, LegCo., 27th Session, 12/2/53, p. 175.
4. Although most of the areas were relatively unpopulated, they could and sometimes did become hotly contested. African protest over the Sanya Corridor, which blew up into the famous Meru Land Case, was presented before the United Nations in 1952.
5. Governor Twining, LegCo., 30th Session, 20/4/55, and 33rd Session, 17/9/57, p. 19.
6. By 1958 there were ten farmers' associations: five were geographical in representation, four related to specific crops, whereas the Tanganyika National Farmers' Union was a general association of farmers. All of these were represented in the newly formed Northern Province Convention of Associations, founded as a forum for political and economic discussion in the run-up to independence.
7. *Daily News* 9/6/72 cited in Fimbo, G.M., 'Land, Socialism and the Law', in Ruhumbika, G. (ed.) *Towards Ujamaa* (DSM, East African Literature Bureau, 1974) p. 252.
8. Raikes, P., *The Development of Mechanized Commercial Wheat Production in North Iraqw, Tanzania* Stanford Ph.D. thesis, (1975) p. 134.
9. Kjaerby, 'Agro-Pastoralism', p. 32.
10. Awiti, A., 'Economic Differentiation in Ismani, Iringa Region', *African Review* 3 (1973) p. 213.
11. Lunan, M. and Weir, J., 'Maize-Growing at Ismani, Iringa, Tanganyika', *EAAJ* 20 (1954) p. 92.
12. Feldman, R., 'Custom and Capitalism: Changes in the Basis of Land Tenure in Ismani, Tanzania', *Journal of Development Studies* 10(3/4) (1974) p. 315.

13. Raikes, *Wheat Production*, p. 244.
14. Raikes, *Wheat Production*, p. 39–40.
15. The 1967 Population Census enumerated 3043 employers in the agricultural industry of cereal production, which constituted only 0.06 per cent of all people engaged in non-sisal estate agriculture and 22 per cent of all employers in non-sisal estate agriculture. Only a portion of these 3043 would have been operating on a scale sufficiently large to be considered capitalised farmers (Tanzania, *1967 Population Census*, vol. 4, Table 314, p. 357).
16. Department of Agriculture Annual Report 1956, p. 38; Minister for Natural Resources, LegCo., 34th Session (1959) p. 7.
17. Only Sukuma peasants were observed to be reliant on market purchase for a portion of their food needs (Economist Intelligence Unit, *A Survey of Wholesale and Retail Trade in Tanganyika* (London: EIU, 1962) p. 105).
18. Nyerere, *Socialism and Rural Development* (1967).
19. Translated 'politics is agriculture'.
20. Tanganyika, 'Proposals of the Tanzania Government on the Recommendations of the Special Presidential Committee of Enquiry into the Cooperative Movement and Marketing Boards', Government Paper 3 (1966) p. 15.
21. In 1972, food imports amounted to 7 per cent of the total import bill whereas they had constituted only 3 per cent during the previous two years.

15 The Merger of the State and Clientage

1. Tanzania, *The Economic Survey, 1977–78* (DSM, Government Printer, n.d.) Tables 16–18.
2. Bank of Tanzania, *Economic and Operations Report* (DSM, June 1984) p. 83.
3. Clark, W.E., *Socialist Development and Public Investment in Tanzania* (Toronto: University of Toronto Press, 1978) pp. 102, 107.
4. Tanzania, *Analysis of Accounts of Parastatal Enterprises 1972–1980* (DSM: Government Printer, 1983) p. 3.
5. Tanzania, *Second Five Year Plan* (DSM: Government Printer, 1969) pp. 212–13.
6. Tanzania, Bureau of Statistics, *Analysis of Accounts of Parastatals* (1976) p. 5; (1983) p. 13.
7. Moshi, H.P.B., 'Towards Improving the Performance of Public Enterprises in Tanzania: The Missing Factors', Paper presented to an 'Economic Policy Workshop', DSM (February 1986) pp. 5, 20 *Daily News*, 'Public firms accounts poor', 11/11/85.
8. Kim, K., 'Enterprise Performance in the Public and Private Sectors: Tanzanian Experience', *Journal of Developing Areas* 15(3) (1981) p. 474; Barker, C.E., Bhagavan M.R., v.Mitschke-Collande P. and Wield D.V., *African Industrialisation* (Hants: Gower, 1986) p. 123.
9. UNIDO, 'The Potential for Resource-Based Industrial Development in LDC's, No. 3, 'Tanzania' (Vienna, 1982).

10. Parker, I.C., 'NDC Investment Policy and Its Relation to National Industrial Planning Objectives', *ERB* Discussion Paper (December, 1970) p. 5; El-Namaki, M.S., *Problems of Management in a Developing Environment: The Case of Tanzania (State Enterprise between 1967 and 1975)* (Amsterdam: North-Holland, 1979) pp. 196–9; Loxley, J. and Saul, J., 'The Political Economy of the Parastatals', in Mapolu, H. (ed.) *Workers and Management* (DSM: Tanzania Publishing House, 1976) pp. 17–23.
11. Clark, W.E., *Socialist Development*, p. 113; Loxley, J., 'Principles of Financial Management in Capitalist and Socialist Economies', *Rasilimali* (January 1973) p. 15.
12. Shivji, I., 'Capitalism Unlimited: Public Corporations in Partnership with Multinational Corporations', *African Review* 3(3) (1978) pp. 358–81; Coulson, A., *African Socialism in Practice*, (Nottingham: Spokesman, 1979) pp. 179–90.
13. Mwapachu, J.V., *Management of Public Enterprises in Developing Countries: The Tanzania Experience* (New Delhi: Oxford IBH Publishing Co., 1983).
14. Nsekela, A.J., 'The Public Enterprise as an Instrument of Economic Development in Tanzania', in G. Ruhumbika (ed.) *Towards Ujamaa* (DSM: East African Literature Bureau, 1974) p. 115.
15. El-Namaki comments that 'As a result of the heavy politicized nature of the state and the lack of properly trained personnel to man professional and technical posts the process of selection and promotion of top level technocrats in Tanzania tends to be strongly influenced by factors other than sheer professional competence. Although there are no established channels for that selection, as it mostly follows an informal pattern based on contacts and personal knowledge, considerations of political commitment, ideological orientation and patriotic pretentions weigh heavily on the governments decision' (El-Namaki, *Problems of Management*, p. 45).
16. Some individuals were on more than 40 boards (Carvalho, V.N., 'The Control of Managing Agents in Tanzanian Parastatal Organizations with Special Reference to the National Development Corporation', *Eastern Africa Law Review* 5(1) (1977) p. 95).
17. They were recepient to per diem allowances and token honorariums (El-Namaki, M.S.S., 'The Effectiveness and the Managerial Behaviour of Company Boards in Tanzania', *International Review of Administrative Sciences* (December 1976) p. 244).
18. Ghai, Y., 'Law and Public Enterprise in Tanzania', in Ghai, Y. (ed.) *Law in the Political Economy Public Enterprise: African Perspectives* (Uppsala: Scandinavian Institute of African Studies, 1977) p. 228.
19. von Freyhold, M., 'The Workers, the Nizers and the Peasants', Department of Sociology mimeo, UDSM (1972) pp. 18–20, 69.
20. According to the Minister of Finance, 'on average 70 per cent of the over 400 parastatals have questionable standards of accounting'. The percentage of parastatals with annual accounts in arrears grew from 3 per cent in 1976 to 46 per cent in 1983: 'it was clear that the managements in the parastatals in arrears had little or no control over their financial affairs. It

was small wonder that 165 such institutions made a loss of 910.21m/- in 1983. . . . If all the accounts in arrears are available, it is needless to add that the losses incurred by the nation due to poor financial controls in parastatals would be very high' (*Daily News*, 'Minister warns on arrears', 16/3/85). The Chairman of the National Board of Accountants and Auditors revealed that the Government is losing 2.5 bn/- annually by way of subvention due to failure by some parastatal organisations to submit their reports of accounts (*Daily News*, 'Accounting standards poor', 16/3/85).

21. Moshi estimated that 60 per cent of the parastatals had substantial amounts of unvouched and improperly vouched expenditure (Moshi, H.P.B., 'Adequacy of Control in Tanzania's Public Enterprises', *Public Enterprises* 5(1) (1984) p. 36); *Daily News*, 'Over 213m/- unaccounted for', 20/4/85).
22. *Daily News*, 'Public funds theft rises', 5/7/77; 'Corruption is now an epidemic', 20/1/78; 'Millions of Government cash stolen', 18/7/78; 'Surprise checks may reduce fraud-Aboud', 8/9/79; 'Firms Start on Wrong Footing', 8/8/80; 'Watchdog of Public Accounts', 6/9/80; 'NEC bans vibali', 11/1/81; 'Millions spent on car hires', 22/1/81; 'Bankers implicated in bribery bid', 5/5/81; 'Ntagazwa urges good materials management', 16/5/84; 'NDL Workers Told: Don't incite row', 15/9/84; 'CATA losses over 22m/-', 30/11/84; 'Report corrupt workers – RTC', 11/12/84; 'Permits disrupt RTC activities', 21/12/84; 'Essentials supply snags explained', 4/2/85; Moshi, 'Adequacy of Control', p. 36.
23. According to the Director of Operations of the National Institute of Productivity; 'business is mostly conducted on credit, as such by withholding payment of debts to creditors the management is able to show that a parastatal is doing well while in actual fact would have fared badly if it had paid the debts on time' (*Daily News*, 'Give Detailed Reports, Firms Told', 10/9/80). Often there were disagreements over the size of debts and refusals to pay (Moshi, 'Adequacy of Control', p. 37).
24. Moshi, 'Towards Improving Performance', p. 3.
25. *Daily News*, 'How stores men lose millions', 2/10/79. According to the Auditor General's annual report, discovered store losses totalled TSh. 126 million whereas cash losses were only TSh. 33 million (*Daily News*, 'Tight control on funds urged', 18/9/84).
26. Nyerere, *The Arusha Declaration Ten Years After* (DSM: Government Printer, 1977) p. 35; *Daily News*, 'Report on falling discipline', 9/7/80; Nyerere stated: 'We have failed to punish those who fail to do their work. As a result no work is done; and the people do not get what they are supposed to get' ('Be bold, says Nyerere', 12/1/82).
27. *Daily News*, 'Juwata raps corruption', 15/6/81.
28. *Daily News* 'Fire guts Central Bank', 18/5/84. During a National Assembly session, '[t]he MP of Kigoma Urban. . . questioned as to how a case like that involving the gutting of the Bank of Tanzania could have been committed by a mere messenger and clerk' ('Call to fight corruption', 20/4/85).
29. In 1970 the Prevention of Corruption Ordinance was amended to cover parastatal employees charged with bribery, fraud or collusion very

broadly defined. Similarly, a Penal Code amendment set a common minimum sentence for parastatal and government employees convicted of theft in the course of their duties or damage of public property (James, R.W. and Ligunya, S. 'Organizational Relationships and the Control of Parastatals in Tanzania', *Eastern Africa Law Review* 5(1) (1972) p. 43). Carvalho argues that 'the fear in . . . the employees of parastatal organisations has heightened to a point of quite a lot of them attempting to shirk responsibilities as much as possible' (Carvalho, 'Control of Managing Agents', p. 110). This should be compared with El-Namaki's view, some years later, that the 'scope for punitive action' was far too narrow. He maintains that government failed to take corrective measures until matters reached a crisis proportion and suggests there is a limit to the punitive action government can take because the shortage of management personnel makes it relatively futile to fire managers (El-Namaki, *Problems of Management*, pp. 238–9, 251, 254). The enigma of stiff penalties but lax legal enforcement is, in the opinion of Ghai, related to the mode of operation of the party versus the judiciary. The Party is 'happy in the language of moral norms and ethics, not in that of regulations and administration . . . there is an impatience with [judicial] rules and procedures' and 'an anxiety at the unpredictability of the results through the legal process. The underlying principles and procedures of the legal system are among the state institutions in Tanzania to undergo the least change since independence. The independence of the courts has been maintained, and the adversary system as well. . . . The control by the executive over and through the legal system is perceived to be less effective than over the administrative process, and produces the tendency towards either moving the matters in question to the administrative sector or altering the balance in the legal process' (Ghai, 'Law and Public Enterprise', p. 256).

30. Moshi, despairingly, writes that a blind eye was pervasive throughout government and the parastatal sector:

> there is no code of conduct in the operations of the PEs. Some are run like ministries, others like personal empires, still others like cars without drivers. The effect of all these is a situation of nil accountability; public funds are embezzled with impunity, arrogant and irresponsible workers confidently boast that they can't easily be dismissed, errant officials instead of being sacked are transferred from one institution to another, where the sins are repeated and lastly, officials who steal money from the PEs are sacked but never get prosecuted. In short, the Tanzania's softness promotes laxity and corruption whose perpetrators are 'heroes and heroines' rather than a curse for which they should be declared national outcasts (Moshi, 'Towards Improving Performance', p. 25).

31. Personal contacts were especially important in unskilled job recruitment (Knight, J.B. and Sabot, R.M., 'From Migrants to Proletarians: Employment Experience, Mobility and Wages in Tanzania', *Oxford Bulletin of Economics and Statistics*, 44 (3), August 1982, p. 221); *Daily News*,

'Nepotism is rampant – MP', 27/6/81; 'Kawawa denies nepotism', 28/6/81; 'PM discounts nepotism claims', 30/6/81; 'Train workers, employers told', 28/2/84.

32 *Daily News*, 'Corruption: Preventive dose needed now', 4/1/76; 'Okulu is guilty'. 28/5/76; 'Squad to open branches', 24/6/76; 'Beware corrupt leaders, CCM Chairman warns', 16/4/77; 'Comment: Corruption', 18/1/78; 'ATC reservations staff negligent-GM', 19/7/80; 'On swindles and losses', 2/8/81.

33. Some of the more spectacular scandals that were uncovered were: the Air Tanzania Corporation (ATC) contract that resulted in the removal of a Minister, the ATC General Manager and the Chairman of the Board of Directors; the Tanzania Investment Bank scandal involving the sacking of the Chairman and Managing Director and the General Manager; and the Tanzania Elimu Supplies fraud followed by the removal of its General Manager (Mlimuka, A.K.L.J. and P.J.A.M. Kabudi, 'The State and the Party', in Shivji, I.G. (ed.) *The State and the Working People in Tanzania*, (London, Codesria, 1985) p. 79).

34. *Daily News*, 'Corrupt people face hell', 12/2/81. At an Extraordinary National Party Conference in 1982, Nyerere 'said almost all leaders wanted lots of money and were being bribed clandestinely' ('Mwalimu slates corrupt leaders', 24/1/82).

35. Dimsdale, J., 'Rhetoric meets reality', *Africa Report*, November/December 1983.

36. 'Mwalimu . . . said managers of public enterprises must . . . be allowed to operate without undue interference from Party branches and government bureaucrats . . . "Our managers are asked too many questions" . . . like managers of private concerns, public sector managers must enjoy operational freedom provided they operated their institutions profitably, paid dividends to the Treasury registrar and maintained good relations between the management and workers' (*Daily News*, 'Let managers do their job', 30/10/86).

37. Ellis, 'Agricultural Marketing and Peasant-State Transfers in Tanzania', *Journal of Peasant Studies* 10 (4), (1983).

38. Translated 'big-men'.

16 Parastatal Staple Food Management

1. *Daily News*, 7/11/73. In September 1973 the TANU Biennial Conference had passed a resolution that the whole rural population should reside in villages by 1976.

2. '[T]he villages could be conceived of as factories in the field'; Kighoma Malima, then Minister for Planning and Economic Affairs in a lecture at the UDSM, 20/2/79 quoted in Kjaerby, F., 'Scratching the Surface: the Tanzanian Tractor Fiasco, the Undiscovered Oxenization Boom and the Drag of Mixed Farming', Draft, CDR, Copenhagen (November 1984) p. 4.

3. McCall, M., 'Heavier Burdens and Lower Status: Some Implications of Villagisation for Women in Tanzania', Twente University of Technology, The Netherlands (1984) pp. 4–15; Kjaerby, 'Scratching', p. 8.

4. Moore, M.P. and Stutley, P., 'Smallholder Food Production in Tanzania', DSM, Report to SIDA and the Government of Tanzania (1981) pp. 92, 97.
5. i.e. before population growth rates caused them to be so.
6. Kjaerby, 'Scratching', pp. 2–13.
7. Contiguous fields and continuous mono-cropping increased the likelihood of plant infestation and disease. The alarming spread of the 'scania' borer in maize came in the wake of villagisation (Golob, P. and Hodges, R., 'Study of an Outbreak of *Prostephanus truncatus* (Horn) in Tanzania', Tropical Products Institute G164, London, (1982)).
8. Bryceson, D.F., 'Peasant Cash Cropping versus Self-Sufficiency in Tanzania: A Historical Perspective', *IDS Bulletin*, 19(2) (1988) p. 38.
9. In 1981/2 the fertiliser price and transport subsidy amounted to nearly TShs. 750 million (Stewart, F., *Economic Policies and Agricultural Performance: The Case of Tanzania*, Paris, OECD (1986) p. 55).
10. Ndulu, B. and Msambichaka, L.A., 'Agricultural Sector Development in Tanzania 1961–1982', Arne Ryde Symposium on the Primary Sector in Economic Development, University of Lund, Sweden (1983) p. 17.
11. Farmers did not like to rely on hybrid maize for home supply because it did not store as well as the traditional local varieties and they did not like its taste (Schneider-Barthold, W. *et al.*, 'Farmers' Reactions to the Present Economic Situation in Tanzania with Respect to Production and Marketing' German Development Institute, Berlin (1983) p. 78; Rasmussen, T. 'Commercialised Maize Production among Smallholders in the Southern Highlands, Tanzania', CDR 86.3, Copenhagen (1986) p. 11; Friis-Hansen, E., 'An Assessment of Changes in Land Tenure and Land Use since Villagisation and the Impact of the Development of Peasant Agricultural Production in Tanzania', *CDR* Research Report (May 1986) p. 99).
12. Tanzania, Ministry of Agriculture, *The Agricultural Policy of Tanzania* (DSM: Government Printer, 1983) p. 63.
13. Kjaerby, 'Scratching', p. 20.
14. Bantje, H., 'Mechanised Food Production in Tanzania: A Portrait of the National Agriculture and Food Corporation', *IRA* Research Paper 6 (1984) p. 10.
15. Bantje, 'Mechanised Food Production', pp. 22–3.
16. *Daily News*, 'NAFCO', 25/3/84.
17. *Daily News*, 'Farm managers lose jobs', 23/1/82; 'Moshi', 25/9/84.
18. Bantje, 'Mechanised Food Production', pp. 24, 44.
19. Bantje, 'Mechanised Food Production', p. 23.
20. Bantje, H. 'The Impact of Mbozi Maize Farms on the Surrounding Villages, A Reconnaissance', *IRA* 59 (1983) p. 23.
21. Tractor hiring is such a well-established practice that when there was an attempt to abolish it, a massive resignation of staff members followed (Bantje, 'Mbozi', p. 23).
22. Bantje, 'Mechanised Farm Production', p. 44.
23. Personal communication from F. Kjaerby, Anthropologist in Hanang District, 5/12/84.
24. Young, R., *Canadian Development Assistance to Tanzania: An Indepen-*

dent Study by Roger Young (The North-South Institute, 1983) p. 64.
25. Bantje, 'Mechanised Food Production', p. 10.
26. *Daily News*, 'The inside of Mbarali rice farm', 22/1/79; Dumont, R., 'Self-Reliant Rural Development', DSM Draft (1979) p. 34.
27. Tanzania, MDB, *Price Policy Recommendations*, (PPR) I (1984) p. 13.
28. Tanzania, MDB, 'Estimates of 1981/82 Import Requirements for the Production, Processing and Marketing of Major Crops in Mainland Tanzania', DSM (1981) p. 8.
29. Bantje, 'Mechanised Food Production', p. 47.
30. Bantje, 'Mechanised Food Production', p. 29–39.
31. Bantje identifies the technological gulf as a disincentive to peasant agricultural production: 'farmers are exposed to the sight of tractors effortlessly ploughing wide stretches of land at the NAFCO farm, and thus become psychologically turned-off from manual agriculture' ('Mbozi', p. 18).
32. Sometimes the management had to resort to barter arrangements with village leaders in which collective labour of the village was performed in exchange for state farm ploughing services on the village communal farm. These arrangements were frequently expedited by local party and government officials, often on the farm's board of directors, who imposed financial or political penalties on those that did not comply (Bantje, 'Mbozi', pp. 29–31).
33. Bantje, 'Mbozi', pp. 30, 36–7.
34. Bantje, 'Mbozi', pp. 25, 32; *Daily News*, 'Students explain hitches at Ruvu', 13/12/79.
35. Tibenderana, H.K., *The Factors affecting Tanzania's National Milling Corporation's Performance (1968–1981)*, M.A. Thesis, UDSM (1982) pp. 109, 115; Kaberuka, D., 'Evaluating the Performance of Food Marketing Parastatals', *Development Policy Review* 2 (1984) pp. 190–216.
36. Tanzania, MDB, 'Price Policy Recommendations for the 1984 Agricultural Price Review', vol. I, DSM (1984) p. 29.
37. Bryceson, D.F., 'Food and Urban Purchasing Power: the Case of Dar es Salaam, Tanzania', *African Affairs*, vol. 84, no. 337 (1985) p. 518.
38. *Daily News*, 'Distribution affects Dar food situation', 4/6/84.
39. *Daily News*, 'Dar hit by acute food shortage', 29/1/74; 'Maize flour shortage; NMC Chief blames Ugawaji, traders', 20/2/79; 'NDL explains food shortage', 25/4/85.
40. The Minister for Industries and Trade told the *Daily News* that 'none of the shop operators followed the city ration regulations, neither did the divisional and ward functionaries make serious supervision to ascertain equitable distribution of the commodities' (*Daily News*, 'Dar Distribution snags explained', 12/6/84); 'Check food leakages- Machunda', 10/2/84; 'Distribution is the problem', 16/1/84.
41. Tibenderana reported: 'According to NMC's records from 1972 till 1977 the corporation lost Shs. 1 856 813/65 through staff misappropriation of funds and stocks, but the incidence of misappropriation reached astronomical proportions between May 1977 and July 1979, when the corporation lost a total sum of Shs. 11 504 027' (Tibenderana, *Factors*, p. 140);

In 1977/8 stock losses were estimated at 16.8 per cent (TShs. 148.6 million); 7.5 per cent due to deterioration and 9.3 per cent from stock disappearance (Tanzania, MDB, 'Report on Investigation into the Financial and Operating Position of Kilimo Crop Authorities: NMC', DSM (1979) pp. 27, 32).

42. *Daily News*, 'NMC man on theft charges', 23/12/78; 'Dodoma', 11/8/79; 'Morogoro', 15/8/81 and 30/12/81; 'Court Round-up', 11/4/84; 'Dodoma', 27/6/84; 'NMC worker jailed 9 years', 3/11/84; 'NDL sacks 7', 8/11/84; *Uhuru*, 'Mwanamke afikishwa mahakamani kwa wizi', 21/3/83.
43. Between 1979 and 1980 the NMC spent TShs. 126 million on hired cars (*Daily News*, 'VP stresses frugality', 18/8/81).
44. *Daily News*, 'NDL sacks 7', 8/11/84.
45. Coopers and Lybrand Associates (1977); CCM party and the Marketing Development Bureau (1979), World Bank (1980), Special Government-appointed Task Force (1981).
46. Tanzania, MDB, 'Proposals for Staple Food Prices under the Structural Adjustment Programme', DSM (1983) p. 1.
47. *Daily News*, 'NMC got 1 bn/- subsidy', 18/7/84.
48. Tanzania, MDB, 'Financial and Operating Position: NMC', p. 3.
49. Tanzania, *The Economic Survey, 1982* (DSM: Government Printer, 1983) pp. 41–5.
50. Tanzania, Ministry of Agriculture, 'Tanzania: National Food Strategy', Second Draft (June 1982) pp. 1–2; Tanzania, Ministry of Agriculture, 'The Tanzania National Agricultural Policy' (DSM: Printpak, 1982) p. vii.
51. Tanzania, MDB, 'Estimates of 1981/82 Import Requirements for the Production, Processing and Marketing of Major Crops in Mainland Tanzania', DSM (1981) pp. 7–8.
52. Cook, K.D., *Dimensions of Food Security/Insecurity: Tanzania, A Case Study*, UDSM, M.A. Thesis (1984) p. 130.
53. Quoted in J.–P. Langellier's feature in the *Guardian* (London) 9/11/80.
54. Tanzania, MDB, 'A Strategic Grain Reserve Programme for Tanzania', vol. II, DSM (1974) pp. 9–10.
55. Tanzania, MDB, 'Price Policy Recommendations', DSM (1984) p. 1.
56. *Guardian* (London), 'Officials accused of "criminal negligence" in face of famine: Tanzania inaction will bring starvation', 28/10/81; *The Economist*, 'The Cupboard is Bare', 31/10–6/11/81.
57. Interview with Martha Honey, journalist, 11/4/82.
58. *Weekly Review* (Kenya), 'Tanzania cabinet changes: agricultural minister sacked', 12/2/82.
59. *Africa Now*, 'Tanzania food scandal', May 1982.
60. Translated 'agriculture for life or death'.
61. Bryceson, D.F., 'Tanzanian Grain Supply', *Food Policy*, (May 1982) p. 117.
62. *Sunday News*, 'Keep your home clean – Sokoine', 7/9/80.
63. *Daily News*, 'Dar valleys for distribution', 15/1/85; 'it would be assumed that those valleys which were not cultivated had no owners, hence their being taken' ('DSM', 16/3/85).

64. *Daily News*, '1000 start farms in Kinondoni', 1/2/84; 'Mwalimu starts Dar tour', 8/2/85; 'Morogoro to develop farming', 20/1/86.

17 Clientage and Crisis, 1979–85

1. Mgaza, O. and Bantje, H., *Infant Feeding in Dar es Salaam*, TFNC and BRALUP, DSM (1980) p. 86; Bryceson, 'Century of Food Supply', pp. 174–5.
2. *Daily News*, 'All private shops in villages must close', 17/2/76; 'Stop it-Nyerere', 23/5/76; 'Operation Maduka: 2000 new shops set up', 30/8/76; 'Ministry clarifies on shops', 23/11/80; 'Village shops', 7/12/80; Tanzania, *Maduka ya Ujamaa*, Prime Minister's Office (DSM: Printpak, 1976).
3. Comparing NMC sales in 1973/4 with those of 1983/4 and assuming that firstly the NMC's distribution of maize, rice and wheat is directed at urban cereal requirements (Table 15), the remaining distributable amounts represented 11.5 per cent of rural requirements in 1973/4 and −0.02 ten years later.
4. Tanzania, Central Statistical Bureau, 1976/77 Household Budget Survey data.
5. Tanzania, MDB, 'Strategic Grain Reserve', II, 10; Tanzania, MDB, 'PPR' (1977) p. 8.
6. This amounts to 15 per cent, 40 per cent and 17.5 per cent of the total production of maize, rice and wheat assuming that 20–25 per cent of all peasant-produced maize, 50 per cent of rice and virtually all wheat was marketed (Tanzania, MDB, 'PPR', I (1984) p. 1).
7. Loft, M. and Oldevelt, J., 'Developments in Peasant Agriculture in Kigoma Region during the Post-Villagisation Years', *ERB* (1981) p. 96.
8. Rasmussen, 'Commercialised Maize', p. 3.
9. *Daily News*, 'Mbilinyi clarifies on food movement', 2/3/84.
10. Translated 'projects', referring to the small-scale trading and farming activities that people undertook as private individuals to help make ends meet in the household budget.
11. Translated 'permission'. Written authorisation by someone in a responsible party or government position allowing the holder to be exempted from normal procedures.
12. *Daily News*, 'Mwanza acts on "urushaji"', 3/11/80; 'Leaders warned on food permits', 7/1/84; 'Ilala bans "social" food permits', 23/2/84.
13. *Daily News*, 'Dar City Council decision dangerous', 19/2/80; 'City to extend its borders', 9/1/82; 'Peasants to win land case', 5/1/84; 'Plot allocation system is faulty', 19/11/85.
14. Furthermore, some towns insisted on enforcing bans on farming within the municipal boundaries ('Keeping Mbeya clean of . . . maize', 19/2/79; 'Bukoba', 23/5/79; 'Moshi Council destroys crops', 4/5/84; 'Mbeya', 18/10/84).
15. Interview with Dr K. Mustafa, 22/6/85; *Daily News*, 'Kibaha', 26/12/81.
16. Mgaza and Bantje, *Infant Feeding*, p. 89.
17. Schneider-Barthold *et al.*, 'Farmers' Reactions', pp. 62, 80.

18. According to one irritated consumer: 'The price depends upon whether the seller knows you or not. If he does well and good, you get it at a normal price. If not you must get it at an exorbitant price' (*Daily News*, 'Bukoba high prices', 2/3/82).
19. e.g. Mwanza, Mbeya and Morogoro (Keeler, A., 'Preliminary Report on the Parallel Market for Grains in Tanzania', Marketing Development Bureau (March 1983), p. 10).
20. e.g. Iringa, Dodoma and Dar es Salaam.
21. *Daily News*, 'Fake traders' days numbered, 14/8/80: 'City to check bogus traders', 7/5/81; 'Axe may fall on bogus traders', 9/9/81; 'City to fight hawkers', 31/12/81; 'Tribunal jails Dar traders', 7/2/84.
22. Cook, *Food Security*, pp. 142–4.
23. *Daily News*, 'Irresponsible workers warned', 26/2/85.
24. Stewart, *Economic Policies*, p. 59.
25. Hanak, H., *The Tanzanian Balance of Payments Crisis*, M.A. Thesis, UDSM (1981) pp. 47–8; The Third Five Year Plan had budgeted 24.2 per cent of investment to industry and only 11.5 per cent to agriculture (Tanzania, *Third Five Year Plan*, I, n.d. [1975], 11).
26. International Labour Office, *Basic Needs in Danger*, Addis Ababa, JASPA, (1982) p. 219.
27. Tanzania, *Economic Survey, 1982*, pp. 41–5.
28. Bank of Tanzania, *Economic and Operations Report*, annual.
29. Singh argues that this project aid worsened Tanzania's balance of payment problem (Singh, A., 'Tanzania and the IMF: The Analytics of Alternative Adjustment Programmes', *Development and Change*, 17 (1986) p. 443).
30. *Daily News*, 'Budget speech', 19/6/81.
31. *Daily News*, 'Don't waver, Nyerere', 8/7/81.
32. *Daily News*, 'Views on trade liberalisation', 18/5/85.
33. *Daily News*, 'Mwalimu warns of hard times ahead', 19/6/79.
34. *Daily News*, 'Heroes get employment', 30/9/79.
35. *Daily News*, 'NEC launches survival plan', 18/5/81. NESP was prepared by the government and launched by the party.
36. Tanzania, *Structural Adjustment Programme for Tanzania*, Ministry of Planning and Economic Affairs, DSM (June 1982).
37. *Daily News*, 'Over 200 projects suspended', 18/6/82.
38. The Tribunal included four judges and eight others, mostly politicians. They tried 372 cases, making 212 convictions as of 3 February 1984 (*Daily News*, 'Police files 1745 cases', 3/2/84).
39. *Daily News*, 'Police swoop nets 1623 Dar "jobless"', 7/1/84.
40. *Daily News*, 'Large-scale farmers welcome', 6/6/81; 'Bohra to start fruit farm', 15/2/84; 'Policy on private sector underway', 13/2/84; 'Now you can build houses for rent . . .', 19/5/85.
41. Nyerere stated: 'When did the IMF become an International Ministry of Finance? When did nations agree to surrender to it their power of decision-making?', *Daily News*, 'NO to IMF meddling', 3/1/80.
42. *Daily News*, 'Nyerere explains stand on IMF Conditions', 23/11/84; 'Nyerere reiterates stand on IMF loan', 8/3/85; 'Nyerere stresses rural progress', 13/3/85.

43. The devaluations that took place measured against the US dollar were: 10 per cent on 20/1/79, 12 per cent on 6/3/82, 20 per cent during June 1983; 26 per cent on 14/6/84, and 33 per cent in June, 1985.
44. In 1985, Nyerere declined to run for president again and Ali Hassan Mwinyi was elected to the position. The following year the IMF and the Tanzanian government reached an agreement that entailed a 100 per cent devaluation against the dollar and the release of approximately $800 million (*Financial Times*, 'Tanzania to receive $800m in aid and loans, 13/6/86; 'Tanzania–IMF agreement ends longstanding feud', 20/8/86).

Bibliography

BOOKS, ARTICLES, RESEARCH PAPERS, THESES AND OFFICIAL PUBLICATIONS

Acland, J.D., *East African Crops* (London: Longman, 1975).

Adam, V., 'Rain Making Rites in Ihanzu', Paper presented at the East African Institute of Social Research Conference, DSM (January 1963).

Allan, W., *The African Husbandman* (Edinburgh: Oliver & Boyd, 1965).

Anderson, D., 'Depression, Dust Bowl, Demography and Drought: The Colonial State and Soil Conservation in East Africa during the 1930s', *African Affairs* (83)332 (July 1984) pp. 321–43.

Arhem, K., Homewood, K. and Rogers, A., 'A Pastoral Food System: The Ngorongoro Maasai in Tanzania', *BRALUP* Research Paper No. 79 (1981).

Awiti, A., 'Economic Differentiation in Ismani, Iringa Region', *African Review* 3 (1973).

Bantje, H., 'Mechanised Food Production in Tanzania: A Portrait of the National Agriculture and Food Corporation', *IRA* Research Paper 6 (1984).

Bantje, H., 'The Impact of Mbozi Maize Farms on the Surrounding Villages, A Reconnaissance', *IRA* 59 (1983).

Bantje, H., 'Food Flows and Dietary Patterns in Ikwiriri Village', *BRALUP* Research Paper No. 74 (1982).

Bantje, H., 'Seasonal Variations in Birthweight Distribution in Ikwiriri Village', *BRALUP* Research Report No. 43 (1980).

Bantje, H., 'Flood and Famines, A Study of Food Shortages in Rufiji District', *BRALUP* Research Paper No. 63 (1980).

Bantje, H., 'The Rufiji Agricultural System: Impact of Rainfall, Floods and Settlement', *BRALUP* Research Paper No. 62 (1979).

Barker, C.E., Bhagavan, M.R., v.Mitschke-Collande, P. and Wield, D.V., *African Industrialisation* (Hants: Gower, 1986).

Bienen, H., *Tanzania: Party Transformation and Economic Development* (Princeton: Princeton University Press, 1970).

Boserup, E., *Population and Technology* (Oxford: Basil Blackwell, 1981).

Boserup, E., *Women's Role in Economic Development* (New York: St Martin's, 1970).

Boserup, E., *The Conditions of Agricultural Growth* (New York: Aldine, 1965).

Brooke, C., 'The Heritage of Famine in Central Tanzania', *TNR* 67 (1967) pp. 15–22.

Brooke, C., 'Types of Food Shortages in Tanzania', *Geographical Review* LVII(3) (1967).

Bryceson, D.F., 'Peasant Cash Cropping versus Self-Sufficiency in Tanzania: A Historical Perspective', *IDS Bulletin* 19(2) (1988).

Bryceson, D.F., 'A Century of Food Supply in Dar es Salaam', in J. Guyer

(ed.) *Feeding African Cities* (Guildford: International African Institute, 1987).
Bryceson, D.F., 'Food and Urban Purchasing Power: the Case of Dar es Salaam, Tanzania', *African Affairs* (84) 337 (1985).
Bryceson, D.F., 'Tanzanian Grain Supply', *Food Policy* (May 1982).
Bryceson, D.F., 'Colonial Famine Responses', *Food Policy* (May 1981).
Bryceson, D.F. and Kirimbai, M., 'Subsistence or Beyond? Money-Earning Activities of Rural Women in Tanzania', *BRALUP/UWT* (1980).
Cameron, Sir D., 'Native Administration in Nigeria and Tanganyika', *Journal of the Royal African Society* XXXVI (1937).
Cameron, D., 'Sessional Paper No. 2: Instructions to Administrative Officers in regard to Native Labour and the Production of Economic Crops' (DSM: Government Printer, 1926).
Carswell, F. *et al.*, 'Nutritional Status, Globulin Titers, and Parasitic Infections of Two Populations of Tanzanian School Children', *American Journal of Clinical Nutrition* 34(7) (1981) pp. 1292–9.
Carvalho, V.N., 'The Control of Managing Agents in Tanzanian Parastatal Organizations with Special Reference to the National Development Corporation', *Eastern Africa Law Review* 5(1) (1977).
Charron, K., *The Welfare of the African Labourer in Tanganyika* (DSM: Government Printer, 1944).
Clark, W.E. *Socialist Development and Public Investment in Tanzania* (Toronto: University of Toronto Press, 1978).
von Clemm, M., *People of the White Mountain: The Interdependence of Political and Economic Activity amongst the Chagga in Tanganyika with special reference to Recent Changes*, Oxford D.Phil Thesis, (1962).
Collier, P., Radwan, S., Wangwe, S. and Wagner, A., *Labour and Poverty in Rural Tanzania* (Oxford: Clarendon, 1986).
Community Development Trust Fund, 'Appropriate Technology for Grain Storage', DSM (1977).
Cook, K.D., *Dimensions of Food Security/Insecurity: Tanzania, A Case Study*, M.A. Thesis, UDSM (1984).
Cory, H., *The Indigenous Political System of the Sukuma* (Nairobi: East African Literature Bureau, 1954).
Coulson, A. (ed.) *African Socialism in Practice* (Nottingham: Spokesman, 1977).
Culwick, G.M., 'Nutrition in East Africa', *Africa* 14(7) (July 1944).
Culwick, A.T. and G.M., 'A Study of Factors governing the Food Supply in Ulanga, Tanganyika Territory', *East African Medical Journal* 16 (1939) pp. 43–61.
Culwick, A.T., 'What the Wabena Think of Indirect Rule', *Journal of the Royal African Society* 36 (1937).
Deane, P. and Cole, W.A., *British Economic Growth 1688–1959: Trends and Structure* (Cambridge: Cambridge University Press, 1962) pp. 7, 16.
Delf, G., *Asians in East Africa* (London: Institute of Race Relations, 1963).
Depelchin, J., 'The "Beggar Problem" in Dar es Salaam in the 1930's', History Department Seminar Paper, UDSM (1978).
Dimsdale, J., 'Rhetoric meets reality', *Africa Report* (November/December 1983).

Dumont, R., 'Self-Reliant Rural Development', DSM Draft (1979).

Dumont, R., *Tanzanian Agriculture after the Arusha Declaration* (DSM: Ministry of Economic Affairs and Development Planning, 1969).

Dundas, A., *Beneath African Glaciers* (London: H.F. & G. Wetherby, 1924).

Durkheim, E., *Professional Ethics and Civic Morals* (London: Routledge & Kegan Paul, 1957).

Durkheim, E., *The Division of Labor in Society* (New York: The Free Press, 1964 (1933)).

East African Statistical Department, 'Tanganyika: Report on the Analysis of the Sample Census of African Agriculture 1950 (revised)', (Nairobi: East African Statistical Department, 1953).

Economist Intelligence Unit, *A Survey of Wholesale and Retail Trade in Tanganyika* (London, 1962).

Egero, B. and Henin, R.A., 'Fertility', *1967 Population Census*, vol. VI (1973).

Ellis, F., 'Agricultural Marketing and Peasant-State Transfers in Tanzania', *Journal of Peasant Studies* 10(4) (1983).

El-Namaki, M.S.S., *Problems of Management in a Developing Environment: The Case of Tanzania (State Enterprise between 1967 and 1975)* (Amsterdam: North-Holland, 1979).

El-Namaki, M.S.S., 'The Effectiveness and the Managerial Behaviour of Company Boards in Tanzania', *International Review of Administrative Sciences* (December 1976).

Feierman, S., *Concepts of Sovereignty among the Shambaa and their Relation to Political Action*; Oxford, D.Phil. Thesis (1972).

Feldman, R., 'Custom and Capitalism: Changes in the Basis of Land Tenure in Ismani, Tanzania', *Journal of Development Studies* 10(3/4) (1974).

Fimbo, G.M., 'Land, Socialism and the Law', in Ruhumbika, G. (ed.) *Towards Ujamaa* (DSM: East African Literature Bureau, 1974).

Finucane, J.R., *Rural Development and Bureaucracy in Tanzania* (Uppsala: Scandinavian Institute of African Studies, 1974).

Fleuret, P. and A., 'Nutritional Implications of Staple Food Crop Successions in Usambara, Tanzania', *Human Ecology* 8(4) (1980) pp. 311–27.

von Freyhold, M., Sawaki, K. and Zalla, M., 'Rural Area-Moshi District', *The Young Child Study in Tanzania* (Dar es Salaam: UNICEF, 1973).

von Freyhold, M., 'The Workers, the Nizers and the Peasants', Department of Sociology mimeo, UDSM (1972).

Friis-Hansen, E., 'An Assessment of Changes in Land Tenure and Land Use since Villagisation and the Impact of the Development of Peasant Agricultural Production in Tanzania', *CDR* Research Report (May 1986).

Furse, Sir R., *Aucuparias: Recollections of a Recruiting Officer* (London: Oxford University Press, 1962).

Ghai, D.P. and Y.P. (eds) *Portrait of a Minority, Asians in East Africa* (Nairobi: Oxford University Press, 1970).

Ghai, Y., 'Law and Public Enterprise in Tanzania', in Ghai, Y. (ed.) *Law in the Political Economy Public Enterprise: African Perspectives* (Uppsala; Scandinavian Institute of African Studies, 1977).

Gillman, C., 'Population Problems of Tanganyika Territory', *EAAJ* 11 (October 1945) p. 86.
Gillman, C., 'A Population Map of Tanganyika', *Geographical Review* XXVI(3) (1936) pp. 370–2.
Goldthorpe, J.E., 'The African Population of East Africa: A Summary of its Past and Present Trends', in *East Africa Royal Commission 1953–55 Report*, app. VII (London: HMSO, 1955).
Golob, P. and Hodges, R., 'Study of an Outbreak of *Prostephanus truncatus* (Horn) in Tanzania', Tropical Products Institute G164, Overseas Development Administration, London (1982).
Gulliver, P., *Neighbours and Networks: The Idiom of Kinship in Social Action among the of* Tanzania (Berkeley: University of California Press, 1971).
Gulliver, P., *Labour Migration in a Rural Economy: A Study of the Ngoni and Ndendeuli of Southern Tanganyika* (Nairobi: East African Literature Bureau, 1955).
Hanak, H., *The Tanzanian Balance of Payments Crisis*, M.A. Thesis, UDSM (1981).
Hartnoll, A.V., 'Praying for Rain in Ugogo', *TNR* 13 (June 1942).
Havnevik, K.J., 'Economy and Organization in Rufiji District: The Case of Crafts and Extractive Activities', *DERAP* No. 112, Bergen, Norway (1980).
Henin, R.A. and Egero, B., 'The 1967 Population Census of Tanzania: A Demographic Analysis', *BRALUP* Research Paper No. 19 (1972).
Heussler, R.W., *British Tanganyika, An Essay and Documents on District Administration* (Durham, N.C.: Duke University Press, 1971).
Hitchcock, E., 'Labour and Employment in an African Plantation', *Inter-African Labour Institute Bulletin* 6 (1958).
Hofmeier, R., *Transport and Economic Development in Tanzania* (Munich: Weltforum Verlag, 1973).
Honey, M.S., *An Economic History of Asians in Tanzania and Zanzibar c. 1840–1940*, Ph.D. thesis, UDSM (1982).
Hyden, G., *Beyond Ujamaa in Tanzania* (London: Heinemann, 1980).
Hyden, G., *Cooperatives in Tanzania* (DSM: Tanzania Publishing House, 1976).
Iliffe, J., *A Modern History of Tanganyika* (Cambridge: Cambridge University Press, 1979).
Iliffe, J., 'The Creation of Group Consciousness among the Dockworkers of Dar es Salaam 1929–1950', in R. Sandbrook and R. Cohen (eds) *The Development of an African Working Class* (Bristol: Longman, 1975).
International Labour Office, *Basic Needs in Danger*, (Addis Ababa: JASPA, 1982).
International Labour Office, *Studies and Reports. Series b Social and Economic Conditions*, No. 23, Workers' Nutrition and Social Policy (Geneva, 1936).
James, R.W., *Land Tenure and Policy in Tanzania* (Nairobi: East African Literature Bureau, 1971).
James, R.W. and Ligunya, S., 'Organizational Relationships and the Control of Parastatals in Tanzania', *Eastern Africa Law Review* 5(1) (1972).

Jerrard, R.C., *The Tribes in Tanganyika, Their Districts, Usual Dietary and Pursuits* (DSM, Government Printer, 1936).
Kaberuka, D., 'Evaluating the Performance of Food Marketing Parastatals', *Development Policy Review* 2 (1984).
Kajumulo-Tibaijuka, A., 'An Economic Analysis of Smallholder Banana-Coffee Farms in the Kagera Region, Tanzania', Report 240, University of Agricultural Sciences, Uppsala, Sweden (1984).
Kavishe, F.P., 'A Safari Report on the Food Crises in Central Mwanza and Shinyanga Regions', TFNC Report No. 883, Project 15, DSM (1984).
Keeler, A., 'Preliminary Report on the Parallel Market for Grains in Tanzania', Marketing Development Bureau (March 1983).
Keen, B., 'Presidential Address by Sir Bernard Keen, Director, E.A.A.F. R.O. at the Conference of the Medical, Agricultural and Veterinary Aspects of Food Production in East Africa,' *EAAJ* 20 (July 1954).
Kerblay, B., 'Peasant Family Economy in the USSR Today', in E.J. Hobsbawm, W. Kula, A. Mitra, K.N. Raj and I. Sachs (eds) *Peasants in History: Essays in Honour of Daniel Thorner* (Calcutta: Oxford University Press, 1980).
Kim, K., 'Enterprise Performance in the Public and Private Sectors: Tanzanian Experience', *Journal of Developing Areas* 15(3) (1981).
Kjaerby, F., 'Scratching the Surface: the Tanzanian Tractor Fiasco, the Undiscovered Oxenization Boom and the Drag of Mixed Farming', Draft, Centre for Development Research, Copenhagen (November 1984).
Kjaerby, F., *Problems and Contradictions in the Development of Ox-Cultivation in Tanzania*, Centre for Development Research, Copenhagen, No. 66 (1983).
Kjaerby, F., 'The Development of Agro-Pastoralism among the Barbaig in Hanang District', *BRALUP* Research Paper No. 56, UDSM (1979).
Knight, J.B. and Sabot, R.H., 'From Migrants to Proletarians: Employment Experience, Mobility and Wages in Tanzania', *Oxford Bulletin of Economics and Statistics* 44(3) (August 1982).
Kocher, J.E., 'Rural Development and Fertility Change in Tropical Africa: Evidence from Tanzania', *BRALUP* Research Paper No. 53 (1979).
Kreysler, J.V., 'Nutrition', *The Young Child Study in Tanzania*, UNICEF, DSM (1973).
Langellier, J.-P., 'Tanzania's Socialist "Choice": Peasant Power', *Guardian*, 9/11/80.
Latham, M. and Stare, F.J., 'Nutritional Studies of Tanzania (Tanganyika)', *World Rev. Nutritional Dietetics* 7 (1967) pp. 31–71.
Latham, M.C., 'A Clinical Nutrition Survey of Certain Areas of the Dodoma and Kondoa District', *East African Medical Journal* 41(2) (1964).
Latham, M.C., 'A Clinical Nutritional Survey of Certain Areas of the Rufiji District of Tanganyika', *East African Medical Journal* 40(3) (1963).
Leslie, J.A.K., *A Survey of Dar es Salaam* (London: Oxford University Press, 1963).
Lewin, R., 'Matetereka', *Mbioni* 5(3) (1969).
Lewis, W.A., *Growth and Fluctuations 1870–1913* (London: George Allen & Unwin, 1978).

Lewis, W.A. (ed.) *Tropical Development 1880–1913* (London: George Allen & Unwin, 1970).
Lewis, W.A., *The Theory of Economic Growth* (London: George Allen & Unwin, 1955).
Liebenow, J.G., 'Tribalism, Traditionalism, and Modernism in Chagga Local Government, *Journal of African Administration* 10(2) (1958).
Liebenow, J.G., 'Some Problems in Introducing Local Government Reform in Tanganyika', *Journal of African Administration* 8(3) (1956).
Loft, M. and Oldevelt, J., 'Developments in Peasant Agriculture in Kigoma Region during the Post-Villagisation Years', *ERB* (1981).
Loxley, J., 'Principles of Financial Management in Capitalist and Socialist Economies', *Rasilimali* (January 1973).
Loxley, J. and Saul, J., 'The Political Economy of the Parastatals', in Mapolu, H. (ed.) *Workers and Management* (DSM: Tanzania Publishing House, 1976).
Lunan, M. and J. Weir, 'Maize-Growing at Ismani, Iringa, Tanganyika', *EAAJ* 20 (1954).
Maguire, G.A., *Toward 'Uhuru' in Tanzania* (Cambridge: Cambridge University Press, 1969).
Mair, L., *An Introduction to Social Anthropology* (Oxford: Clarendon, 1983).
Maletnlema, T.N., Mhombolage R. and Ngowi, G.E., 'Family Food Consumption Surveys in Rural Tanzania', *TNR* 73 (1974).
Malthus, T.R., *An Essay on the Principle of Population and Summary View of the Principle of Population* (Middlesex, Penguin, 1970 (1798 & 1830)).
Mangat, J.S., *A History of the Asians in East Africa c. 1886–1945* (Oxford: Oxford University Press, 1969).
Mascarenhas, A.C., 'Agriculture, Food and Population Change in Tanzania', in J.E. Kocher (ed.) 'Social and Economic Development and Population Change in Tanzania', *BRALUP* Research Paper No. 36 (1975).
Mascarenhas, A.C., 'Aspects of Food Shortages in Tanganyika, 1925–1945', *Journal of the Geographical Association of Tanzania* 3 (1968).
Mascarenhas, O., 'Women's Control of Resources and Its Implications for the Food and Nutrition Status of their Family', Tanzania Food and Nutrition Centre/UNICEF Workshop on 'Hunger and Society', Soliwayo, Tanzania.
Masefield, G.B., *Famine: Its Prevention and Relief* (London: Oxford University Press, 1963).
Mbilinyi, M., 'The Changing Position of Women in Peasant Commodity Production: The Case of the Shambaa Kingdom', Symposium on Women and Work in Africa, University of Illinois at Urbana-Champaign (1979).
Mbogoni, L.E.Y., *Labour Migration and Famine in Dodoma District*, B.A. History Dissertation, UDSM (1977).
McCall, M., 'Heavier Burdens and Lower Status: Some Implications of Villagisation for Women in Tanzania', Technische Hogeschool, Twente, The Netherlands (1984).
McCallum, D., 'Rain-making in Taganyika', *TNR* 52 (March 1959).
Mgaza, O. and Bantje, H., *Infant Feeding in Dar es Salaam*, TFNC and BRALUP, DSM (1980).

Mgeni, A.Y., *A Prospective Study of Pesticide Effects (Particularly Anticholinesterases) on Health of Exposed Workers in Tanzania*, Universtiy of Zagreb Masters Thesis, (1978),

Migot-Adholla, S.E., 'Power Differentiation and Resources Allocation: The Cooperative Tractor Project in Maswa', in Hyden, G. (ed.) *Cooperatives in Tanzania* (DSM, Tanzania Publishing House, 1976).

Migot-Adholla, S.E., 'The Politics of a Growers' Cooperative Organisation', in Cliffe, L., Lawrence, P., Luttrell, W., Migot-Adholla, S., Saul, J.S. (eds) *Rural Cooperation in Tanzania* (DSM, Tanzania Publishing House, 1975).

Migot-Adholla, S.E., 'Traditional Society and Co-operatives', in Widstrand, C.G. (ed.) *Co-operatives and Rural Development in East Africa* (New York: Africana Publishing Corporation, 1970).

Miller, R.W.R., 'Rations for African Labour', *EAAJ* 12 (October 1946).

Mitchell, Sir P., *African Afterthoughts* (London: Hutchinson, 1954).

Mlimuka, A.K.L.J. and Kabudi, P.J.A.M., 'The State and the Party', in Shivji, I.G. (ed.) *The State and the Working People in Tanzania* (London: Codesria, 1985).

Mohamed, S.A. and McKeag, J., 'The History of Human Nutrition Activities in Tanzania', Human Nutrition Unit, Ministry of Health, DSM (1970).

Molohan, M.J.B., *Detribalization: A Study of the Areas of Tanganyika where Detribalized Persons are Living* (DSM, Government Printer, 1957).

Moore, J.E., 'Rural Population Carrying Capacities of the Districts of Tanzania', *BRALUP* Research Paper No. 18 (1971).

Moore, M.P. and Stutley, P., 'Smallholder Food Production in Tanzania', DSM, Report to SIDA and the Government of Tanzania (1981).

Mosha, A., 'Kuhifadhi na Kudunduliza Mazao Yaliyo Muhimu', *Tanzania Food and Nutrition Journal* 1 (1976).

Moshi, H.P.B., 'Towards Improving the Performance of Public Enterprises in Tanzania: The Missing Factors', Paper presented to an 'Economic Policy Workshop', DSM (February 1986).

Moshi, H.P.B., 'Adequacy of Control in Tanzania's Public Enterprises', *Public Enterprises* 5(1) (1984).

Mwaluko, E.P., 'Famine Relief in the Central Province of Tanganyika, 1961', *Tropical Agriculture* 39 (1962) pp. 163–8.

Mwapachu, J.V., *Management of Public Enterprises in Developing Countries: The Tanzania Experience* (New Delhi: Oxford & IBH Publishing Co., 1983).

Ndorobo, B., 'Famine Problems in Dodoma District', *Journal of the Geographical Association of Tanzania* 8 (1973).

Ndulu, B. and Msambichaka, L.A., 'Agricultural Sector Development in Tanzania 1961–1982', Arne Ryde Symposium on the Primary Sector in Economic Development, University of Lund, Sweden (1983).

Ngalula, T.K.F., *Women as Productive Force in the Tanzanian Rural Society: A Case Study of Buhongwe Village in Mwanza District*, M.A. thesis, UDSM (1977).

Nieuwolt, S., 'Seasonal Droughts in East Africa', *EAAFJ* 43(3) (1978) pp. 208–22.

Nsekela, A.J., 'The Public Enterprise as an Instrument of Economic Devel-

opment in Tanzania', in G. Ruhumbika (ed.) *Towards Ujamaa* (DSM: East African Literature Bureau, 1974).
Ntundu, Y., 'The Position of Rainmaker among the Wanyiramba', *TNR* 7 (June 1939).
Nyerere, J.K., *The Arusha Declaration Ten Years After* (DSM: Government Printer, 1977).
Nyerere, J.K., *Socialism and Rural Development* (DSM: Government Printer, 1967).
Nyerere, J.K., 'Ujamaa – the Basis of African Socialism' (1962) in *Freedom and Unity* (Oxford University Press, Oxford, 1966).
Oomen-Myin, M.A., *Involvement of Rural Women in Village in Tanzania: A Case Study in Morogoro District*, Department of Agricultural Extension, UDSM, Morogoro (1981).
Orde-Browne, Major G. St. J., *Labour Conditions in East Africa* (London: HMSO, 1946).
Orde-Browne, Major G. St. J., *Labour in the Tanganyika Territory* (London: HMSO, 1926).
Parker, I.C., 'NDC Investment Policy and Its Relation to National Industrial Planning Objectives', *ERB* Discussion Paper (December 1970).
Patton, M., 'Dodoma Region 1929–1959: A History of Famine', *BRALUP* Research Report No. 44 (1971).
Perham, M., 'The System of Native Administration in Tanganyika', *Africa* 4 (1931).
Petit, A., 'Report of a Nutrition-Status and MCH-Coverage Baseline Survey in Nainokanoka Ward, Ngorongoro District, Arusha Region, Tanzania', Oxfam (1984).
Preobrazhensky, E. (trans. B. Pearse; intro. by A. Nove) *The New Economics* (Oxford: Clarendon, 1965).
Raikes, P., *The Development of Mechanized Commercial Wheat Production in North Iraqw, Tanzania*, Stanford, Ph.D. thesis, (1975).
Rald, J. and Rald, K., *Rural Organization in Bukoba District, Tanzania* (Uppsala: Scandinavian Institute of African Studies, 1975).
Ranger, T., 'European Attitudes and African Realities: The Rise and Fall of the Matola Chiefs of Southeast Tanzania', *Journal of African History* 20 (1979).
Rasmussen, T., 'Commercialised Maize Production among Smallholders in the Southern Highlands, Tanzania', Centre for Development Research 86.3, Copenhagen (1986).
Reining, P., 'Social Factors and Food Production in an East African Peasant Society: The Haya' in P. McLoughlin (ed.) *African Food Production Systems* (Baltimore: Johns Hopkins Press, 1970).
Ricardo, D. (ed. and intro. by J.H. Hollander and T.E. Gregory) *Notes on Malthus and Principles of Political Economy* (Baltimore: Johns Hopkins Press, 1928).
Ricardo, D. (ed. J. Bonar) *Letters of David Ricardo to Thomas Robert Malthus, 1810–1823* (Oxford: Clarendon, 1887).
Rigby, P., *Cattle and Kinship among the Gogo* (Ithaca: Cornell University Press, 1969).
Robson, J.R.K., 'Malnutrition in Tanganyika', *TNR* 58/59 (1962).

Rudengren, J. and Swantz, M.-L., 'Village Skills Survey: Report of the Pre-Pilot and Pilot Surveys', *BRALUP* Research Paper No. 42 (1976).
Rutaguza, G.H.M., 'The Cooperative Leadership', in Hyden (ed.) *Cooperatives*.
Sachak, N., 'Creating Employment Opportunities for Rural Women: Case Study of Dodoma Rural District', *BRALUP* Workshop on Women's Studies and Development, Paper No. 6, UDSM (1979).
Sahlins, M., *Stone Age Economics* (London: Tavistock, 1974).
Savile, A.H., 'A Study of Recent Alterations in the Flood Regimes of Three Tanganyika Rivers', *EAAJ* 11 (1945).
Schneider-Barthold, W. *et al.*, 'Farmers' Reaction to the Economic Situation in Tanzania with Respect to Production and Marketing: A Case Study of Five Villages in the Kilimanjaro Region's', German Development Institute mimeo, Berlin (1983).
Seshmani, L., 'Food Consumption and Nutritional Adequacy in Iringa – A Case Study of Four Villages', *ERB* Paper 81.5 (1981).
Shivji, I., 'Capitalism Unlimited: Public Corporations in Partnership with Multinational Corporations', *African Review* 3(3) (1978).
Shorter, A.E.M., *Chiefship in Western Tanzania: A Political History of the Kimbu* (Oxford: Clarendon, 1972).
Singh, A., 'Tanzania and the IMF: The Analytics of Alternative Adjustment Programmes', *Development and Change*, 17 (1986).
Stewart, F., *Economic Policies and Agricultural Performance: The Case of Tanzania*, Paris, OECD (1986).
Storgaard, B., 'Women in Ujamaa Villages', *Rural Africana* 29 (1976).
Sumra, S., 'Changes in Agricultural Practises among the Peasants of Handeni District during the British Colonial Period', Social Science Conference of E.A. Universities, UDSM (December 1976).
Swantz, M.-L., 'Strain and Strength among Peasant Women in Tanzania', *BRALUP* Research Paper No. 49, UDSM (1977).
Swantz, M.-L., Henricson, U.-S. and Zalla, M., 'Socio-Economic Causes of Malnutrition in Moshi District', *BRALUP* Research Paper No. 38, UDSM (1975).
Swynnerton, R.J.M., 'Some Problems of the Chagga on Kilimanjaro', *EAAJ* 14 (January 1949).
Tanganyika, Department of Agriculture Annual Reports.
Tanganyika, Department of Cooperative Development Annual Reports.
Tanganyika, Department of Labour Annual Reports.
Tanganyika, Legislative Council Proceedings, various sessions.
Tanganyika, 'Proposals of the Tanzania Government on the Recommendations of the Special Presidential Committee of Enquiry into the Cooperative Movement and Marketing Boards', Government Paper 3 (1966).
Tanganyika, *Report of the Presidential Special Committee of Enquiry into Co-operative Movement and Marketing Boards* (DSM: Government Printer, 1966).
Tanganyika Territory, *Second Convention of Representative Chiefs of Tanganyika* (DSM: Government Printer, 1958).
Tanganyika Territory, *Report on the Census of the Non-Native Population taken on the Night of 25 February, 1948* (DSM: Government Printer, 1953).

Tanganyika Territory, Circular Letter No. 45 of 1947.
Tanganyika Territory, *Tanganyika Transport: A Review by J.R. Farquharson, Chief Engineer, Tanganyika Railways and Ports Services* (DSM: Government Printer, 1945).
Tanganyika Territory, *Report of the Committee Appointed to Consider and Advise on Questions relating to the Supply and Welfare of Native Labour in the Tanganyika Territory* (DSM: Government Printer, 1938).
Tanganyika Territory, 'Commission for Human Nutrition: Preliminary Survey of Nutrition among the Natives of Tanganyika Territory', Government Report of Committee, DSM, (1937).
Tanganyika Territory, Government Notice No. 144 of 1936.
Tanganyika Territory, *Labour: The Recruitment, Employment and Care of Labour* (DSM: Government Printer, 1933).
Tanganyika Territory, (by P.E. Mitchell) *Labour: Notes on Labour in Tanganyika* (DSM: Government Printer, 1933).
Tanganyika Territory, Circular No. 33 of 1930.
Tanganyika Territory, *Native Administration Memorandum No. I* (DSM: Government Printer, 1930).
Tanganyika Territory, *Native Authority Memorandum, No. III* (1930).
Tanganyika Territory, *Native Authority Memorandum No. VIII* (DSM: Government Printer, 1929).
Tanganyika Territory (Cameron), *Instructions to Administrative Officers in regard to Native Labour and the Production of Economic Crops*, Legislative Council Sessional Paper No. 2 (DSM: Government Printer, 1926).
Tanganyika Territory, *Non-Native Census, 1921, Report* (DSM: Government Printer, 1921).
Tanganyika Territory, Bukoba District Annual Report, 1920/1.
Tanganyika Territory, Tukuyu District Annual Report, 1919–20.
Tanner, R.E.S., 'Subsistence Agriculture on the Tanganyika Coast', *EAAJ* 24 (1958).
Tanner, R.E.S., 'Land Tenure in Northern Sukumaland, Tanganyika: An Analysis of Present-day Trends in Two Parishes', *EAAJ* 21 (October 1955).
Tanzania, *Analysis of Accounts of Parastatal Enterprises 1972–1980* (DSM: Government Printer, 1983) p. 3.
Tanzania, *The Economic Survey, 1982* (DSM: Government Printer, 1983).
Tanzania, *Structural Adjustment Programme for Tanzania*, Ministry of Planning and Economic Affairs, DSM (June 1982).
Tanzania, *The Economic Survey, 1977–78* (DSM: Government Printer, n.d.).
Tanzania, *Maduka ya Ujamaa*, Prime Minister's Office (DSM: Printpak, 1976).
Tanzania, *Third Five Year Plan for Economic and Social Development 1st July 1976–30th June 1981*, (DSM: Government Printer, n.d. [1975]).
Tanzania, *Second Five Year Plan* (DSM: Government Printer, 1969).
Tanzania, 'Annual Manpower Report to the President 1969' (DSM: Government Printer, 1969).
Tanzania, Bank of Tanzania, *Economic and Operations Report* (DSM: June 1984) p. 83.

Tanzania, Bureau of Statistics, *1978 Population Census*, vols VI and VIII (DSM: Bureau of Statistics, 1983).
Tanzania, Bureau of Statistics, '1976/77 Household Budget Survey', (HBS), Unpublished Computer Print-out Tables, 1983.
Tanzania, Bureau of Statistics, *Analysis of Accounts of Parastatals* (1983) (1976).
Tanzania, Bureau of Statistics, *Agricultural Census of Tanzania 1971/72*, vol. I, *Peasant Farming* (DSM: Bureau of Statistics, 1979).
Tanzania, Bureau of Statistics, *1969 Household Budget Survey: Income and Consumption*, vol. I (1972).
Tanzania, Bureau of Statistics, *1967 Population Census*, vols I–VI (DSM, 1970–3).
Tanzania, Marketing Development Bureau, 'Price Policy Recommendations for the 1984 Agricultural Price Review' (PPR), vol. I, DSM (1984).
Tanzania, Marketing Development Bureau, 'Proposals for Staple Food Prices under the Structural Adjustment Programme', DSM (1983).
Tanzania, Marketing Development Bureau, 'Estimates of 1981/82 Import Requirements for the Production, Processing and Marketing of Major Crops in Mainland Tanzania', DSM (1981).
Tanzania, Marketing Development Bureau, 'Report on Investigation into the Financial and Operating Position of Kilimo Crop Authorities: NMC', DSM (1979).
Tanzania, Marketing Development Bureau, 'Price Policy Recommendations', Dar es Salaam (1977) p. 8.
Tanzania, Marketing Development Bureau, 'A Strategic Grain Reserve Programme for Tanzania', vol. II, DSM (1974).
Tanzania, Ministry of Agriculture, *The Agricultural Policy of Tanzania* (DSM: Government Printer, 1983).
Tanzania, Ministry of Agriculture, 'The Tanzania National Agricultural Policy' (DSM: Printpak, 1982).
Tanzania, Ministry of Agriculture, 'Tanzania: National Food Strategy', Second Draft (June 1982).
Tanzania and UNICEF, 'Analysis of the Situation of Children and Women and the Priorities for Child Survival and Development', UNICEF, DSM (1985).
Temu, P., *Marketing Board Pricing and Storage Policy with Particular Reference to Maize in Tanzania*, Stanford, Ph.D. thesis, (1975).
Thiele, G., 'State Intervention and Commodity Production in Ugogo: A Historical Perspective', *Africa* 54(3) (1984).
Tibenderana, H.K., *The Factors affecting Tanzania's National Milling Corporation's Performance (1968–1981)*, M.A. Thesis, UDSM (1982).
United Nations Industrial Development Organization, 'The Potential for Resource-Based Industrial Development in LDCs, No. 3, Tanzania' (Vienna, 1982).
Unomah, A.C., 'Indirect Rule and the Nyamwezi Traditional System in the Tabora Province of Tanganyika', *Tarikh* 3(3) (1970).
Walker, P.T., 'A Survey of the Use of Maize Stalk Borer Control Methods in East Africa', *EAAJ* 25 (January 1960) pp. 165–8.
Weber, M., *Economy and Society* (Berkeley: University of California Press, 1968).

Westergaard, P., 'Analysis of the Accounts of the Co-operative Societies in Tanzania for the Years 1967–69', *ERB* 73.2 (1973).
Wright, F.C., *African Consumers in Nyasaland and Tanganyika* (London: HMSO, 1955).
Young, R., *Canadian Development Assistance to Tanzania: An Independent Study by Roger Young* (The North-South Institute, 1983).
Young, R. and Fosbrooke, H., *Land and Politics among the Luguru* (London: Routledge & Kegan Paul, 1960).

ARCHIVAL SOURCES

Public Records Office, London

CO691/78/152 – Letter from Cameron, Governor of Tanganyika to Secretary of State for the Colonies.
CO852/428/17600/II – 'Food Supplies, Crop Failure, East Africa', 1943.
CO852/428/17630 – 'Food Supplies to Tanganyika', 1943.

Rhodes House, Oxford

Aplin, H.D., *Report on Native Administration in Tanganyika Territory* (Zomba, Nyasaland Protectorate, 1931), [RH], G18.
Bagshawe, F.J.E., 'Private Diaries', RH Mss. Afr.s.281–9.
Brinkworth, H., 'Tanganyika Safari Diary, 1946', RH Mss. Afr.s.788.
Chambers, D.V., 'Food and Cashcrops', RH Mss. Br. Emp.s.476.
Dickson, J., 'Lupa Diary, 1925', RH Mss. Afr.s.738.
Dudbridge, B., 'Report on the 1949/50 Famine in the Maswa District', RH Mss. Afr.s.880.
Elliot, Sir H.F., 'Food Situation in the Western and Southern Areas of Mwanza District', Safari Report addressed to the DO, Mwanza, 3/3/38, RH Mss. Afr.s.1430.
Fosbrooke, H.A., 'Tanganyika, the Application of Indirect Rule to Chiefless Societies', Rhodes-Livingstone Conference Proceedings, RH (1959).
Gillman, C., 'Diary', RH Mss. Afr.s.1175.
Hall, Lady Lorna, 'A Bushwife's Progress: The Life of a Colonial Officer's Wife in Tanganyika, 1932–53', RH Mss. Afr.s.1834 (1982).
Holmes-Siedle, Bishop J., Transcript of 'Conversation between Bishop Holmes-Siedle, Bishop of Kigoma in Tanzania, the White Fathers – and John Tawney', RH Mss. Afr.s.1595.
Leslie, J.A.K., Transcript of 'Interview upon his Service as D.O.; Commissioner, Social Development; and Permanent Secretary in Tanganyika, 1946–54', RH Mss. Afr.s.1516, 42–43; Hall, RH Mss. Afr.s.1834.
Longland, F., 'Answers to Heussler's Questions' in 'Heussler's British Tanganyika Papers', 1960–1974, RH Mss. Br. Emp. s.480/4.
Malcolm, D.W., 'Correspondence, Reports concerning Land and Agriculture in Tanganyika, with Diary and Photos as Private Secretary to Lord Hailey when Director of the Africa Resource Survey, 1926–1960', RH Mss. Afr.s.1445.
Pearson, N., 'Trade Unionist on Safari, 1949', RH Mss. Afr.s.394.

Rowe, E.G., 'Interview concerning Colonial Service in Tanganyika, 1928–1958', RH Mss. Afr.s.1698 (1969).
Savory, B. in Heussler, R.W., 'British Colonial Service in Tanganyika', 1965, RH Mss. Br. Emp.s.480/4.
Stenhouse, A.S., 'Memoranda on Agriculture, Tobacco, Groundnuts, etc., in Tanganyika 1933–1948', RH Mss. Afr.s.417.
Sturdy, D.S., Transcript of 'Interview concerning Agricultural Services in Tanganyika, 1926–45', RH Mss. Afr.s.1331 (1969).
Tomlinson, G.A., Miscellaneous Papers: 'Memorandum on Indirect Rule', RH Mss. Afr.s.370 (1937).
Wakefield, A.J., 'Address to Colonial Office Summer School, Cambridge, August 1948', RH Mss. Afr.s.348–53.
White, E.G., 'Brief Domestic Reminiscences of Life in Tanganyika, 1929–34', RH Mss. Afr.s.172 (n.d.).
Winnington-Ingram, C., Miscellaneous Papers: 'N. Mara district annual report', RH Mss. Afr.s.1749 (1950).

Tanzania National Archives, Dar es Salaam

TNA Acc. 7 – Bagamoyo district files.
TNA Acc. 61 – Dar es Salaam district files.
TNA SMP 3998 – 'Trading Centres in Districts', 1922–6.
TNA SMP 10138 – 'System of Marketing of Produce', 1927–45.
TNA SMP 11306 – P.C. Mitchell to Governor, 1/11/30.
TNA SMP 13252 – 'Shortage of Foodstuffs. Famine Relief', 1929–42.
TNA SMP 19417/3 – 'Sisal Industry', 1946.
TNA SMP 19454 – 'Food Shortage – Eastern Province', 1930–6.
TNA SMP 19533 – 'Maize Industry', 1930–41.
TNA SMP 23544 – 'Labour Matters in Sisal Areas', 1936.
TNA SMP 25908/1/66 – 'Labour Inspection', 1938.
TNA SMP 25987 – 'Report of Nutrition Committee', 1940.
TNA SMP 27245 – 'Re-organization of Native Administration', 1940.
TNA SMP 29549 – 'Control of Foodstuffs', 1941–50.
TNA SMP 30598 – 'Cost of Living of Africans in Townships', 1942–51.
TNA SMP 30626 – 'Crop Production', 1942–5.
TNA SMP 35181 – 'Cereal Storage', 1947–51.
TNA SMP 38804 – 'Maize Prices in Relation to those for Export Group and the Stimulation of Agricultural Production Generally', 1948–53.
TNA SMP 39114 – 'Retail Prices and Subsidization of Grain', 1949.

University of Dar es Salaam, East Africana

Wright, A.C.A., 'The Transition from Native Administration to Local Government', Paper prepared for the Government of Tanganyika (1952) 3 (Cory Collection No. 402, UDSM).

NEWSPAPERS

Africa Now, London.
Africa Report, London.
The Economist, London.
Financial Times, London.
Guardian, London.
Daily News, Dar es Salaam.
Sunday News, Dar es Salaam.
Uhuru, Dar es Salaam.
Weekly Review, Kenya.

Index